Col. Hankins

Dakota Land

An Original, Illustrated, Historic, and Romantic Work on Minnesota and the Great

NorthWest. Second Edition

Col. Hankins

Dakota Land
An Original, Illustrated, Historic, and Romantic Work on Minnesota and the Great NorthWest.
Second Edition

ISBN/EAN: 9783744679176

Printed in Europe, USA, Canada, Australia, Japan

Cover: Foto ©ninafisch / pixelio.de

More available books at **www.hansebooks.com**

Col. Hankins

Dakota Land
An Original, Illustrated, Historic, and Romantic Work on Minnesota and the Great NorthWest.
Second Edition

ISBN/EAN: 9783744679176

Printed in Europe, USA, Canada, Australia, Japan

Cover: Foto ©ninafisch / pixelio.de

More available books at **www.hansebooks.com**

Yours Truly
C. Hankins

DAKOTA LAND

OR THE

BEAUTY of St. PAUL

BY
Col. Hankins.

Entered according to Act of Congress, in the year 1868, by
COL. HANKINS,
In the Clerk's Office of the District Court of the Southern District of New York.

DAKOTA LAND;

OR,

THE BEAUTY OF ST. PAUL.

AN ORIGINAL, ILLUSTRATED,

HISTORIC AND ROMANTIC WORK

ON

MINNESOTA,

AND

THE GREAT NORTH-WEST.

BY COL. HANKINS,

EDITOR OF "THE NEW YORK HOME GAZETTE,"

And Author of "Agnes Wilto," "Maniac Father," "The Apostate Quaker,"
"The Idiot of the Mill," "The Orphan's Dream," "The Banker's Wife,"
"The Mother's Prayer," "The Beautiful Nun," "Hearts That Are Cold,"
Besides innumerable Serial Productions of Truth and Fiction.

SECOND EDITION.

1869:
HANKINS & SON, PUBLISHERS,
Office of the "New York Home Gazette,"
NEW YORK CITY.

TO THE

CITIZENS OF ST. PAUL, GREETING.

AN ACCEPTANCE OF THIS VOLUME,

RESPECTFULLY DEDICATED

AS A

MARK OF SINCERE ESTEEM

FOR YOU PERSONALLY,

AND ALSO AS A

TOKEN OF ENTHUSIASTIC ADMIRATION

FOR YOUR

BRIGHT NEW CITY,

WILL BE VERY GRATIFYING TO

THE AUTHOR.

PREFACE.

My first visit to Minnesota was not until the latter part of September, ——; and then it so happened that I could tarry but twenty-four hours in the vicinity of St. Paul. With the popular disbelief of all strangers to that region, I anticipated the real existence of no very great attractions there, and accordingly had made arrangements for returning to New York the first week in October. However, I saw and felt enough during the speedy lapse of that one day, to convince me of my error. And although I could not then prolong my stay, there was much comfort in hopefully promising myself the pleasure of a more extended visit some other time. But the next day after my departure down the river, on board a "white collar" steamer, and while dreamily gazing upon the lovely scenery of Lake Pepin, and musing upon the marvelous enchantment of the Great North-west, I was suddenly inspired with the idea of publishing a Dioristic and Statistical History of the bright, new city which I had so recently seen. And that inspiration eventually terminated in a fixed resolve. For even though a stranger there, I could not fail to perceive how greatly such a book was needed, and also the prospective surety that the publisher thereof would be well compensated by its ready sale.

The result was that I hastened back to St. Paul early in November. And on arriving there, the editors of the *Daily Pioneer* and the *Daily Press* kindly encouraged me by complimentarily noticing my intention. But very soon afterward, they also noticed the similar individual purposes of several *native* "brothers of the scissors and the quill," whom my *coming* effectively roused to a full sense of the "golden opportunity" which I had in view. And as I prudently declined any rivalry or contest with those who were so much better qualified to successfully accomplish the proposed undertaking, it only remained for me to "interpret well that meaning cry of 'Ship ahoy,' and into smoother waters quickly steer." (See page 397.)

Yet, one pleasant evening before I sailed from the port of St. Paul, the *Spirit* of "Good Dame Fortune" appeared to me with her charming face all dimpled in a patronizing smile. And, while a sweet, hope-beguiling expression stole out of her coquettish eyes, she said to me, "Come, disheartened mortal, cheer thee up! Be of good heart, and listen! With the aid of my magic power, ere to-morrow's sun goes down, thou shalt have the *Key* to a Mystery that's been long concealed. With that talisman in thy hand, and the story of the beautiful, golden-haired *Fleurette*, whom thou know'st so well, strange fatalities may be revealed! Come; get thee to thy task! And remember that we shall meet again! Farewell!"

So, having acted upon the *Spirit's* suggestion, I am now vain enough to believe that this Volume of "DAKOTA LAND; or, *The Beauty of St. Paul*," will prove both interesting and instructive to every reader who may honor it with a fair perusal through.

Dakota Land proper, originally included nearly all the territory which is now occupied in part by the States of Wisconsin, Iowa and Minnesota—only that distant section north of Nebraska and west of Minnesota, yet retaining the Dakota name. So after all, Dakota Land and the Great North-west are simply different appellations for the same region. The former was chosen for the title of this volume, because it harmonized more pleasantly with the peculiar character of the objects and themes which I purposed treating upon. Whether that choice may have been an appropriate one, the reader will now determine unknown to me and regardless of my opinion.

THE AUTHOR.

INDEX TO CONTENTS.

A Synoptical Reference to Scenes and Events of the Volume, Necessarily or Incidentally Connected with the Remarkable *Denouements* of "LOST, and FOUND!"

CHAPTER I.

The Solitary Pine...A Strange Fancy...Upon a Lofty Hill...A Sunset View...The Bright New City...Children of the *Bois brule*...Round Blue Stones...A Curious Mound...No More Crimson Hues...A Twilight Dream...Church Spires and Council Fires...The Plowman's Whistle, and the Farm-house Dinner-horn...The Red Man's Blood...Enchanted Ground...A Lost Spirit...Theory of the Past...A Weird Sentinel of Time!.. 17

CHAPTER II.

Magic Arts...The Prophet's Tomb...A "Shrine of Life"...The Franciscan Adventurer...Cavern of Wakan-tebee...Back Two Hundred Years...The Gospel Missionary...A Temple of Ruin..."Pig's Eye" **Pandemonium**...Hell of Virgil and Dante...Incantation of the Fiends...Poison **for the Aborigine**...The Dawn of Light...Finding a *Lost Key*...Parrant's Fate to be Revealed...Consulting the Stars...The "Angel of Love," and the "Eye of God!"............................ 27

CHAPTER III.

Northern Wilds...An Ambitious Earl....The Marquis Dupontavisse...From Paris to Red River..."Morganatic Ties"...A Singular Town...Unknown *El Dorado*...Beauty Will Fade...History of a Life...Widowhood and Despair...The Fair Adventuress...A Fur Trader's Love...What Jealousy Will Do...Kaskadino, the "Medicine Man"...A Heartless Nurse...Cool Draughts and Poison...The Mother Dies...Hear that Voice!... 41

CHAPTER IV.

The Grave-Digger's Mound...Marriage *a la mode du pays*..."No Pedigree, no Nation, no God!"...What History Does Not Tell...Approach of "The Destroyer"...Wooing a Brother's Child!...Staking a Human Soul...Marvelous Coincidence in Life....Prodigal Coquettes...."God Bless that Man!"....Farewell to Mother's Grave....The "Ox-Train" Moving....Intoxicating Sounds...Modern Sons of Ishmael...Encampment at Night...A Novelty more Primitive than Tubal Cain!.. 57

CHAPTER V.

Imaginary Fears..."Voice of the **Bells**"...When Graveyards Yawn...The Tavern Keeper's Son...Something About Cats...A Country School...An Idiot's Love...Village Superstition...A Deed of Blood...The Haunted House...Challenge Accepted...A "Million Sighs!"...Journey in the Dark...The Forest of Pines...Unearthing a Ghost...Did the Devil Enter Swine?...Moonrise in Minnesota...An Enchanting Scene...The Yawning Chasm...A Devious Path!...... 71

CHAPTER VI.

Delicious Repose...Flight with Morpheus...Back to the Solitary Pine...That Curious Mound...Presentiment of Evil...Philosophy of Fear...Natural Melodies...An Imbecile Statue...The Sobbing of Grief...Spell-bound...In the Claws of a Demon...A Stygian Imp...Prince of Darkness..."Was it of Woman Born?"...The Paralyzed Arm...A Gorgon Laugh...One of God's Creatures, after all...A Wild "Ha, ha!"...The Vision Dissolves!............................ 87

CHAPTER VII.

Hah-zah-ee-yun-kee-win..."Running Injun with Big Moon"...St. Paulians Should all Have Wives...An Old Squaw's Grief...Alas, "Me Choonkshee!"... Angry Wakan Stole her Child away...Beautiful Lament...Round Blue Stones, from Minne-in-ee-o-pa...Mystery of the Curious Mound...A Balm for Sorrow... Strange Beliefs...The Land where Spirits Dwell...Scalps and Love...A Mother's Superstition...Strange Adventure, and Terrific Fall!.................... 95

CHAPTER VIII.

Shoulder-straps and Champagne...Drawing it Mild...Tea *versus* Wine...The Two Canoes...St. Paul in the Year 1845...Unexpected Recognition of Parrant... Scene in his Shanty...A Fair Acquaintance..."Go, I want to be free!"..."Give it to me, or you die!"...A Mystery Unexplained...Rescued by Old Betz...In the Cavern of Wakan-Teheei...The Rendezvous...Square Rock below Mendota... The Indian Assassin...Parrant Left to Die!................................ 113

CHAPTER IX.

Kaskadino in Disguise...A Death Struggle...The Body not Found...Friendship of Old Betz...Disappointments all Around...Philosophy of Erratic Love...The "Old Story" That's Often Told...Gone...Other Destinies to Fill...Nuptial Vows...A Painful Suspicion...The False Priest...Desertion...Phineas O'Brien, the Inebriate Attorney...Uncertainty of the Law...The Grandmother's Affection...Justice or Revenge!.. 125

CHAPTER X.

Indian Summer in Minnesota...Dreamy *Seance* of Nature...St. Paul by Moonlight, in November...New York City at Night, in a Storm...Colossal Tombs... Gloom Without; What's Within?...Prayers for the Dawn...A Girl-Mother and her Babe...The Palace and the Attic Room...The Gold Screen and the Broken Pane... A Heart of Stone...Three Common Wrongs...Portrait on the Wall...An Evil Spirit Hovering Near!.. 139

CHAPTER XI.

The Infant Heiress...Marriage without Love...Love without Marriage...Precept and Example for Ambitious Young Girls...The Two New Mothers...A Bitter Heart...The Dark Resolve...Saved by a Picture...Bribes Refused...Everything to Gain, and Nothing to Lose...A Housekeeper's Letter...Warning for Rich Mothers...Counterplotting....Expiation for The Destroyer....More than Revenge...A Cruel Wrong...Wonderful Instinct of a Mother!................. 153

CHAPTER XII.

Personal Charms...Beauty and Mind...Belle of the Crescent City...Wedded Life...Nothing we have or enjoy can ever remain the same!...The Unhappy Husband...A Loving Wife...The Poor Old Slaves...Who Remember Levasseur...The Financier and Ladies' Man...Nobles in Disguise...Social Laws...Theory of Love...Marriage Often a Fraud...Festered Hearts and Souls...Duty and Desire...The False Go-between...The Apostate's First Repentance...Searching for his Lost Love...Gyneocracy and Divorce!.. 167

CHAPTER XIII.

The Shadows Falling...Torture and Despair...The Apostate Warned...Marvelous Daring...Gathering of the Storm...The Stolen Child...Trick and Stratagem...Unconscious Meeting of the Rival Mothers...The Abyss of Ruin...A Distressing Scene...The Fatal Truth Revealed...The Destroyer and Avenger face together...The *Affecting Denouement* of Lost!...A Compact and the Oath!...Behold the Sacrifice, now!.. 183

CHAPTER XIV.

The Desecrated Sanctuary...Last Link Broken...The Betrayed Wife..."Oh, let me die!"...The Adventuress' Last Hope...The "Beautiful Snow!"...Where Cobwebs Grow....The Deserted Dwelling...Inquisitive Old Maid...."Them blasted Niggers!"...The Chamber of Mystery...Something Wrong...Bells Tolling Fire...Burning of Levasseur's City Mansion...McJudas, the Detective, in Search of Crime Concealed!.. 193

CHAPTER XV.

Satan Panting for Souls....The Dismal Palmetto Tree....Jupiter Dim'd by Mars...Juno in Tears...The Siren Spy...Potency of Gold...Out of Rebeldom into the Union Lines....A "Consumptive Invalid and her Slaves"...."Hear that cough!"...The Great "Dr. Passion;" a Christian Quack...A Jersey Farmer, whose Dog "Goliah" has an "Opinion"...The Farmer's Strange Suspicion that he sees "Mini," the Convict, who escaped many years ago...Going to Minnesota...The Four Sisters..."O, must she die?".. 207

CHAPTER XVI.

The Deserted Wife....Her Slaves' Affection...."O, when his heart grows sad!"...Doom of the Fair Adventuress...A Sectarian Asylum...The Poor Little Orphans...Those Sad Blue Eyes...A Sweet Foundling...The Necklace of "Job's Tears"...Something to Love...The Hectic Flush...Old Mortality...The "Two Lands of Flowers"...See the Vampire Smile...Pure Air better than Medicine...Force of Example...Steamboat Captains in the East and in the West...Arrival at St. Paul...Dr. Passion in the River!.. 223

CHAPTER XVII.

A Piercing Scream...Goliah quickly Flies to the Rescue of Fleurette, and coolly Leaves the Vampire to Drown...A Grand Ovation to Goliah...The Widower's Heart...Friends Must Part...Sincere Regrets...Sancho and the Quacks...Southern Ideas of Cold...Spring and the Blue Bird's Song...Rosy Cheeks when the Butter Cups Bloom...The Sioux War-whoop!...A Sea of Blood...The "Turkey and the Crow!"..."*Is* there *Such* a Man?"...The Captive Girls...Horrors Untold...The Escape...Poor Goliah..."Father is dead!"............................ 239

CHAPTER XVIII.

Tradition of the "Flood"...The Three Sons of Noah...A Chief's Power...Family Relations...Indian Laws...Prisoners of War...Caligula Outdone...Obsequies of their Dead...**Marriage**..."Plenty of Wives!"...Virtue and Divorce...Utility of Squaws...**In and** Around the Teepees...Brutal Feelings...Immortality of their Souls..."Dog Pie"...Mounted for the Chase...Cunning of Wolves...Voracious Gluttons.....The Blanket "Carryall".....The **Red** Man's Redemption!... 257

CHAPTER XIX.

Anti-Sectarian Germans...Churches Forbidden...The Girl-Captives saved by a Whisky-Keg...Execution of "Bad Injuns"..."Good Injuns" Sent Away...Amusing Interview with Old Betz...Phrenological Inquisition...Kosh-popee *all the time*...The Marvelous Creature Sings a Song...Indian Etiquette...Ghastly Toys....Plumes of the Brave....Classic Aborigines....God's Handiwork Gone Astray...The Dying Squaw!.. 273

CHAPTER XX.

Smoldering Ruins...Goliah Not Dead; but Saves his Master's Life...A Joyful Return..."We're beggars now!"...Prospects of the Future...A Friend in Need..The "Scare," and Fall in Real Estate...A "Dog-Train" from Red River...Farmer Denton's "Sledge" Adventure...Worse than Dr. Bartlett's Camels...Novel Journey Over the Snow...Dogs and Wolves..."Playing 'Possum"...Canine Hotels...The Hunger of a Blighted Heart...An Old Ardor Anew..."I ne'er again shall wed!"... 278

CHAPTER XXI.

The "Angel Heart" Proves Faithful Still...Wooing the "Beauty of St. Paul"...The Prodigals of Stolen Bliss in Paris yet...But God has heard the Wife's Prayer, and at length the **Husband's Heart** *does* grow sad...The Grandmother's Affection proves a Fatal Curse...Jealousy and the Result...A Pleasure Dream of Sixteen Years at its End...Darkest before Dawn...The Forsaken, Penitent Man...Sleep of Remorse and Vision of Joy...And then, instead of Love Returned with Life, only a Corpse is Promised to the Wife...Put Flowers on his Grave...Moonbeams from Above!.. 305

CHAPTER XXII.

"He comes!"..."Ma, dear, God is always near!"...The Coffin on board the Steamer...Strangers in St. Paul...Hospitality Accepted...A Solemn Scene...Prayer of the "Angel Heart"..."Let our Graves be One!"...The Dead Alive...*Startling Denouement* of FOUND!..."Your corpse; what of that?"...The Prototype Beauties!...Wonders Multiplied...Truth Stranger than Fiction...**The Joy of** "*Lost Love Returned!*".. 321

CHAPTER XXIII.

A Speculation...Four Crimson Blushes...The Three Brides..."She's my only boy!"...Jane "Counted In."...Up in the World...Elegance of St. Paul...Nothing Like Money Anywhere...The Citizens of St. Paul...Who Live in the Palaces, and What's "Behind the Scenes"...Under the Gaslight Glare...The Distinguished and the Wealthy...A long List of Eminent Names in full...Smiles of Welcome...

Getting into "Society!"...The Same Man Still...Fighting the Cold...A Word to "Consumptives!"...The "Beavers"...Their Habits and Customs...A Curious Study...Real-estate "Financiers!" 335

CHAPTER XXIV.

Summer Resorts...Pharaonic Apollyons, and Cytherian Decoys...Where Souls are Prepared for Hell...*No* "Black Crook" in the Retreats of Dakota Land, where Virtue Sweetly Breathes...Scenery on the Mississippi River...Castellated Bluffs...**Mountain Graves**...The "Lake of Tears"...Traditions of the Past... When the Bottom of Lake Pepin *Fell Out*...The Garrard Estate...Society of Frontenac...A Summer Paradise in Embryo...The Abode of Happiness...Mysterious Boiling River...A Terraqueous Problem for Geologists to Solve!......... 353

CHAPTER XXV.

Winter in Minnesota...Consumptives in the "Promised Land"...Celestial Phenomena...Sun-Dogs; Moon-Dogs, and *Lumen Boreale*...Nicollet House, in Minneapolis..."Louise" and the Author Laughing **at** Zero...*L'Hotel de Shantie*...The Mystic Tree...Shivering Romance...A Frozen Beauty...**The** "Weeping Waters" Entombed in Ice...A World of Pure White Glass...Rendezvous of the Great... Where Lovers Can Woo...Boulevard of St. Paul...What Strangers Desire to Know...Skeleton of Tah-o-ah-ta-doo-ta...Po-go-na-ghe-shick *On a Spree!* 369

CHAPTER XXVI.

Delightful Drives...The "Round Trip"...Legend of **Anpetusapa**...Devotion of Scarlet Dove...Fast Horses...Race to Lake **Como**...A Genius in St. Paul...The "**Calumet of Peace**"...A Happy Home...Exhuming a Skeleton...The Knife and Pistol...Scene in 'Alpine Cottage"...Solving a Mystery of the Past...Bones of Old "Pig's Eye"...*The "Lost Key" Found!*...Editors Playing "Bluff"...Story of Parrant's Ghost...The very Best of Men...Burning of Barnum's Museum... Among the Ashes of Snakes and Bears!... 383

CHAPTER XXVII.

The Grandmother's Repentance, and the Granddaughter's Grief...Pursuit of the "Forsaken Husband"...The Beautiful Maniac..."My child, not hers!"...A Misspent Life...The Self-willed Man...Flight of "Irene"...The Wife's Prophecy **Fulfilled**...Memories of the Past...The Dead-house...Fate **of Leonore**...Dying Confession of the Avenger...The Beautiful Prototype Sisters...One *Accursed*, and the other a *Happy Bride*...Revisiting St. Paul...The Vampire Caught at last... Pity of the "Angel Heart"...The Destroyer's **Remorse**...A Tomb in Greenwood Cemetery...Now, and *Forevermore!!* 405

ILLUSTRATIONS.

Illuminated with over One Hundred Engravings of Descriptive Scenery, Authentic Portraits and Dramatic Tableaux.

1.	ENGRAVED PHOTOGRAPH OF THE AUTHOR	(*Frontispiece.*)
2.	PORTRAIT OF FLEURETTE, "THE BEAUTY OF ST. PAUL"...	(*Illuminated Title.*)
3.	The "Solitary Pine," beyond the wide river.........................*Page*	17
4.	Sunset View of the "Bright New City"	17
5.	A Rolling Prairie in Dakota Land	26
6.	View of Upper Fort Garry, on Red River	27
7.	Portrait of "Winneshiek," with his "Pipe of Peace"...............	27
8.	Old Indian Graves, near the town of Crow Wing......	32
9.	Aboriginal method of traveling "On Rail"	36
10.	Portrait of the Sioux Chief "Little Crow".............................	40
11.	A Fur Trader wooing "Leonore's" Mother	41
12.	Moonlight View in Dakota Land..	44
13.	Lovely Night Scene in the Red River Region.........................	48
14.	Church and Mission School at Pembina	52
15.	The Great "Golgotha" of Dakota Land	56
16.	An "Ox-Train" from Red River to Mendota............................	57
17.	Fort Pembina, with Ox-Train and Half-breed Teepees	64
18.	An Ox-Train Encampment at Night	70
19.	The Idiot tormenting his Favorite Cat...................................	71
20.	Portrait of 'Cut Nose," or "Me Good Injun"	76
21.	Portrait of Ex-Governor Ramsey	82
22.	An Object but vaguely suggesting a "Habitation"................	86
23.	Primeval View on Lake Minnetonka.......................................	87
24.	Traditional Throne of the Spirit of War	87
25.	An Indian Burial Scaffold..	92
26.	Portrait of "Old Betz," the Centenarian Squaw....................	98
27.	Marriage Ceremony of the Chippeways	99
28.	Moonlight View of Burial Scaffolds on Dayton's Bluff	107
29.	A Naudowessian Sibyl, or "Imaginary Witch".....................	112
30.	The Lovely Ideal of a Youthful Dream	112
31.	Scene on White Bear Lake, near Murray's Hotel	113
32.	A First-Class Hotel, during the Reign of "Pig's Eye".............	113
33.	The Surroundings of Fort Snelling.......................................	124
34.	Near the "Square Rock" below Mendota.............................	125
35.	The Assassination of Old Parrant..	125
36.	Portrait of "Standing Buffalo" ("Sweet Corn's" friend)	131
37.	Fancy Portrait of "One Good Little Injun Boy"	138
38.	The "Girl Mother" and her Babe, in the Attic Room.............	139
39.	Cathedral of St. Boniface, near Fort Garry...........................	146
40.	Landscape at "Red Wood," with an Indian Camp................	153
41.	Scene in the Rich Wife's Luxurious Chamber	153

ILLUSTRATIONS. 15

42.	A Life Saved by the Eyes of a Picture	153
43.	The "Laughing Water," or Minnehaha Falls	160
44.	View of Fort Abercrombie, on Red River	166
45.	*Soire Dansante*, in Washington City	167
46.	The Recreant Husband, a Ladies' Man	167
47.	City of St. Paul, viewed from Dayton's Bluff, in 1853	176
48.	Pembina Settlement, Mouth of Pembina River	182
49.	The Desecrated Sanctuary	183
50.	Oath of the Apostate Husband	183
51.	Portrait of "Red Iron," an "Ugly Savage"	190
52.	View of Otter Tail City and Lake	196
53.	The Deserted Mansion and the Beautiful Snow	197
54.	Indian Girls Engaged in Useful Occupation	202
55.	The "Magic Ferry" across Rum River	206
56.	A Convict's Family, and the Necklace of Bear's-Claws	207
57.	Lake Pepin, with Distant View of "Maiden Rock"	207
58.	Rock Island, where the Sioux Monsters are confined	216
59.	Party of Summer Tourists "Camping Out"	222
60.	The Inside of a New York City Orphan Asylum	223
61.	View of Castellated Bluffs, near Lake Pepin	230
62.	Romantic Scenery on the Upper Mississippi River	238
63.	A "White-Collar" Steamer at the St. Paul Levee	239
64.	The Dog "Goliah" rescues "Fleurette" from Drowning	239
65.	View at Crow Wing, Minnesota, in 1853	250
66.	The Widowed Mother, and Her Heroic Boy	256
67.	Mounted Indians, chasing a Herd of Buffalo	257
68.	View of Pelican Lake, near Otter Tail River	266
69.	Countless Mounds of the "Ancient Dead!"	272
70.	A Scene During the Sioux Massacre of '62	273
71.	The Dog "Goliah" Killing the Assassin of his Master	273
72.	Portrait of a Murderous Indian	280
73.	White Women attacking the Captured Sioux	286
74.	A "Dog-Sledge" Train, approaching at full speed	287
75.	Tourists enraptured at the sight of Red River	294
76.	Picturesque View of "Wild-Goose-Nest" Lake	304
77.	A Sunbeam on the head of the Penitent Man	305
78.	The Dream of Remorse and Vision of Joy	305
79.	An Eccentric Horse giving his Rider a Bath	312
80.	Wild Scenery on the "Assouri" River	320
81.	The "Angel heart" expecting the Corpse of her Husband	321
82.	View of St. Paul and River, as seen from the Western Heights	321
83.	St. Andrew's Church, at Selkirk Colony	328
84.	Tourists fording the "Calumet" River	334
85.	Fleurette, "The Beauty of St. Paul," riding her Pet Horse	335
86.	A View of St. Paul, looking toward Dayton's Bluff	335
87.	Spontaneous Strawberry Festival, in Dakota Land	342
88.	The modest "Claim" of Johannes Oberhoffer	351
89.	View of "Devil Lake," where "Little Crow" was Killed	352
90.	Bennett, the Red-Wing Artist, and his Sister	353
91.	A Lovely Scene on the Upper Mississippi River	353
92.	The Peculiarity of "Sandstone" Hills	360
93.	A Panoramic View of River Islands	368
94.	The Grand Plaza, in the City of Minneapolis	369

ILLUSTRATIONS.

95.	Tourists enjoying the "Round-Trip" Drive	369
96.	Suspension Bridge, at the Falls of St. Anthony	3 4
97.	Portrait of Po-go-na-gbe-shich, **or** "Hole-in-the-Day"	382
98.	**A Ride** to Lake Como, with "**Beauty** and Fashion"	383
99.	"Webb's" Team distancing "Farmer Denton's"	383
100.	**The "First** Shanty" erected **where** the "Bright **New City**" now stands.	390
101.	*View on the* Ash-ki-big-isibi, **or** "Green-Leaf River"	404
102.	Scene in Greenwood Cemetery, **New York City**	405
103.	The Graves of "Zorah and Leonore!"	405
104.	Distant View of Pembina Mountain.	414
105.	The "Silver Cascade," a beautiful waterfall.	426
106.	**Impatient** "Sight-Seers" *Starting* on a Tour.	378
107.	River-Side View "Where the Iron Horse Runs in Dakota Land"	344
108.	An Ex-Consumptive Invalid, taking it Easy	402
109.	A *Hungry* Tourist Left Behind	379
110.	Portrait of Governor Marshall, of Minnesota	377
111.	The old Flag-tower of Fort Snelling	319
112.	*Happy* Tourists Homeward Bound!	403

Also, (finely engraved on copper-plate, and nicely colored,) a Large and Accurate
Map Of The Entire Great North-West!

CHAPTER I.

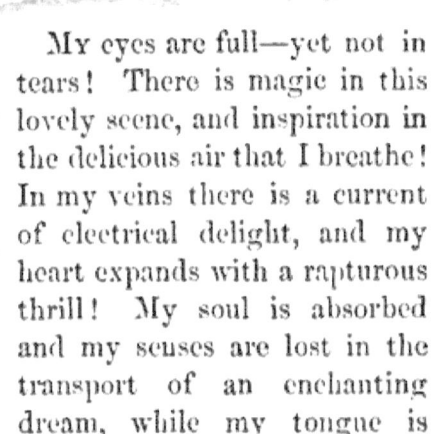

My eyes are full—yet not in tears! There is magic in this lovely scene, and inspiration in the delicious air that I breathe! In my veins there is a current of electrical delight, and my heart expands with a rapturous thrill! My soul is absorbed and my senses are lost in the transport of an enchanting dream, while my tongue is eagerly dancing to utter wild words of joy! But where am I, and what do I see?

I live not here. My home is far away! They told me of a bright realm of flowers, of beautiful lakes and winding streams, where health and happiness might dwell forever! Then, with the lightning speed of modern travel, I journeyed hither, this paradise to see.
And yonder, where the gray stone walls and the church spires are gleaming, I arrived a few days ago.

Away in the distance, beyond a wide river, I beheld a dark bluff towering upward high. And upon the dark bluff I saw a lonely pine! The people, in their daily rounds of leisure or of business strife, could behold the bluff, and they might perceive the pine. I scanned their faces well, yet saw not one who paused to glance that way. But, musingly, I said, why should they pause, when to them the sight was nothing new? For just there, the same from day to day, the dark bluff ever reared its form. And as all novelties lose their attraction when constantly seen, so the people thought not of what I saw. Thus, how true it is that we often undervalue or overlook the greatest blessings which are given us to enjoy. Even beauty must be scarce or new to gain notice more than common things!

And as the passing multitude strode or rode along, I stood lost in contemplation of the scene. Pensive I was and my heart grew sad. I could not help imagining that I saw the giant form of a sorrowful and weary sentinel, who had been left standing there upon the bluff by some strange long-past decree, to count the lapse of time, and then to guard the bright new city which was to be!

And how forlorn it appeared to me! Without regard from any one, for days and nights unnumbered, in summer suns and winter snows, there it had been for many, many years!

Solitary and alone! No comrades near. Not so much as a little dwarf oak, or a scraggy bush, could I then discern upon the rocky summit where it grew.

The longer I mused upon the mournful tree, the more I wished to hie me thither and cheer it with a human smile. And puerile as that impulse may seem to other minds, I could not resist it then. We all have little fancies at certain times, which might be sneered at by the world, if they were disclosed without a redeeming cause. Neither the wisest, nor the very great, are exempt from the general rule.

But to sympathize with a solitary tree, would sound so silly in adult ears that I quietly resolved to indulge my weird fancy, without consulting any one. Thus,

>At the close of a lovely autumn day,
>In "Dakota-land," I wander away
>To the solitude of a lofty hill,
>Where the throbbing of life is hush'd still—
>And here, upon this bleak and barren stone,
>Amid the solemn silence, all alone,
>As the evening shadows, lengthening, fall,
>I sit and gaze in rapture on St. Paul!

Reclining upon the brow of this gigantic bluff, beneath the solitary pine, with great hill-tops around me, all rearing toward the steel-blue sky; and

>From doubtful-meaning smiles apart,
>My soul is unrestrained and free
>To linger sadly with my heart,
>Or sail out on a pleasant sea!

But I came too late for a grand view in the full blaze of day. Even now the sun is disappearing behind a dark promontory which seems to defy the hostile frowns of old Fort Snelling, whose gloomy walls across the river overshadow the "meeting of the waters!" The western horizon is glowing with gorgeous crimson hues, and the little cloudlets are brightly fringed with luminous tints of gold, while a pleasant murmur in the soft and mellow air hushes nature to repose!

>Below the rock whereon I am sitting,
> Away down there, four hundred feet and more,
>Millions of golden ripples are flitting
> Along the Mississippi's pebbly shore—
>Flowing on thousands of miles to the sea,
>Like Time rolling into Eternity!

In the edge of a small forest, further back upon the bluff, a mile or so away, I behold a slender volume of smoke curling up from the mud chimney of a rude cabin. And down in the sloping ravine, near that great spring of water bubbling all the year, I can perceive three objects, half concealed among the bushes. Moving slowly around, they presently emerge upon the bare rock; and now I can distinguish a woman and two little ones.

An old Indian squaw had a favorite daughter who married the son of a *bois brule;* and she is now with her grand-children there upon the rock above the ravine. The children live with their parents in that abode where the volume of smoke is curling up in the air. The cabin itself is in the edge of the forest and scarcely visible from here.

There they go up the steep, and then down again into the ravine. The old squaw leads the way, and the little ones cling to her blanket as they scramble through the briers.

She reminds me of a hen quail or a maternal turkey, skulking out of sight to screen her young ones from impending harm. The children hover each side of their old grandma just as I have seen timid young birds nestle up to their dam, when the hunter and his dogs were near.

And I can not help fancying that she is actually clucking to the little chicks, while leading them through the bushes, up and down among the stones. Perhaps she is cherishing a desire which she can not realize. It occurs to me that she is yearning to entice those children away to the haunts of her tribe. She loves them, and they are fond of her. And impelled by that unconquerable habit or instinct of nature which characterizes her race, I imagine her to be wishing within her heart that she could lead them hence and have them all her own. Yet that can never be. Civilization has partly reclaimed their father, and he has taught their mother to live in a manner less barbarous than she did in the wigwam, or *tee-pee*, of her parents before he made her his wife. But there they go down into the narrow glen, and are soon entirely out of sight!

And now I discover an object of much greater interest quite near. With vague conjectures I try to account for the origin of that huge pile of round blue stones not many rods from the edge of the bluff! It seems to have been the work of human hands. The stones are nearly all of the same shape and size, and evidently heaped up there for some particular purpose and with great care— like one of those Indian mounds, but entirely of stones, and to all appearance more recently formed. I have not seen any stones precisely like those anywhere about St. Paul. Can it be possible that they were all brought by the Indians from some distant place and piled up here in such a shape? Really, I would like to know why they were placed here thus. But it is useless to study out any theory—for these prairies and hills, and lakes, and rivers, are full of mysterious evidences of the past, which neither history nor science will ever unseal!

Again I turn my eyes upon the beautiful city to perceive that its walls are no longer gleaming. The flood of sunlight that made them look so bright when I first gained the top of this elevated wild, has now entirely gone. Even the lurid fires that seemed to blaze from the window-panes of glass have lost all their glow.

But what a tranquil scene! The hush of silence is sublime!

A TWILIGHT DREAM.

> The bright glory of sunset is dying
> Upon the gilded expanse in the west,
> And the hawk and the crow both are flying
> To the far-off hills for a place of rest.
>
> No more golden hues, nor a sign of red—
> The lingering twilight is lost in gloom—
> Silently it mourns for the day that's dead—
> Then softly slumbers in its airy tomb!

And now stars bedeck the great blue arch above. But the surface of the river is still in sight. A little archipelago divides the stream lengthwise between; and the waters resemble a great white ribbon, in the centre all rent and torn, and stretching westward until lost behind the black outline of invisible hills.

Sharp gleams of gas-light are plainly seen over in the city where vacant space admits a view, and feebler lights are glimmering among the humble abodes down on the plain between the base of this great bluff and the water's edge.

In the distance, there is a monster light, with many smaller ones spread around. They belong to a packet just coming up the river with passengers and merchandise. I hear the steam-pipe signal howling fierce and wild, and mark its echoes far and near.

Would I were among the throng now gathering on the *levee* there to see the passengers step ashore; for I have already learned that strangers least expected are coming hither every day. All the world is beginning to think and talk of Minnesota—because it offers some attraction or inducement to every one. But I shall not leave this pleasant solitude yet awhile.

One night, many years ago, I sat upon Bergen Hights, before Hudson City became a town, and gazed at the immense metropolis across the North River. That scene was grand, but then I did not feel the indescribable charm experienced by me now. There never was anything around New York so peculiarly romantic as the scenery connected with St. Paul. At least I never knew it, if there was.

New York is mighty and grand, as an emporium of commerce, an abode of luxury, and a reservoir of misery and want—while this bright new city seems to be an enchanted rendezvous for the acquisition of joyous health and buoyant hope.

A new city, because less than a quarter of a century has elapsed since all this region was an uncultivated wild. Just there where the city now sleeps in repose, only rocks and trees were seen but a few years ago. And in the identical spot where I am sitting now, doubtless many a savage sat long before the first paleface came this way. It was but yesterday that the red man's canoe glided noiselessly to and fro upon the pellucid lakes and the Father of Rivers that beautify this wonderful land. Wonderful, because so unlike countries elsewhere.

Church-spires are now gleaming in the light of day where council fires then burned at night. Instead of the savage war-whoop "on the prairies and in the hills," we now hear the "plowman's merry whistle and the farmhouse dinner-horn." The scenes and sights of twenty-five years ago nearly all have past away. Only a few tame savages remain prowling hereabout to beg or to steal. The multitude have been sent further to the West. The revengeful Chippeways and the insatiate Sioux no longer are permitted to fight their terrible battles here.

The soil of Minnesota is rich with human blood! Many a thrifty farmer is accumulating wealth from the products of land made fertile by the carcases of warriors long since slain! Here it was that a deadly strife between the aboriginal Algonquin and the encroaching Sioux waged incessantly for a period of at least three hundred years!

Tradition tells us that the Sioux came hither ten times three hundred and fifty moons ago. From which I infer that their advent had some connection with the conquest of Mexico. When the Spaniards occupied the halls of the Montezumas, a large and powerful host of Indians were driven to the North. And the marked dissimilarity of the Chippeways (who declare that their Algonquin ancestors have been here forever) and the encroaching Sioux (who came from afar), is some evidence in favor of the hypothesis I suggest. Indeed, the relationship of the Sioux and the older native Indians of Minnesota must have been like that of the Greeks in Asia, the Romans in Greece, the Goths in Italy, and the English in Ireland. Conquest gave them a strong footing.

Another Thermopylæ was here!

Dakota land is really classic ground. And though no chiseled marble leaves a trace to mark any spot where heroes lie, innumerable mounds of buried dead are seen to prove that a race far superior to the miserable red man lived and died here in time long since past.

When I first beheld the great rolling prairies of this region my mind was filled with wondering retrospection. The rich soil is filled with roots of esculent production that have deteriorated in the course of time. Millions of acres are silently waiting for the plow to come and bring forth immense harvests of grain! And I can not resist the conviction that the timber was removed from the land now forming these immense prairies by a race of agricultural antediluvians, or an industrious and, perhaps, civilized nation existing and extinguished since the flood! The surface of Minnesota is found by settlers precisely in the shape and condition that the cultivated farms of the East might be thousands of years hence, if the inhabitants were to leave them now. Long-continued decay would remove every vestige of houses, barns, fences and walls. All the improvements would crumble to dust and totally disappear. But after an agricultural pulverization of the earth for years and years, the fields would remain cleared of timber to the end of time. With an annual decomposition of spontaneous crops perpetually increasing the fertility of the soil, in the course of incalculable time, abandoned farms would become quite as rich as the land of Minnesota.

So far as I have seen, there is no doubt of the correctness of this theory. I am aware that some great scholars will sneer at my deplorable ignorance of the learning which they pride themselves in. Yet the conclusion here stated, is happily established in my humble mind, and I record it without any fear of unanswerable contradiction.

But, hark! The stillness in yonder thicket is disturbed by a voice of complaint. A melancholy owl gives vent to his feeling by an occasional utterance that is very unpleasant to my ear. And in the distance, other birds of the same feather, and eyes, are amusing themselves with similarly unmelodious sounds. Then from the pine tree-top, high above my head, there comes a breathing of sorrow!

> In the sobbing of the wind,
>   Methinks I can hear the deep sigh
>   Of some lost spirit who can find
>   No place of rest up in the sky!

There is something about this solitary tree that makes me sad. I can not help thinking how long it has been standing sentinel here, cruelly neglected by the living world. And were I of that persuasion who believe in the transmigration of souls, I might imagine that it had been imbued with the spirit of a departed mortal—perhaps one of that extinct race who lived here and cultivated these great prairie fields long before even the red man claimed them for his hunting grounds. And when my musings wander into a mystic vein, it is quite easy for me to interpret that weird voice of sadness up there among those ever-green boughs, as articulated grief which has not been answered since the hour when its last kindred spirit fled!

A Rolling Prairie, in Dakota Land.

CHAPTER II.

ALADDIN'S magic lamp produced upon the instant all that his capricious fancy might suggest. But Aladdin and his wonderful lamp existed only in story. No magic arts, nor charms, nor incantations ever built a city where mankind could live. And that "God made the country, leaving men to build the towns," is a significant allusion submitted to infant minds at school.

In the usual course of progress, it requires considerable time to build a town of only moderate size. Many towns have been building ever since architecture was known to the inhabitants of the world, and a majority of them are not completed yet. Settlements are frequently made and towns begun in a rude wooden style, which never rise beyond the dignity of their beginning. Numerous cities have been founded in eligible situations and elaborately mapped out upon paper with prodigious expectation. Some of those paper cities continue to exist only in imagination, or with a melancholy display of failure evident at every door.

And before visiting St. Paul I amused myself with catechetical exercises of mind as to a repetition of sights previously seen. Hearsay indicated perfection; but experience has taught me not to rely upon all that I am told—while different people see the same object and regard the same subject in various lights according to the prejudice of their minds or in conformity with the pecuniary interests they may have in view.

Invalids came hither to regain their health. I was well aware of that. Many of them found what they sought. Some were doomed to die! A few continued to reside here after the recovery of their health, and a majority of them accumulated riches in addition to their worldly store. A number of the wealthiest citizens of St. Paul came to Minnesota with scarcely a dollar left in their pockets, after distinguished physicians had made significant allusion to the certainty of a premature grave. I heard all that some time ago. But seeing is believing; and I am now convinced beyond a doubt. The history of St. Paul could not be written without including innumerable instances of regained health and acquired wealth.

Devout pilgrims journey to Mecca for the salvation of their souls, to be made certain by prostrating their weary bodies near Mohammed's tomb. That is a pious delusion in Arab-land—while here the sick and the needy are sure to find redemption from disease and want by breathing the atmosphere and participating in the rare advantages peculiar to this beneficent shrine of life!

Two hundred years ago, a couple of Canadian *voyageurs* paddled Father Hennipin's canoe up the Mississippi River. Near Lake Pepin the Indians captured him and his men. They confiscated his goods and smashed the fragile bark in which he came. And then he was taken to lodge near the "Lake of Tears," so called because Aquipaguatin, the chief, wept half the night and finally compelled one of his own sons to participate in that recreation until morning.

Nearly a hundred years later, a venturesome Yankee trader, known as Captain Carver, also came up the Mississippi River in a canoe. Carver was the first white man to discover that mysterious subterranean council-chamber, or incantation hall, which the Indians called *Wakan-tebee*. The unexplored magnitude of that wonderful cavern was then said to contain a curious lake of transparent water and a fathomless abyss. It is under Dayton's Bluff, just beyond Trout Brook, a lively stream, fed by perpetual springs and gurgling amid the railroad improvements in the lower suburbs of St. Paul.

When Father Galtier, a missionary from the Catholic diocese of Dubuque, passed this spot, on his way to Fort Snelling, in April of the year 1840, he saw only a solitary log-cabin upon the site where the bright new city of so many thousand inhabitants now stands beyond the river there with its gas-lights gleaming in the darkness of night.

Soon after then, a number of families from Red River built their shanties near the solitary cabin; and the priest erected a log-house in which they might worship God. Fancying the need of a powerful protector, he named the new church "St. Paul," after his patron model of patience and courage. And then he desired that the settlement should take the same name.

But a very baneful influence was retarding the happy results labored for by the priest. Two great spirits were at war in the neighborhood of the new St. Paul's Church. While Galtier solicited salvation for the souls around him, the inspiration of a fiend caused his labors to be treated with scorn—and he found his field a hard one to till.

One Pierre Parrant, who was in the service of the fiend, opened a temple for his followers to worship in. Parrant was a Canadian *voyageur*, who acquired some notoriety from a facial deformity not very dissimilar to that of Caliban. Many people believed that he had but one eye. That was a mistake. He had two eyes. But the singularity of defect in his optical expression was so swinish, that even the Indians as well as the whites, unanimously bestowed upon him the derisive title of "Pig's Eye." Yet he cared not for that so long as they were his deluded slaves. He had a miserly heart, and loved nothing better than gold.

Parrant's temple became a popular resort. There was no sign over the door, nor any emblem of Deity or God to be seen upon the outside of the temple; and yet it was thronged with Dakotas and pale-faces who thirsted for *minne-wakan*—which is called "whisky" in our less poetical vernacular idiom. Parrant was a frontier rum-seller. No excise law could reach his jugs, his kegs, or his barrels. Business was lively in his groggery. It was lively during the day, and more than lively at night.

"Injun love rum!" I heard a Chippeway chief boasting that. And he added, "Injun's father love minne-wakan great many moons ago!"

The Dakotas, *couriers de bois, voyageurs, bois brule*, and degraded adventurers hanging around, soon elevated Parrant to the exalted position of chief liquor merchant in the place. Numerous other white skins, with heart-feelings figuratively darker than the color of their mangy hides, also established groggeries hard by. But none of them were patronized so liberally as Parrant. And indeed, if the recollection of my informant is correct, all the merchants who first opened stores in the settlement, sold as much whisky as they could.

I may say that whisky formed a great part of the early history of St. Paul; and for some years after, the place was spoken of only as "Pig's Eye," in honor of Parrant, the rum-fiend, rather than "St. Paul," out of respect to the church there of that name. And the small flock who availed themselves of pastoral teaching were almost hourly shocked by the terrible doings among the groggeries down near the water's edge.

The drunken Indian hordes, and the inebriate white men, went on carousing, until their own conduct threatened to exterminate them all together. Their orgies were frightful! They must get drunk. And Parrant and his brothers in evil were eager to drench them with liquid ruin!

Dakotas then called St. Paul the "place where Injun get minne-wakan!" Some would tramp hundreds of miles, in the worst of weather, to procure a keg full of the fire-water, so delicious to them. Without minne-wakan they were unhappy, and with it they were dangerously savage. If possible, they would be drunk months at a time—and, in all probability, until death terminated their existence entirely, if the liquor held out to the end. They would have minne-wakan; and to obtain it, barter away the very garments they wore—just as the miserable drunken creatures in some dismal precincts of New York are doing now while I am tracing these lines.

"Big Injun need much minne-wakan. Made to drink! Must have him now!" And as every Dakota fancied himself big, each one drank all he could get.

Old Indian Graves, found near Crow Wing, Minnesota.

Savages, when sober, must necessarily become demons under the inspiration of intoxicating drink. Pure whisky would have been bad enough for them to swallow. But Parrant and his colleagues in crime did not always sell even an inferior grade of that. Intent only upon enriching themselves at all hazards, the traffickers in ruin sold the ignorant red men a horrible liquid, which, by its virulent concitation of the mucous membrane, inflamed all their passions.

Into an ordinary barrel of thirty-two gallons capacity they placed at least a bushel of rank "black-twist" chewing tobacco, three or four gallons of bad whisky, and a quantity of raw vitriol, with river water sufficient to fill the cask! After standing some time the destructive fluid was served out to thirsty Dakotas, who almost immediately demanded dram after dram to satisfy those cravings produced by the inflammatory corrosion at work upon their intestines and organs of digestion! And I might add that this "Injun whisky" is still sold to the aborigines wherever they are found.

I once heard of an old toper who abandoned rum and took to camphene a short time before he murdered his wife and children! But the juice of rank tobacco, tinctured with any ingredient like vitriol, is unquestionably worse than burning fluids of ordinary kind.

Parrant poured out the poison and clutched his pay with an exulting smile! He sneered at the entreaties of the poor man's wife, and made no reply to the pursuasion of those who feared the danger that was brewing! And the wretched inebriates rolled out of his shanty into the mire, when they could find that soft and agreeable material to lie in.

And then they quarreled and fought! They bit off noses, broke craniums, dislocated spines, gouged out eyes and disemboweled each other with knives! They went raving mad, and killed each other with guns, billets of wood, stones and axes, and burned each other with bundles of blazing straw, and drowned themselves or their opponents in the river! They died from suicide, from freezing, and in all manner of ways!

The Furies, the Eumenides, Medusa, and all the monsters of history or fiction, were eclipsed in the frightful exhibitions produced by inebriated men and women! The hell of Virgil and of Dante was not more impressive than that created by ferocious passions, boiling with hatred, jealousy, old quarrels, and deadly antipathies in full blast! Shrieks from women and children, mingled with the yells of demons, and the howling of terrified dogs, added the terrors of hearing to the appalling sights enacted in "Pig's-Eye Pandemonium!" And it required the strenuous co-operation of the "people" to abate the "increasing cause" of alarm. Finally, respectable merchants began to arrive and erect stores, and a number of wealthy strangers were looking around for pleasant places.

And yet the whisky traffic continued until "Little Crow," chief of the Lightfoot band, who occupied the Indian village of Kaposia, on the opposite side of the river, some miles below, was shot by his own brother while in an inebriated condition. The chief did not die, but he began to foresee the terrible danger that threatened himself and his people, and thereupon solicited the mediation of the Indian agent stationed at Fort Snelling, which resulted in establishing a school!

And one dark, rainy *Sunday* morning in July, 1847, the first school in Minnesota was opened by Miss Harriet E. Bishop, a young lady of Eastern origin, who seemed to have been born purposely and educated expressly for the trying and thankless vocation of intellectual and moral preceptress. She migrated nearly two thousand miles from her native home, with the intention of devoting herself to the task of enlightening the red-skin papooses of the wild Dakota, and also teaching the progeny of the pale-face who shied away from the approach of civilization, as well as instructing the children of Christians seeking a habitation in what then appeared to be an unreclaimed earthly elysium. She "opened to a slim house," in a little log hovel covered with bark and chinked with mud, and previously used as a blacksmith shop. One apartment, ten by twelve feet square, with pegs driven into the logs on three sides to support board seats. Another seat was made by placing one end of a plank in a crack between the logs and then on a chair. This was for visitors. A rickety cross-legged table in the centre, and a "hen's nest in one corner," completed the "fixtures and goodwill."

Seven scholars came—three whites and four half-breeds, with a half-breed female visitor. One half-breed acted as interpreter. Thus, Miss Bishop not only established the first Sunday school in Minnesota, but she sustained it for at least one year without any assistance. And from that rude hovel of simple tuition, since then have nucleated countless school edifices which even surpass those of the older States. A bright future was dawning there.

The vulgar appellation of "Pig's Eye" grew intolerably odious to the ears of the better class of new-comers, and even the Dakotas were learning to grunt *Sip-all* instead of *Im-in-i-jas-ka*, which in their language signifies *white rock*. They had always called the place so because of the white, sugar-like color of a singularly beautiful

A Primitive Mode of Travelling "On Rail," as accomplished with the laborious assistance of Taurus, and uncomfortably enjoyed by Juvenile or Infirm Dakota Indians.

sandstone which lies beneath the top stratum of grayish rock forming the bluff upon which the city now stands.

But one night Parrant mysteriously disappeared, and none of his patrons could tell why he did not return. Some said he had made money enough, and wanted to find a place for the enjoyment of his wealth. Others contended that he went away quite poor. Many questions were asked which none could answer.

Very few cared to know why he went, and some were glad that he had really gone. Singular as it may seem, he had no enemies. All sober or pious people disliked him because of his nefarious traffic, but in other respects he escaped personal malice. In short, he loved no one, and no one loved him. His acquaintances only knew that he had gone. How he went and where his destination might be, never transpired to the knowledge of the pale-faces whom he left behind. And until they read this volume, the people of St. Paul can not tell what became of old Parrant. For now that nearly twenty-five years have elapsed since his mysterious departure, it remains for me to disclose his singular fate!

By the merest chance one day I trod upon a "*Lost Key.*" I always pick up whatever I am lucky enough to find; and perhaps my readers would laugh to see me in the humble attitude of search for a pin in the carpet or on the floor. However, that key unlocked the mystery so long concealing Parrant's grave!

But what terrible noise is that I hear? It is like the rumbling of far-off thunder, coming nearer at every growl! Now a wild scream startles the hooting owl, and it flutters to another bush. Louder roars the noise, and then a double scream, piercing enough to rouse the ancient dead who lie in dust upon these hills!

Hah! It is the wild neighing of an "iron-horse" and

the roar of a train of cars upon the track of the Milwaukee, St. Paul, and Minneapolis Railway, bringing the Eastern passengers and mail. Nearer comes the noise. The train is dashing down from Mendota Junction, and will presently arrive at its final destination, opposite the city.

Before the sun went down, I noticed that the depot in the distance was plainly seen from this lofty cliff—while now, in the feeble starlight, I can only imagine the arrival of the train. But presently I see the lanterns darting around and bobbing up and down, and fancy an undiscerned multitude of people, all travel-worn and eagerly impatient for their suppers.

But the iron horse is puffing and snorting again. Perhaps he, too, is impatient to enter his smoky stable and enjoy a night of repose. And by the dispersion of the flitting lights, I presume that the omnibuses, the baggage wagons, the carriages and the pedestrians are now ascending the great inclined bridge to the pavements of the city.

There! They have all gone, and quietude prevails once more upon this side of the river.

The sky is deeply blue and serenely clear. Like solitaire diamonds of colossal magnitude set in a sapphire ground, the planets fairly blaze, and the little orbs of borrowed light intensely shine. I am not addicted to star gazing, but the entire firmament has unusual attractions for me to-night. Surely I never saw so many celestial luminaries at one time before.

Venus is my favorite among the stars. I remember asking questions about her when a very small child. Somebody then told me that the "Evening Star" was the beautiful eye of the "Angel of Love!" The same person had previously impressed upon my infantile mind that the Sun was the "Eye of God!" And I also remember how I hid myself one day in a dark cellar, so that "God's Eye" could not see me while devouring a nice mince-pie which I had been tempted to purloin from the pantry in the house of my aunt. And then, when the pie was all eaten, I went out and skulked beneath the *arbor vita* bushes and the Norwegian pines that decorated the lawn—a miserable, trembling thief—with a penitent resolve never to steal any more pies!

But what is Jupiter now doing so near the "Angel of Love?" I never saw him in such close proximity to Venus before. I wonder if the astronomers will note this fact? It is certainly a rare phenomenon. The old fellow has gone away down into the southwestern horizon to meet her there. And he must have left one of his satellites behind, for I can perceive only three attending him now. Oh, if I had a powerful telescope in my hands, what a treat it would be to look at them while thus so near together! So near, did I say? I had forgotten that they are yet millions of miles apart!

How wonderful are the works of nature—the creations of Almighty God!

Learned astronomers tell us that we can not see more than a thousand stars in the clearest atmosphere, although from the first to the sixth magnitude inclusive, there are precisely three thousand one hundred and twenty-eight actually visible to mundane eyes. How exactly the science of astronomy can estimate numbers and size! And then, besides the visible stars, there are countless millions that shine throughout infinite space beyond the reach of mortal vision.

It is also said that those orbs of light emit a vast amount of warmth for the benefit of the planet upon which we live. Without their assistance the heat of the sun would not be sufficient to sustain either vegetable or animal life upon the surface of the earth. And if we credit the assertion of Pouillet, who has formed an ocular acquaintance with all the heavenly bodies, the heat furnished by the stars during a single year would be enough to melt a crust of ice seventy-five feet thick!

But the pretty stars do not deter me from thinking of the past—and my mind again reverts to this sphere of human life. And here I will present a likeness of "Little Crow," the chief whose misfortune resulted in the dawn of light!

Tah-o-a-doo-ta; or "Little Crow."

CHAPTER III.

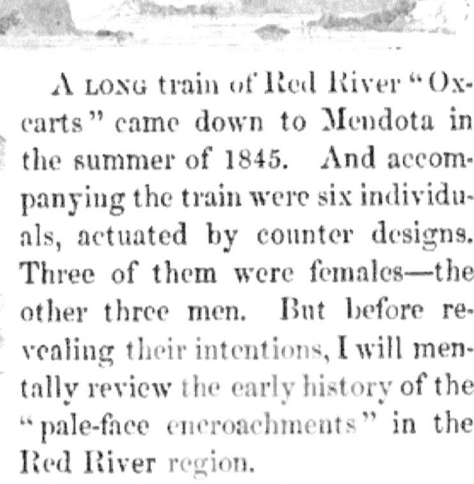

A LONG train of Red River "Ox-carts" came down to Mendota in the summer of 1845. And accompanying the train were six individuals, actuated by counter designs. Three of them were females—the other three men. But before revealing their intentions, I will mentally review the early history of the "pale-face encroachments" in the Red River region.

I think it was Prince Rupert who obtained a charter from Charles II., about two hundred years ago, covering the "rights of territory" bordering upon all the waters flowing into Hudson Bay. But the treaty of Utrecht, in 1714, somewhat divided the operations of the English and the French, who had both been competing for the fur traffic with the Indians. The French subsequently turned their endeavors more particularly in the direction of "The Lakes," the Assineboine and the Saskatchewan Rivers, until by the treaty of Versailles, they were compelled to retire with mortification and disgust. British subjects then had it all their own way—and in 1803, a wealthy organization was formed to establish a lucrative trade across the continent, by way of the "line of lakes," from Montreal to the Pacific Ocean.

Then followed a savage contest between the Hudson Bay Company and the new Association, which finally resulted in the erection of a fort on Red River—and also the establishing of a colony by "Earl Selkirk, a Scotch nobleman of high rank and large fortune"—as the flaming prospectus of his scheme at that time stated. But the ambitious Earl was not quite as successful as he anticipated. And yet a great number of Europeans were enticed thither by false representations. Some of the emigrants perished with hunger and cold; others escaped as best they could—and if they survived the hardships of a journey to the more hospitable settlements of "Brother Jonathan Pioneers," their future was generally made comfortable with realized hope and plenty.

Notwithstanding the sad fate of so many victims, the colony grew, and it became the chief source of agricultural supplies for the numerous trappers and traders employed by the Hudson Bay Company. The few hundred survivors made concubines of the Indian squaws, and with continual accessions of Irish and Scotch, the population went on increasing, until it now includes some ten thousand. Part of them are British Protestants, and part half-breed French of the Catholic faith—while many of them have no religion at all!

Selkirk Colony, with its ten thousand or more inhabitants, is perhaps the most curiously arranged settlement in the world. It consists of "strip-divided" farms, each having a narrow frontage of only six chains upon the banks of the Red River and Assineboine—thus extending for nearly a hundred miles! And those men who are pecuniarily interested in the fur trade, have good reasons for jealously guarding that wonderful El Dorado, which is almost entirely unknown to the more civilized people of the "outer" world.

But I may add that the British Government is now taking possession of the entire domain hitherto controlled by and belonging to the Hudson Bay Company. This is of some importance to the people of the United States, who have recently acquired such a vast territory beyond there. The fur-trading grant covers an area of more than two millions of square miles, lying east and west from the Atlantic Ocean to the Rocky Mountains, and north and south from the Arctic Ocean to Canada, and is intersected in every part by large rivers. A great portion of it abounds in agricultural and mineral wealth, and means of communication with the United States and the Atlantic Ocean may be easily established at every point by its numerous lakes and streams. The cession of this territory to the British Crown means the establishment of a regularly organized government there instead of the domination of a few trappers, who of course are only concerned about their own private interests, and therefore have made no attempt to develop the immense resources of their possessions. Whatever may be the ultimate disposition of the territory, the people of the United States should be interested and gratified in its development and eventual civilization.

In its early existence, many ladies of refinement and education were taken to the Colony. Some of them are said to have been quite beautiful. But the most charming was the wife of a gentleman having a consanguinity

The Beautiful Moonlight in Dakota Land.

with the Earl. Her husband had been sent out as an agent to look after the interests of his noble relation, and he took her with him. She was also accompanied by her daughter Leonore, and her aged mother, who was called Zorah. A name similar to that of her husband may be seen in the recently published business directory of St. Paul.

Madame Zorah, the wife's mother, was of Scotch birth. But she spent the best part of her youth in the gay city of Paris, where her beauty attracted the notice of the old Marquis Dupontavisse. She became the wife of the Marquis according to the rites of "morganatic" marriage—a popular institution among European noblemen who find it inconvenient to assume the responsibility of "cherishing" a beloved or an admired "object" for life. While her noble morganatic husband continued alive, he denied her nothing. But when he died, she had no further claims upon his estate. For awhile she subsisted upon the fragments of her lost position.

But as beauty fades from the cheek, so vanish the charms of many a belle who foolishly imagines that her powers of fascination will endure to the end of existence—and the morganatic widow of the deceased Marquis eventually found herself nearly destitute in the beautiful city of pleasure and the frightful city of want. And then she wept in anxiety, how she might also provide for the maintenance of her young daughter.

Trouble, misfortune, sickness—a thousand asperities, were not long in changing her appearance, so that nearly all the acquaintances of her youth and prosperity turned their eyes away. Her effeminate face and graceful person were gradually transformed into a masculine exterior, and finally she was bereft of every charm that might inspire love. The multitude coldly passed her by, and scarcely a smile encouraged her to live. Yet she was not of that desponding nature which seeks to end its sorrow in death. Suicide did not enter her mind then. She would rather fight than die. If her fellow-mortals jostled her rudely, she could try to jostle them in return. When fair means did not avail, other plans might succeed. At all events, she existed through the variations of sorrow that is unavoidable to her class and position, with at least one pure and holy feeling ever actuating the best impulses of her heart—and that was entwined around her child, whom she loved with almost an idolatrous devotion.

Circumstances induced her removal to London, where, through the patronage of a wealthy family, her child was not only reared and educated, but afterward admitted into society as an accomplished and beautiful lady. And almost the first thing she did was to fall in love with and marry a young exile from France. Soon after marriage, her husband ventured back to his native country, and there he died!

The Marquis Dupontavisse left two grandsons whom Zorah had never seen. And, unknown to her, one of those grandsons actually married her daughter—who, according to the denomination of consanguinity, thus became the wife of her nephew! But the singular circumstance was not revealed for many years after. The fruit of that unnatural alliance was a daughter.

It seemed useless to expect anything from her husband's estate—for, in the fashion of noble exiles, he had even concealed his proper name and title. There was no clue to aid her in establishing the just claims of a widow, and she finally married again.

She resided with her second husband for some time in Quebec, Canada. Eventually he became the Earl's agent to the Red River Colony, and she accompanied him thither. Thus her daughter Leonore was really the grandchild of the Marquis Dupontavisse by a double line of pedigree!

On their way to the Colony, they were joined by a lady from Montreal, who expressed a determination to journey thither with them. The Agent was rather pleased to have her society, and so she went along.

An agreeable traveling companion is not obnoxious at all times. Her name was Florinda. But she said very little about her previous history. Whether she had been married or always single, was a question that she left unanswered, for her new acquaintances to solve if they could. None failed to recognize her accomplishments and personal charms.

Madame Zorah did not like her any too well, nor did the Agent's wife. However, they fraternized with tolerable satisfaction to the end of their journey.

Soon after their arrival at the Colony, the Agent was recalled to Quebec—and he persisted in leaving his wife and her daughter, Leonore, to the care of Madame Zorah. His wife begged hard to accompany him; but replying that he would return in a short time, her tears and entreaties were all of no avail. Cheerfully she would have undergone any hardship or privation rather than be separated from him for a single day. It was love and devotion that induced her to brave the fatigue and the exposure of going with her husband from the comforts of a city residence to a rude wilderness habitation in the centre of America, and surely she would go back with him if he consented. But he positively refused. She must remain in the Colony to weep until his return.

She wept a long time. Many days came and went without even an affectionate letter to cheer her drooping

Lovely Night-Scene, near Fort Garry, on the Red River of the North.

heart. Three whole months passed in expectation, and still her husband did not return. Numerous strangers arrived, but none brought tidings from him.

At length one of the *voyageurs* who accompanied her husband, returned to say that he was drowned in Lake Superior. She then determined to leave the wilderness without further delay. Her mother asked how that was possible, when they were utterly destitute of money. She replied that she would borrow money of the *factors*; for they were her husband's friends. And she did try; but without success. Then she wrote a letter to his relations in Montreal.

It was easy enough to write, but an answer would be a long time coming. She wrote six letters—one a month—in succession, without getting any response. Then she wrote the seventh, to which an answer promptly came. But instead of getting consolation and relief, she was filled with deeper anguish by a curt intimation that the benevolent father of her deceased husband could not think of acknowledging her claims of relationship, for reasons which he vaguely named!

Such a letter very naturally sent her to bed heart-sick and nearly bereft of reason. And while her mother and her daughter did all they could to cheer and comfort her, Florinda showed even greater solicitude than previous circumstances might seem to warrant. And those previous circumstances were questionable to a great extent.

An opulent man named Tashae, connected with the fur-trading interests of that region, after having enjoyed quite an animated flirtation with Florinda, gave unmistakable signs of admiration for the widow, whose husband had very evidently gone forever. Indeed, from the conduct of Tashae, it was evident that he correctly surmised or really knew more about the actual position of the grief-stricken widow than she did herself. But his sentimental addresses had been strictly confined to Florinda, until the reported death of the husband gave him an opportunity for transferring them. And as Florinda and the widow lodged beneath the same roof, the former was quick to perceive a decline of her influence with Tashae. Then she watched them closely in and out of doors.

Jealousy does not always exhibit a violent demonstration. In some hearts there lurks a subtile deceit particularly adapted for safe concealment of the direst purposes of revenge. Hence it frequently occurs that an innocent victim is unconsciously fettered in the toils of hate. And thus for some time Florinda had been industriously planning evil. Quite probably she understood domestic intrigue, though it did not appear certain that she would succeed in becoming the wife of Tashae. She tried hard enough—and it was a very laudable intention for an unprotected woman; but not properly appreciated by a less anxious individual of the opposite sex.

The "green-eyed monster" has ever been a prime instigator of ruin alike to the evil and the pure-minded believers in that juvenile god who does so much mischief with his bow and arrows, and it was not surprising that Florinda should increase her malice toward the innocent widow in proportion to the growing preference which Tashae made no effort to conceal.

But the widow cared nothing for Tashae's admiration. She was insensible to every feeling save grief for the loss of her husband, and distress from the tone of that cruel letter—and therefore did not perceive the alarming exigency of her position. Her only remaining wish was to leave the Colony forever. Yet she could not accomplish that without friends or money.

Despair knows no law but that of self-preservation; and, counting upon Tashae's friendly attentions, the sorrowing widow reluctantly solicited him to loan her sufficient means to convey herself, her daughter and her aged mother, to any locality within the bounds of civilization, where they might obtain employment, and thereby earn enough to repay him and eventually recross the ocean.

Florinda was heartily pleased with that proposition. But Tashae did not intend to part with the widow yet. He and Florinda had different opinions regarding the widow's health. Tashae contended that she would not be able to endure the fatigue of an "Ox-cart" journey for thirty or forty days. Florinda declared that it would completely restore her. As a rival, she wished her at the other side of the world—and then she might have the field all to herself.

And even before the period of mourning was over, Tashae asked the widow to become his wife. He would then gratify her every wish. His presumption brought a flat refusal. And still he persisted. Arguments and persuasion were used upon one side, while resentment or scorn was hurled from the other.

Tashae was a bold, bad man, with plenty of money; and he disliked to be baffled. He could and he would do whatever he pleased, where neither religious influences, nor courts, nor juries compelled a strict adherence to moral laws. But an influence which he could not control was already at work.

The unhappy widow fell sick, and Florinda became a very attentive nurse.

Physicians of great knowledge or skill were scarce in

A Quaint Little Church (and Mission School) at Pembina, in the Far North-west.

the Colony; and Florinda suggested that Kaskadino, a half-breed, who had some reputation as a "medicine man," should be called in to prescribe.

The medicaments of an Indian doctor are very simple, and precisely those used by Chiron and Esculapius, in olden time. The half-savage physician may be ignorant, but I have read that when Hippocrates began to mix theories with medicine, its healing powers grew less. And while some sneer at the mummery of the "medicine dance" and manipulative pow-wows of the savage, I contend that such imposture is not a tenth as bad as the frauds of sectarian "systems" or antagonistic "schools" of *materia medica*, as practiced in the midst of civilization. The Indians know of certain herbs or roots that will cure almost any disease they are liable to contract; and with all their unnecessary juggling over the sick, or the "possessed," they maltreat and kill fewer than do our pretending quacks.

But Indian doctors are sadly ignorant of physiology. They only know that a particular remedy is generally efficacious in certain diseases or injuries. In their opinion, all maladies are bilious; and they administer either the emetics or cathartics of their humble pharmacopœia. External wounds or eruptions are speedily cured. The small-pox is an exception. Some years ago, that horrible disease was sent among them by goods from Canada; and, despite all their remedies, it carried off whole bands!

A "medicine man" is supposed to possess some mysterious influence beyond the curative power of the pharmaceutical ingredients that he may compound. The early French explorers used the word "medecin" for doctor, and since then "medicine" has signified anything of a mysterious meaning. But "medicine men" are prophets and conjurers, who claim to perform wonderful miracles through charms and incantations. A sick Indian imagines that he is afflicted by the spirit of some animal, or, more likely, by the spirit of an enemy; and he sends a horse or a blanket for the doctor to come and turn it out. The messenger is stripped to run swiftly, retaining only his "breech-cloth" and carrying a bell. Entering the doctor's teepee, he kicks him with his foot and rings the bell. Then there is a race back to the sick man's lodge. If the doctor overtakes the messenger and kicks him in return, he will keep his fee and stay at home until sent for again. However, Kaskadino was not summoned in that way to attend the widow.

Florinda had already agreed with the rascal. She not only suggested his services, but proceeded to act without the delay of consultation, and at once began to administer the remedies prepared by him.

The grandmother and the daughter were too intent upon the condition of their loved one, raving in delirium upon her bed, to scrutinize the conduct of Kaskadino and Florinda. And if there was a peculiar look of inquiry in the face of the latter as the former delivered his potions, it escaped observation!

Florinda smoothed the pillow for the sufferer's head, bathed her temples with cold water, and presented the draughts for her to drink.

It did not take long to wear out a frail remnant of existence with fever and doubtful remedies given. And not even the neighbors were able to interpret the strange flashing of exultation in Florinda's eye as she daily witnessed the ebbing of life.

The pale forehead became smoother, and the blue veins might be traced under the skin. The eyes grew dim, and occasionally wandered with a vacant stare, showing that reason had gone. And the pinched nostrils and the parched lips were drawn tighter each succeeding day.

One night the dying mother tried to speak, but it was only an incoherent whisper. A convulsion and a shiver, and then a deep sigh announced that her spirit had gone forever!

In the brief silence, Madame Zorah bowed her head to weep. But Leonore rose gasping for breath, and frantically shrieked, "Mother!"

A voice was heard in response. It came from Kaskadino, the medicine-man, who, unobserved, had been watching at the outer door.

In a hollow tone he said, "I can do no more!"

As the dark man spoke those words, a tremor disturbed the composure of Florinda. She could not meet his piercing gaze; and with a sign of fear, her head was turned away. When she ventured to look at him again, he pointed at the corpse; and then pressing one hand against his heart, in a significant manner, abruptly quit the house!

The "Great Golgotha," in "Devil Lake" Region, where the Bones of Buffalo, slaughtered by the Indians a long time ago, are bleaching for miles around.

CHAPTER IV.

Past suffering and endurance for the sake of her darling child, had given Madame Zorah an expression of features somewhat older than she really was. But most of her trials were experienced before little Leonore came into the world to share the love she had to bestow.

With the anxious solicitude of a mother, she watched the maturing of her beloved offspring into a lovely woman; and, after seeing her twice a bride and once a mother, it was hard to look upon that young mother lying in death!

She kissed her forehead the last time, when it was icy cold, and then saw the dismal coffin-lid screwed down, before they put it away in the damp earth!

The *sœurs grises*, or "gray nuns," came out of their cloister in the Colony, and assisted in the sad preparation of the corpse. They were "Sisters of Charity," and such missions self appointed to perform.

The obsequies were simple and plain. Only grandma

and the orphan wept in mourning! They were frantic with bitter woe, while other eyes calmly looked on in sober silence, undimmed by a sign of tears!

The grave was in a quiet corner of the field of the dead, near the grove at the river side, where many others had been buried before. And when the heavy clods fell in upon the coffin with that appalling sound, the mourners' hearts almost ceased to beat, so suffocating was their grief!

The old grave-digger reverently heaped up a little mound; and with his spade he patted the fresh earth into shape! And then they all slowly turned away!

O, how cruel it seemed to leave the loved one there to feed the worms, and dissolve in eternal decay!

But Florinda desired not to accompany the mourners when they followed the coffin to the grave. She stayed at home to brood over her crime—and to wonder if the living would ever discover the wrong done to the dead!

And Tashae did not look upon her with any more favor after her rival's death. He then began to woo the daughter, whose greatest inheritance was her mother's magnificent eyes.

Leonore was scarcely sixteen, and beautiful enough to inspire a purer heart than Tashae's with admiration and love. But Tashae could not appreciate such love as Leonore might give. His mind was gross and his heart was cold. Strange that he interested Florinda! But whether she loved him or not, her ambition was to be his wife. One life had been sacrificed with that object, and another would leave her mistress of the situation.

Kaskadino quickly perceived her thoughts, and shook his head with a hoarse grunt, which signified a very emphatic "No!" He was a cunning as well as a wicked demi-savage. Well aware that she aspired to be Tashae's wife, he easily understood why the widow had been in her way; and it became equally as evident that the life of the innocent daughter was in danger, too!

Kaskadino lent his aid in the first crime, hoping to get Florinda in his power. Moreover, according to his theory, what he had already done, should induce her to follow him ever after as his obedient slave. And perceiving that her regard for Tashae continued as strong as it was before he conspired with her against the widow, he not only grew jealous himself, but firmly resolved that the daughter should not be harmed, while there remained the least prospect of his rival continuing to woo her.

Tashae and Kaskadino were said to be friends. But I will not believe that any tie of friendship could actually exist between two men of such widely different origin and position. However, they were not enemies, to judge from the pleasant words exchanged by them whenever they met.

It soon became necessary for Tashae to visit Mendota in person, upon business of great importance connected with the settlement of pecuniary affairs controlled entirely at that place. And Kaskadino would accompany him thither. The half-breed was very familiar with the route. In summer, he often traveled it with an "Oxcart," and in winter with "Dog-sledges" and snow shoes.

From Kaskadino's great interest in Florinda, a stranger would infer that he was an unmarried man, while he really had a gigantic wife and half a dozen robust children, all living within half a mile of her abode. For, in conformity with an established rule of the Hudson Bay fur-trading interests, all their vassals are required to appropriate squaws—and he long ago married *a la mode du pays*, just as his father did before him.

Kaskadino was only a simple *bois brule* and a rough teamster—one of those mongrel beings of illegitimacy and miscegenation, who have no pedigree, no nation, and no God!

If the true history of Selkirk Colony should ever be written, it would reveal every species of fraud, crime and atrocity that is enacted in a populous city, made hideous there by its isolation from the civilized world. A naturally beautiful region—but the unfortunate settlers were controlled by relentless speculators and surrounded by insatiate savages, in the midst of a wilderness, where the summer is very short and the winter so intensely cold that the mercury freezes in the thermometer, and large trees and great rocks are split asunder with the frost! There is no probability that its history will ever be written.

It was the middle of summer when Tashae found it necessary to visit Mendota. Of course he would accompany the Ox-train then preparing to start. Had it been in the winter time, dogs would have taken the place of oxen.

A week or so before the Ox-train was ready to start, Major Levasseur arrived from Fort Snelling. That was not his real name, but it answered every purpose. He bore the stamp of a gentleman. His cultivated demeanor and distinguished personal appearance commanded the profound deference of all whom he met. He spoke English fluently, though that was not his native tongue.

Major Levasseur's mission there was to perfect a negotiation of commercial importance with the so-called Governor of the Colony. And consummating which almost immediately, he gave notice to his small retinue that he intended to return the next morning. But hearing that an Ox-train would soon go down, he resolved to wait and join the expedition.

The Governor referred him to Tashae, through whose courtesy he made the acquaintance of Florinda; and she, in turn, could not avoid introducing him to Madame Zorah and Leonore, the beautiful orphan, who were still crushed with grief.

There certainly was some strange fatality following in the path of Madame Zorah. One grandson of her noble morganatic husband made her daughter his wife in London, and then away there in the far-off wilderness of America, the other grandson came to besiege the heart of Leonore! But Madame was ignorant of that. Had she known the truth, Major Levasseur would have been less welcome. As it was, she hoped that Leonore's beauty might prove their salvation. Should she captivate him, he would remove them from the Colony.

Levasseur had seen his brother's bride in London, and indistinctly remembered her magnificent eyes. But when he tried to recollect where he had seen such eyes as Leonore's, it was impossible to tell. Little did he dream of their real origin!

Florinda went to work again. She seemed to entertain the most prodigal views of flirtation. In her opinion, every individual of the opposite gender was legitimately a fair prize, if she could catch him. I have encountered similar birds of passage in various grades of society. And how unaccountable it is that they so seldom marry. It is also a notable fact that when one of these prodigal coquettes succeeds in nabbing a husband, the unfortunate individual almost invariably and speedily seeks consolation from celibate companions, who, after ridiculing his folly to their heart's content, kindly receive him as a tolerated *protege* for a butt of reference when the bliss of matrimony is brought into question.

However, Levasseur's skillful address quickly disarmed Florinda. He effectually assumed a strictly paternal interest in the gentle orphan, without the remotest idea that she was really his own niece. But he understood the art of wooing too well to fail when the object was so richly worth the pure love of a noble heart in return.

The grave held Leonore's mother, and yet it seemed to Madame that she was with her still. Leonore's presence kept that love alive. Nevertheless, the resemblance between Leonore and her mother was noticeable in nothing except her eyes. Those were precisely like her mother's. Perfectly black, and remarkably large, with a melting lustre that the beholder would hardly ever forget. Her mother's eyes captivated her father, and now his brother came to fall in love with hers! A marvelous coincidence in life! Not an imaginary position—but an actual misadventure in social life!!

Madame was not aware that the grandson of the proud old Marquis Dupontavisse stood ready to kneel at her granddaughter's feet. But she smiled when Levasseur said that Leonore's lustrous black eyes recalled another pair he had seen somewhere before. She had no reason to suspect that Levasseur ever saw the eyes of Leonore's mother!

Had Levasseur arrived before her mother died, there might have been a recognition. But entirely ignorant of all that, Madame congratulated herself on the probability of realizing the scheme which suddenly inspired her heart. She would let the stranger woo Leonore until he took them back to the civilized world, and there he must either marry her or go his way, and leave them to pursue theirs.

Thus the grandmother planned—to lose or to win! In that desperate game she was staking at least one pure human soul!

Tashae obliged Levasseur with such arrangements as he required to accompany the Ox-train; and Florinda exerted herself to look captivating. But while merely thanking them for their good nature, Levasseur became deeply interested in the sorrows of the beautiful orphan. He listened to her story, and generously offered to convey them hence.

Tashae was sorely vexed when Levasseur made known his magnanimous intention, and would have opposed it if he dared. But he feared to displease a man whose influence could remove him from his position. So while chafing beneath compulsion, he put on a smile of approbation, and hoped for a favorable result during their long journey.

The evening before their departure, Levasseur accompanied Leonore and her grandmother to take a last look at her mother's grave!

It was a sad picture to see those stricken hearts weeping over the little mound of earth that covered the remains of their dear one gone forever! And when Levasseur raised Leonore from the crouching posture in which she wept with her head buried in her grandmother's arms, and kissed her as a father might a darling child, an observer would have ejaculated, " God bless that man !"

The night passed, and morning came. Already the Ox-carts were moving. One after the other they fell into line. And when the last started, the foremost was far away.

Fort Pembina, with Half-breed Teepees; and the Arrival of an "Ox-train."

Madame Zorah's hollow cheek was not so pale, nor were Leonore's beautiful eyes so red, when their benefactor kindly and tenderly lifted them both upon easy riding horses. A long and a rough road lay before them—but hope urged them on!

The sun rose bright and fair, the wild birds were caroling in the trees, and the delicious odor of neglected flowers perfumed the air.

Adieu, Selkirk—adieu!

And mother's grave? Dear mother! Farewell!

Then also good-by to the "land of windmills" with their grotesque wheel-sails whirling upon giant arms, or hanging motionless when there was no breeze to give them motive power. They are a feature of antiquity blended with the other romantic associations peculiar to Selkirk Colony.

At the junction of the Assineboine and Red Rivers, they passed Fort Garry, floating above the gloomy walls of which a blood-red flag revealed the monogrammatic *signum* of the Hudson Bay Company. And opposite the fort, they saw the half-ruined walls of the cathedral which was erected many years before and never finished outside or in. The rough stone abutments and facades were surmounted with two steeples. And the heavy chime of bells in one of them seemed to jar the dingy timbers in the open tower with its framework still naked to the eyes of every passer-by. All those quaint objects faded from the travelers' sight as they journeyed on in hope of enjoyment yet to come.

Kaskadino had duties to perform. But while trudging along at the side of his oxen, he now and then hurled a revengeful glance far to the rear, where Tashae was riding on horseback accompanied by Florinda.

That wicked woman had become one of the party

through the skillful exercise of her cunning. She did not want to lose sight of Tashae, while Leonore was near him; and he acquiesced in her going, for the sake of a pleasant traveling companion on his return.

The Red River Ox-cart has wheels at least six feet high. Such a great diameter is to facilitate their progress over roads that would seem utterly impassable to a citizen's eye. The shafts are similar to those of an ordinary dray, but extend from the animal's shoulder beyond the rear of the box and rest on a level. Thus, the load is not easily displaced by violent jolting nor liable to dip into the muddy sloughs. The spokes pass entirely through the deep, wide rim of the wheels, and slant out some inches beyond the hub, thus forming a brace at each side of the vehicle to prevent it upsetting. Only a single ox is attached to each cart—though sometimes a lazy driver has been known to tie the horns of his patiently toiling beast to the rear end of the cart ahead; and so on, stringing a lot together—in which position their poor necks must suffer at any unexpected jolt.

The most singular feature of the cart and harness is that not a particle of iron need be used in their construction. Only ash or swamp-oak wood, roughly hewn with hatchets, forms the vehicle. The harness is similar to that used in more civilized parts of the world two hundred years ago. A buffalo-hide collar, stuffed with moss, supports the hames, which are connected with the shafts by short traces of rawhide and wooden pins. A band passes entirely around the animal's body, resting upon a small rude saddle at the back, after wrapping the shafts to keep them from shaking about. The hold-back strap passes over the hips and connects with the shaft on each side in a peculiar way.

Nine hundred pounds is considered a good load for

an Ox-cart, and thirty miles far enough to travel in one day. Every six or eight miles, the oxen are allowed to feed. Prairie grass is the only food they get. While the oxen crop the grass, the people lunch on wild game or *pemican*. After an hour's delay, they resume their journey as before.

An army of one hundred thousand crazy soldiers, marching with a *calithumpian* band, could not surpass the awful noise made by a train of several hundred Ox-cart wheels when in motion. The axle-trees are greased with a composition of lye and buffalo fat, which quickly slushes out, leaving the friction to produce the most doleful sounds ever devised to torture human ears or to demoralize a sensitive mind. A lazy, creaking whine, as if all the imps of pandemonium were singing themselves to sleep after a high old spree.

At Red River, a cart costs from fifteen to thirty dollars, and, with proper care, may be used five or six years, providing a new axle-tree is put in every spring. They are employed in carrying merchandise out to the British possessions and bringing in furs. The Hudson Bay Company use at least eight hundred at the present time; and individuals are running a thousand or so more. Each load is packed under a second-quality buffalo hide, which is first soaked to be tightly drawn—thus forming a sure protection against the weather.

The train that brought down Madame Zorah and Leonore, included nearly fifty carts, and quite as many people. The Captain had his wife, and some of the drivers had their wives and children with them. At sunset, the flag was pulled down. And then the cattle were unharnessed, and the carts all backed up in a circle around the camp-fires, inside of which they and the people, and dogs and horses, were comparatively secure from external harm. The evening was spent in telling stories and card-playing, or whatever might suit their fancies. After a horrid sleep, the flag was hoisted again; and they were all up and away the next morning an hour before the sun appeared in the sky.

But as if the "wheel melodies" of the previous day were not abundantly sufficient for the extreme enjoyment of the organic sense of human hearing, two other styles of music were introduced at night. Purely natural, both of them. The barking of prairie wolves not unfrequently deterred the inexperienced travelers with the caravan from sleeping as soundly as they might in bed at home. Indeed, the close proximity of significant growls had some tendency to produce a trifling sensation in the minds of the half-breed ox-drivers who were accustomed to such lullabies to intensify their dreams. The wolves not only growled and barked, but they seemed to be carnivorously inclined. And the traditional theory of their indiscriminate appetites has been well established by them devouring mankind, regardless of age or sex. The ladies were somewhat alarmed when they heard a retaliative whine between the dogs inside the circular camp, and their uncivilized cousins who prowled hungrily without. Then the exquisite song of the mosquitoes that filled the air in quest of nourishing subsistence, also disturbed the composure of Madame in particular. She violently abominated that species of insectile torments, and mentally vowed never to incur similar punishment by a second journey in the land where they exist at certain, or rather uncertain, seasons to an extent entirely beyond the conjectural scope of people who have not been there to realize the truth by personal experience.

With the primitive simplicity of conveyances, invented before the existence of Tubal Cain, the quaintly-fashioned carts creaking, and the bovine hoofs clattering upon the trail—and with men, women and children in romantic attire, the winding cortege-caravan somewhat resembled a procession of crusaders foraging for plunder, or a horde of pilgrims in quest of promised rewards that lie afar.

The captain's authority is absolute when once in command, and the multitude all obey. As the pillar of cloud was to the camp of the children of Israel, so is the flag of these modern sons of Ishmael to them. When it is hoisted at dawn, every one must rise and be moving. It flutters in the breeze all day upon the march, and goes down with the sun at night. A leading ensign, a guide—an animated signum of life, in the tramp, tramp, over the hills and far away!

Hah! Again my reverie is broken by a startling sound. Now I hear the tolling of a bell beyond the wide river! The strokes are regular and solemn—and I count ten, eleven, twelve! Precisely the midnight hour!

And while the multitude of people in the city are nearly all slumbering comfortably abed, I am lingering here alone upon this uninhabited hill. An irresistible impulse brought me up here to enjoy a sunset view, and for seven long hours since then, some strange spell has kept me chained to these rocks.

Midnight View of an "Ox-train" Camp.

CHAPTER V.

I am not addicted to imaginary fears; but, at this particular moment, a very unpleasant sensation disturbs the usual placidity of my nerves. To be candid, I am suddenly and seriously impressed with a vague comprehension of the weird-like scene surrounding me at such an hour. Midnight solitude in a spot like this, does not tend to inspire a common mortal with the most exhilarant feelings.

The tones of that bell must have produced this strange emotion. I can not tell why, but the tolling of a bell is sure to make me sad. Even those "holiday chimes" in the church towers, sound doleful to me. And then, too, the "merry marriage bells," so often meant for joy, seem to say in my ear, "Come and laugh with us to-day, for perhaps to-night we'll die!"

What if an inebriated savage, either Sioux or Chippeway, should chance to wander this way and ruthlessly despoil me of my scalp? Having "no hair upon the top of my head," might not save me from his sanguinary intention. And what if half a dozen aborigines, filled with the evil inspiration of minne-wakan, should surprise me here? Yet that is not possible now—for the "bad Injuns" have all been sent away.

And then that mournful breathing up in the pine tree-top, is so sadly suggestive of a lost spirit hovering near! Nevertheless, I am not fearful of a ghostly apparition. Even when a child, I could not be taught to dread spectral horrors, nor to shun grave-yard terrors, the darkest night in the year. Indeed, I once slept at night upon a marble tomb.

Strolling through a grand old cemetery on a pleasant evening, I sat down to muse. Sleep overpowered me; and, instead of a visit from ghosts or goblins, I realized a marvelously romantic dream, in which there was much more truth than fiction.

Haunted houses are very terrifying to morbidly superstitious people, whose absurd fancies lead them to suspect that a spiritual emissary of evil is lurking in every dark nook and gloomy retreat. And now I remember a ghost adventure, or rather a ghost hunt, in which I participated some years ago.

The sighing of the breeze among the branches of the solitary pine, recalls that adventure. It was in a deserted school-house standing at the edge of a small forest of pines. A little edifice of stone, erected long before I came into the world, was standing somewhat remote from any habitation; but in the midst of a thickly-populated agricultural district, so that it might be convenient to the farmers living in either direction. Not far distant was the shire town with its stores, and its shops, and a particularly shabby tavern. The tavern was all the more unpleasant in consequence of the landlord having a nearly grown-up idiotic son, who frequently terrified the neighbors and the guests by malicious depredations or raids of lunatic diversion. He had, nevertheless, learned to read and write—but mathematics he could not understand.

His favorite amusement was industriously tormenting the neighbors' cats. So far did he carry his diversion in the feline community, that nearly all the affrighted Tommies and Tabbies would scamper out of sight the instant he appeared or even his voice was heard.

This tantalizing propensity of the imbecile, in such a delightful pursuit, won for him the appropriate *sobriquet* of "Cattey"—by which he was familiarly designated among the more *compos mentis* inhabitants of the town. I believe that all villagers select some particular individual of the community upon whom they unanimously crack their jokes and play their tricks. In conformity with that popular rule, Cattey was made the acknowledged *butt* of those who were addicted to ridicule or fond of fun.

He never killed any cats, but displayed a marvelous talent for devising novel methods of annoying and torturing them. One old masculine rather disputed his right to "hiss and skat!"—and frequently inflicted gashes upon his legs, arms, hands and face, *pugnis et calcibus*. But instead of exasperating the Idiot into a violence that might have resulted in his own destruction, the spunky old cat thereby won the admiration and esteem of his foolish tormentor.

This theme reminds me of the ethical discourse of "one old maid in a thousand," who cherishes an abhorrence for the entire feline race. She compares their characteristics to everything mean in human nature—

and says, "I hate cats. They havn't one of the virtues, but all the vices. They are deceitful and ungrateful—and they'll steal. You can't bribe them to be faithful, nor can you arouse their pride by ill-treatment. Spurn a dog's friendly advances, and it will shy off insulted; but you may kick a cat out of the house ten times a day, and it will sneak in and pur-r-r-r around you hypocritically whenever it smells cream. It will caress you without any love. It will return to the house you have left because it has been comfortable there. But it will never follow you like a dog does through sickness, sorrow and want, and then lie moaning on your grave when your friends have all gone off and forgotten where you lie. I tell you that I abominate them all—from the old gray cat squalling out of doors after people have all gone to bed, to the Maltese kitten on the rug in front of the parlor fire."

The old school-house near the forest of pines, had been managed by a male pedagogue in the winter and by an exemplary "marm" in the summer, from year to year, until eventually a young lady of New England origin filled the vacant chair.

The tavern-keeper's silly son saw the new teacher, and fell in love with her. He said he was old enough to have a wife. But she declined his offer of marriage, and repulsed him so harshly that he resolved to seek revenge. She thought lightly of his threat, and went on in the even tenor of her way without the least fear of harm.

Her school consisted of only nine pupils, all told. Six little girls, two little boys, and Jane, a large wench, made up the number. In Jane, the teacher had a very warm friend.

The Idiot was frequently seen lurking about in the

pines. But Jane kept on the alert. One day he approached the school-house and looked in at the window near Jane's seat. After frightening the little children and winking at the teacher, he wrote with a pencil on the window-sill. Then laughing in a strange manner, he slowly walked off out of sight among the pines.

When the Idiot was gone, Jane read in the large characters plainly written upon the window-sill:

"I'll come when that nigger aint here, and fix you off then. If you resist me, I shall take out your heart and keep it to carry on my watch-chain. My knife is a new one. Yesterday I sharpened it up on father's grindstone. Its edge is as keen as Uncle Josh's razor."

A few hours afterward school was dismissed for the day, and the children scampered off to their homes. But, suspecting danger, Jane lingered to accompany the teacher.

They closed up the shutters as usual, and were just ready to emerge from the door, when the Idiot stood before them. His face was distorted with an exulting grin, and uttering an incoherent exclamation he grasped the teacher's arm.

Totally paralyzed with fear from his sudden reappearance after what he had written upon the window-sill, she could neither resist nor scream. And with mouthing, maniacal chuckles, the Idiot dragged her back into the dark room! The struggle was quickly over!

Two blows from an axe and a heavy fall! A long moan and gurgling sounds! And then all was still!

A stream of warm, crimson blood ran across the floor and gathered in a pool where the light shone in at the open door!

"You have killed him!" shrieked the teacher. "He is dead!"

Cut Nose; or "Me Good Iujan." A Tender-hearted Sioux Convict, who was executed for Butchering Nineteen White People.

A long, loud, wild scream came from Jane as she darted out of the school-house, and fled into the pines! The teacher called and called, but Jane did not return! Flying, whither none could tell, she disappeared forever!

A farmer then chanced to be passing along that way, and, lifting the corpse into his wagon, he carried it to the village tavern.

The teacher's story was believed in consequence of Jane's flight. But after the corpse of the Idiot was laid in the ground, she departed for a distant town. And there was no more school in the old stone house at the edge of the forest of pines!

I slept in that miserable village tavern eight or ten years after the school-house tragedy had been performed. Business connected with the opening of a new railway called a friend of mine thither, and I accepted an invitation to accompany him. While there, a villager related to me the whole story, with a declaration that the house was haunted.

After the Idiot's funeral it had not been visited by any one. But groans, such as he was supposed to have uttered with his last breath, were frequently heard at night-time by persons obliged to journey that way. It was generally believed that a ghost must be there at such hours, in just the same condition which the Idiot's body was when he struggled in the agony of death.

I laughed at the villager when he related the ghost part of his story; and a very large, swarthy teamster thought to intimidate me by saying that I was "afeered" to enter the old school-house after night. He boasted that the neighbors dare not go in; and also assured me that the window-shutters still remained closed precisely as the teacher and Jane had left them.

I accepted the teamster's challenge upon condition that he and some of his comrades should accompany me and point out the location of the house. To this he very reluctantly assented. There was no moon at the time; and so we started off in the twilight, followed by nearly all the villagers who knew what was going on. We soon came to the edge of the forest, and there the teamster stopped short. He said that I might easily find it by continuing on through the pines, which seemed impenetrable to me. I heard a million sighs among the ocean of green boughs as they responded to the wafting of the evening breeze! A doleful requiem that would express all the grief in the world! And the narrow road was shrouded in gloom! I could not think of groping my way alone through such a dreary place to confront the ghostly inhabitant of a haunted house.

I spent some time trying to ridicule the teamster's fears, and he finally concluded to "see me through," as he expressed it, if first allowed to "wet his whistle" with the whisky-bottle carried in a comrade's pocket. And when his whistle was in tune, he insisted that the "whole crowd" should go along. They finally consented; and we marched on through the sighing pines to the air of Yankee Doodle, which the teamster whistled with marvelous skill.

But as we approached the far edge of the pines, his whistle grew fainter, and finally ceased altogether. He then squeezed my arm tightly, and informed me in a whisper that the haunted house was not more than a hundred yards ahead. I peered through the opening among the trees and saw a dim outline of something.

Having an axe and a dark lantern, I made them promise not to desert me while I reconnoitered. Silently and cautiously I drew near the dilapidated edifice—and, sure enough, I distinctly heard a heavy groan! But it seemed to me that the sound came from under the house; and so I very quietly proceeded to walk around the premises with minute inspection. At the rear I discovered, by the aid of my lamp, an open passage-way leading down into the cellar; and just at that moment a repetition of the mysterious noise caused me to halt.

It occurred to me that such groans could not proceed from a ghost, or from anything unnatural. I noticed a peculiar cadence that was familiar to my ear; and at once turned the full light of the lantern through the opening in the wall, to behold what brought a peal of laughter from me loud and merry enough to inspire the trembling villagers with courage to approach. And then the teamster frankly admitted that they were all "darned fools" for imagining the lamentations of swine to be those of an Idiot's ghost!

The cellar door was unclosed at the time of the tragedy, and a small herd of "wood-hogs" found therein a very comfortable retreat. And as it is impossible for those eccentric animals to lodge together without a perpetual indulgence in piteous complainings about each other's selfish encroachment in bed, the unknown tenants of the old school-house cellar quite innocently and very naturally disturbed the stillness of the night with their doleful griefs. The villagers all laughed very heartily over their long-entertained supposition of a ghost; and two or three of them emphatically declared that they never believed in "hants" of any kind.

While one of the disbelievers was vehemently reiterating his contempt for the foolish superstition of his neighbors, he suddenly ceased talking and stood petrified with terror, caused by a nimble scratching up in the eaves of the house. Instantly every one of the hilarious villagers ceased their blabbering and ran away at the top of their speed. Assuring them that the cause of their alarm was merely the noise made by the claws of a raccoon climbing out of the garret in fright at our presence and the glare of the lantern, they returned laughing and vociferating all together.

The wood-hogs (wild swine) "boo-hoo'd" and left their stye. Escaping into the pines, we subsequently heard them there in grunting and grumbling consultation.

We explored the cellar, and then pried open the door, which had been closed ever since the last teacher turned the key in the lock that night after the farmer carried out the Idiot's dead body. Everything stood precisely as it was left. There lay the rusty axe; and when the thick accumulation of dust was brushed away, the blood stains were yet to be seen. The mice and woodchucks had eaten the books. Cobwebs filled the corners, and a dozen scared bats flew down from the walls.

My friend revisited that neighborhood last June; and he says that the walls of the old school-house were long since torn down. And a very remarkable fact which he heard in connection with the demolition of the house, was that a white man had purchased the stone to build a residence for himself and his "colored wife," in which they now live together!

Perhaps that old school-house ghost was really as genuine as a majority of other apparitions, or manifestations of supernal or infernal spirits, which are supposed to exist in gloomy or deserted places, where any unusual sound might occur to suggest associations with a previous crime or some traditional mystery.

But, see! While I am reviewing my ghost adventure, a paler tint of azure is suffusing all the Eastern horizon! It comes like the dawning of day, only not so ruddy as a reflection from the rays of the sun. A pleasant glow, softly expanding in brightness, until the twinkling stars totally disappear and the larger ones are scarcely seen. And as the lovely radiance spreads far and wide, a new sensation accelerates the throbbing of my heart! My feelings are jubilant with an emotion such as might be inspired by a beautiful dream. I seem borne aloft and soaring in the sky!

Lost in admiration, I gaze with anxious inquiry for a solution of the bright phenomenon, and presently catch a glimpse of the rising moon! It is peeping up slowly from behind Dayton's Bluff, all red, and huge in size, strangely unlike what I have seen it elsewhere. In the clear, dry atmosphere on this part of the globe, the magnitude of the rising moon is wonderfully strange! With its features so plainly defined, I can hardly convince myself that it is not merely just beyond the bluff, instead of being so many thousand miles away.

Travelers who have been in those exotic lands where undying summer continues all the year, assure me that the glory of the rising moon is more sublime there than pen can write or tongue can tell. A view of the moon coming up out of the sea, has often inspired poetical minds with emotion which could find expression only in glowing rhymes. I once saw the moon rise amid mountains in a clime where cold winds never blow. That was a beautiful sight; but the vision I now behold is more charming than any similar scene in my recollection. A friend told me that the moonlight beneath these skies was beyond my conception, and truly I find it so to-night. In this transparent air, the firmament itself seems nearer to the earth than it does in any other

Hon. Alexander Ramsey, First Governor of Minnesota.

region where I have been. The very stars appear close enough to be reached with the hand!

But as the moon ascends toward the zenith of the sky, it turns paler and decreases in size until its color and its magnitude are familiar to my eye. And now the eastern side of the bluffs are almost as light as day. Scattered over that semicircular range of hills, and nestling among vines and trees, I catch glimpses of many a palacious villa in which wealthy citizens abide, with the elegance and the refinement that distinguish the more antique habitations of their peers who dwell near cities and towns existing long ago. And down in the bright, new city, among the thoroughfares of trade, I can distinguish the gray stone walls, filled with costly merchandise, and that contain plethoric vaults of undoubted currency, if not silver and gold. Between the warehouses in which busy men traffic during the active hours of the day, and the superb villas grandly reposing along the continuous hill, I behold the undulating outline of variform houses that constitute the great magnitude of the growing city, spread out for miles around.

And above the river's surface, silver'd o'er
With quiv'ring ripples that reach from shore to shore,

I plainly see the complicate frame-work of that immense *inclined bridge* which reaches from the towering front of the city down to the low flat bordering this side of the mighty stream.

Great shadows are behind the rocks which surround the lofty cliff where I am sitting, and thin, airy phantoms seem to lie in waiting under those bare-armed bushes above the gorge. The street-lamps over in the city have lost their sharp gleam, and dimly flicker beneath the resplendent brightness of the moon. Even the hooting owl in yonder thicket has ceased to complain; and up in the pine tree-top I do not hear such a mournful sighing of the wind as I did before this new light came to smile upon nature in repose.

The entire universe seems utterly still! A solemn enchantment hovers around. Experiencing a feeling of awe, I am also at the same time filled with a strange delight. I mentally ejaculate as light as day! But it is not so. For even in this rarefied atmosphere, the smiling face of Luna is but a mirrored reflection of the rays of light borrowed from Sol, whose eternal living fire is now shining down upon our antipodes in China and in Japan, while their enterprising and prosperous cousins in Columbia-land are nestled in the arms of Morpheus, the consoling god of sleep.

And, behold! Newspaper print is quite legible to the eye! for I actually peruse a paragraph of "leaded brevier" type in the St. Paul "Daily Pioneer"—at midnight by the light of the moon!!

Removing the paper from before my eyes, I unavoidably perceive the moonbeams playing amid the confusion of rocks far down beneath me. At the bottom of the yawning chasm, there is a deep pit, all in darkness like an abyss of oblivion, over which I have been sitting with my nether limbs dangling in the frightful void, entirely unconscious of the peril of my position. I saw the precipice before the sun went down, and, though its depth seemed immense by daylight, it is a thousand times more appalling now!

With a shudder, I very cautiously work further back from the smooth edge of the projecting cliff—and, nervously and carefully drawing up my limbs, I do not breathe until I gain a safer footing a few yards nearer the solid centre of the great rock.

When I reflect how many hours I sat so carelessly

perched out at the very point of that thin ledge of stone, I tremble with fright. The tiny projection might have snapped off at any moment and precipitated me into the air, to be dashed among the chaos of rocks, down there so far below!

Recovering from fright at the dangerous position I unconsciously had been in, I find all my romantic aspirations absorbed in a new desire. I now want to go home! I've had enough midnight solitude in this unfrequented mountain. Even the joyous moonlight now seems melancholy. Every object wears a mournful expression.

These reactions of feeling will occur at times; and now I would give something considerable to know that I was safely lodged in the cozy bed that is waiting for me at the International Hotel. Indeed, most people would say that it was very foolish to stroll away up here among these rugged rocks to spend seven hours alone with Nature, when I might have remained in the city surrounded by gas-light and social companions.

And now I am somewhat doubtful about finding the right road back to town. It is at best a very devious path. First I must cross yonder glen, and pick my way through the small forest sloping down into the gloomy gorge. Then I shall be obliged to clamber and stumble among the broken rocks to the open lawn, where the low-roofed farm-house stands a mile from here. At that point I shall try to find the wagon-track of a blind road, which, after winding up and down, apparently at random, to shun a rock or to avoid a clump of trees, will lead me to a mountain brook. I crossed the stream with some difficulty before sunset, by leaping from one stone to another; but now the dense growth of trees on the other side will hide the crossing from the rays of the moon. Doubtless I shall there experience the pleasurable sensation of very wet feet. After ascending the very steep hill beyond the stream, and walking half a mile further, I can reach the public highway. Then on, around, down—continually around, down, for a mile or so, I shall emerge from the wilderness and receive fresh courage by treading upon a more civilized level of the earth, with a good macadamized thoroughfare leading to the great inclined bridge, over which I can cross the river and ascend to the streets of the city. Arriving there, I shall breathe much easier than I do now in this solemn wild!

An Inexpensive Edifice, called a "Claim Shanty," not unfrequently seen in remote parts of Minnesota.

CHAPTER VI.

My peregrinations of the day and part of the night are ended, and at length I am once more snugly couched for repose. To an exhausted body and a weary mind, I know of nothing more pleasurable than the sensation of a horizontal attitude upon a cosy bed with the prospect of quiet slumber. And I fully realize that enjoyment now. It is nearly two o'clock in the morning ere I have attained a recumbent position between these nice linen sheets. It is unnecessary to say that my "carnal" sensibilities are eagerly yearning for beatific repose. After such a protracted reverie on the wild hill-top, terminating with an extended detour over dark, rugged and uncertain paths in the night air, I am not at all surprised to experience a "goose flesh" creeping outside, while a chill reaches my very vitals within. However, a few extra blankets piled on top of me will soon dissipate all that.

Heigho! Such gigantic yawns! The shivers perceptibly decrease, and oscitant wandering lulls me into a pleasant unconsciousness of sleep—to dream!

And now my spirit goes back again to that great bluff. Entirely forgetful of having returned home and come to bed, I seem to be lingering there yet. I am in the same spot beneath the solitary pine, and can plainly hear the whispering sobs and sighs among its green boughs. The moon is calmly smiling, and all the objects around me are reposing with the quietude in which I left them an hour ago.

Receding from the edge of the cliff, I am sensible of the night chill, and give my coat an extra button. I am perfectly conscious of all that passed through my mind while here in person, during the evening, up to the moment of my departure for the city. At that point, my double identity has lost its impression, and I am about to start on a devious journey, unconscious of having actually passed through the tiresome ordeal. But ere proceeding ten paces, I suddenly pause with a disagreeable presentiment of evil. Perhaps it is all fancy; but a voice of lamentation seems to issue from that curious mound of round blue stones which I noticed so intently in the light of day.

I experience a numbness in my veins, and then a warm nervous thrill makes my head feel as if the hair all stood stiff on end. What can it mean? Were I awake, such a feeling would scarcely put a tremor in my knees. But I am dreaming and powerless to resist at will. Yet everything appears real. How vividly the past comes up in my recollection. I very distinctly remember never seeing an apparition in all my life. I also recall my juvenile explorations wherever any unaccountable manifestation was said to exist or expected to occur; and all without once having realized the coveted gratification of a personal interview with supernal beings.

Breathlessly I pause to listen. And when I have made up my mind that it is merely imagination, or perhaps caused by the breeze frolicking in sadness among the rocks further on, I am suddenly and seriously startled by its repetition. My hair is now really struggling to get on end, and a distressing weakness is torturing my knees. Is it possible that I have come all the way here to be foolishly frightened? I must banish this cowardly feeling. Yet there it is again! Deep and mournful, like the sobbing of long-fostered grief!

Motionless I stand, in doubt what to think and afraid to start! I can perceive no movement except the gently waving tall dead grass and the small bushes. I hear no noise, save only a faint rustling over in the thicket, where the crisp brown leaves are clinging to their dry parent stems, and the soft murmuring of that tiny cascade down in the gorged ravine, which comes up like a pleasant lullaby that might hush angels to repose. Beside those trivial sounds, which are the purest melodies of nature, whispering their primevous requiems of sorrow and chansons of joy, all else above, below and far around, is sunk in silence, and seemingly at rest. Surely no spirit of evil can be lurking here beneath the lovely moon; and I shall not permit any superstition to haunt my mind. I am ashamed of myself for thus pausing in silly dismay, because the wind chances to frolic with audible sound in a cleft or a fissure of those prodigious broken rocks.

Forward—march! One step—two, three, four, five! Despite my bold resolution, those knees of mine will play the coward! And that crawling numbness is tingling up and down my back, while the hair on my head feels as if it would dislodge my hat and stand stiffly erect. My breathing is difficult; and I do not remember hearing my heart thump so ever before. Instead of taking courage, I stand like a statue representing the stolidity of an imbecile transfixed with fright. I can not go that way—and there is no other path!

It must be something more than a wind frolic in the cavities of rock! Such sounds as I now hear can not be tuned by a random current of the wind. And they surely emanate from that curious mound. It is a breathing lamentation emitted from among those round blue stones—which I am obliged to pass. An unearthly noise that would startle the nerves of any civilized mortal who might hear it in a dreary mountain wild like this, at such an hour of the night.

But I shall not admit a prevalence of anything supernatural, even here. The philosophy of only common sense assures me that the indubitable laws of nature will not permit unearthly manifestations where the living can breathe. With this conviction shaming me to action, and really provoked at myself for credence of what could never be, I once more boldly start in the direction of the curious mound. But as I approach, the mysterious noise becomes louder at every pace.

Facing an open enemy in deadly conflict requires a deal of courage; but I am inclined to the opinion, from my peculiar sensations at this unpleasant crisis, that undue nervous delinquency would quickly incapacitate me for proceeding any further. But I shall go! Avaunt there! Spirit, demon, devil, or mortal of human form! I still hear you; but though I feared your wail a moment ago, I am resolved to brave your presence now!

Tramp, tramp. Firm and steady. And at every stride, the lamentation comes plainer to my ear. My heart will throb quicker than it usually does. But what of that? I am now on a line with the curious mound, out of which the wailing noise seemed to come a moment ago. Hah! Another step reveals a dark object to my sight! It is crouching in a heap at the edge of the round blue stones! What can it be? A wild beast, surely—for it bears no semblance to anything of human form!

And here I suddenly pause once more! In fact, if I continue on that way, my presence will rouse the creature from its apparently unconscious condition. Thus I tremblingly stand. The moonlight throws my shadow almost to where the dark object is crouching, and I half shudder at the thought of its touching even that.

Twisting and writhing, with moans and mournful sighs, it sways from side to side and conceals its head beneath its shapeless trunk. A strangely animated mass of life—whether flesh, fish or fowl! I know it lives and breathes, because I can see it move and hear its piteous noise.

A ghost, if such spirits ever do appear to human eyes, would be too ethereal to utter any sound. A lost soul could not, and in all reasonable expectation would not, inhabit such a hideous material substance as that. A hobgoblin—a spirit damned—would scarcely be allowed to escape from the mythological regions of conflagrant sulphur in that supposed *terra incognita* beyond the grave!

A beast, a brute, a dumb animal of any species or undiscovered kind, would not thus exhibit emotional distress. And yet a wounded animal might roll in agony of body and utter cries of pain. But a beast has

An Indian Burial Scaffold, upon which the bodies of the Dead were placed to decay.

a hide of hair or some other external features devoid of the handiwork of art; while, in the flood of moonlight, I perceive the ends of a textural garment unworn by wolves or bears. And now I discern long tresses of hair streaming down from this creature's head and wiping the dust off the rock. That looks more human! But can a human being double up into a wad or a ball and execute a vocalism so unearthly dissonant as what I hear?

But see! I have done it now! The crushing of a small stone beneath my foot has produced a counter noise, which the creature hears. And, with a startled cry, it suddenly bounds upright on its hind legs. I can perceive its wild stare of surprise, and then I hear a hoarse grunt and a defiant snarl. An instant it pauses; and immediately I experience a chill of horror as it darts upon me, grasping my arm like the pressure of an iron vice. Confused with fright, I have but one distinct idea —and that is to escape the claws of a demon!

Though all my life averse to believing in disembodied devils, a careful study of the dark side of human nature has firmly convinced me that incarnate fiends numerously walk the earth with bold impunity among the best of men. But this monster strikes me dumb. In the beautiful moonlight, I can plainly discern its hideous features—and they are partly human! Its hot breath burns upon my face as it stretches its long, lean neck to peer into my eyes, while I am utterly powerless to struggle, much less to resist. To describe my feelings would be impossible. Like a group from the sculptor's chisel, we both stand transfixed and immovable as stone. I cannot speak, and the demon tightens its grasp without uttering any sound. The terror paralyzing my strength is not greater than the revulsion of my senses from the close contact of the demon's visage—which bears a tomb-like deformity somewhat similar to one of those mummies exhumed from the catacombs of ancient Egypt, where they had lain thousands of years!

Now the monster smiles—a ghastly expansion and contraction of its hard, dry features, from which every particle of flesh and moisture appears to have gone! A repulsive grin—not of rage—but in exultation at my capture and evident fright. A huge mouth, with harsh cartilaginous lips drawn wide apart, disclosing a pale, sickly front of toothless gums. There may be two or three bodkin-shaped snags in the lower jaw, the remote expansion of which is hinged by a square breadth of angle such as bull-dogs are noted for—while but one useless fang is quite pendulous above. Particularly coarse black hair, in cleanliness and texture suggestive of the vertebrate capiliform posterior extremity of the equine or the bovine species, separated into rough stringlets and matted flakes, is dangling before and behind from the frounced and frouzy vertex of the demon's head! The wrinkled cuticle of its face is withered and dry, and tightly drawn across a great Roman nose. It has small black eyes, that glare in the moonlight streaming upon them. They are deeply sunken into its head, and each is surrounded with the protruding rim of a bony cavity, not unlike those huge sockets shown in the front of that noted criminal's skull which I have seen among the phrenological specimens on exhibition at a celebrated academy where they elucidate anatomical wonders!

Doubtless those black eyes were large and luminous when the demon was young; but as all living things must mature and decay, this creature has long since passed its youthful prime. Even a demon's existence can not extend beyond a limited span. Though from external appearances, the longevity of this one is very great. I imagine that some marvelous liberality in the usually inexorable laws of nature has permitted this being to retain a vital tenacity and a herculean strength beyond all the established physiological theories of life. And, without any stretch of my already excited imagination, I can not refrain from comparing those deeply sunken and fiercely glaring small black eyes to the outlets of some mysterious cavern, where the prince of darkness sits upon his cabalistic throne, with grim exultation in mockery of the weeping angel of light, who is a suppliant captive kneeling at his feet!

A dingy blanket is wrapped loosely around the demon's form as far down as the knees, and its slender ill-shaped nether extremities are swathed in what appear to be the shreds of a discarded coat, or a pair of old pantaloons! Male or female, whichever it is, no outward indication now reveals. And I should not be surprised if it had no sex at all! Was it born of woman, the offspring of man? Is it a creature of God, or a gorgon from some purgatorial limbo unknown?

In those theatrical representations of Stygian waters, and in the Tartarean realms over which Pluto and Hades rule, I have seen hideous masks to personate the satellites of that Luciferean dignitary who occupies the honorary position of Beelzebub-in-chief—but none of them were any more hideous than the infernal visage before me now.

In this lonely spot, at the midnight hour, under these circumstances, and in such manner, with a great flood of magical moonlight streaming upon its form and illuminating its horrid face, how could my reason be otherwise than partly overturned? But I am in bodily pain!

What a powerful grasp the demon has! It does not relax in the least. On the contrary, I feel it clutching tighter still! And as its great bony fingers harshly indent my flesh, a strange numbness begins to destroy all sense of feeling. My arm is unnerved and apparently stiff! The blood has ceased to flow in the veins beyond my shoulder, and I fancy that the entire limb is already cold.

In the violent clutch of this demon there seems to be some mythologic power that can paralyze living things with a magic spell, at its will. And if my arm is thus withered by its terrible grasp, what else have I to apprehend? Will the blight extend any further than my arm? With that question, a horrible suspicion enters my mind, and a sickening perspiration suffuses every part of my body. What if I should be transformed into a rock or a tree, and so continue to exist through the lapse of countless ages, without volitive animation, and yet retaining all the consciousness of intellect characterizing a human heart and brain? Is it possible that I am doomed to stand here ever like the solitary pine, among whose green boughs the moaning of a lost spirit is so often heard in response to the night wind and the evening breeze?

Surely there must be some magical influence pervading these hills, as yet unknown to the science of the world. That indescribable sensation experienced by every one when they first breathe the intoxicating atmosphere of this wonderful land, is significantly suggestive of invisible charms which may operate upon the body and even the soul of an individual who sympathizingly yearns for a more intimate acquaintance with that psychological mystery connecting the celestial and mundane spheres.

THE VISION DISSOLVES.

But how strange it is that I can pause to moralize with theory and reflection, while the clutch of this demon is palsying my limbs and evidently depriving me of the natural functions which pertain to life! Perhaps I have been lost in the hallucinatory imagination of a trance, which is gradually dispelled upon discovering the faint gleam of a smile that now lightens up the countenance of the demon. I certainly begin to feel more like myself. The numbness of my arm is abating with the relaxation of that terrible grasp.

Hah! and now I see the demon laugh! Not with pleasurable anticipation of devouring me; but in merriment at my trembling fear. Its tongue moves! It speaks! Thank Heaven!—then it is one of God's creatures, after all! But what does it say?

"Haugh! White man 'fraid of Injun! Hi-augh! Tremble at old Injun squaw! Hoi-augh! White man *big knife*, but don't know *Old Betz!* Haugh! White man sick! Been hurt in head! Ugh! White man lost—can't go to bed!"

At this announcement I am lost in mental oblivion. The bluff instantly disappears, and I grasp at seeming objects that are but empty air! A wild "Ha, ha!" is ringing in my ears while I pass entirely out of the world.—Gone, I know not where!

Presently I awake and find myself lying on my back, scarcely able to breathe, with such a great pile of extra blankets pressing upon my lungs!

Hah-zah-ee-yun-kee-win; or "Old Betz"—That remarkable Centenarian Female Savage, whom the Author first saw in a Singular Dream.

CHAPTER VII.

How strange that I should see Old Betz in a dream! I am not surprised that my spirit flew back to the moonlight scene upon the bluff, after lingering there such a length of time in meditation. But why did I encounter that centenarian squaw? She is the most wonderful living curiosity in Minnesota; and I presume that nearly every one acquainted with the North-west, has frequently heard her name. I had been hoping for a personal interview with her; but did not expect that we should meet in a vision of sleep, or otherwise, at midnight upon a lonely mountain top.

Ah, well! Perhaps these dreams are—Heigho! I am much too drowsy for theorizing now. How I yawn! It may be—that is—and—

My heavy respiration notifies the little mouse skulking in the corner there behind the stove, that I am once more sound asleep.

After a brief lapse in oblivion, while my weary body is reposing upon this comfortable bed, in spirit I fly off on another excursion. Space is no hindrance to my flight. Instantaneously, without even the trouble of conceiving a desire, I am once more on the back of that invisible genii who attends to this mysterious department of human exploits. He wafts me across the river—and again I am in the identical spot where I saw Old Betz awhile ago. Hah! and here she is now!

The moonlight is full upon her face; and as she tries to smile, I notice the expression of her small black eyes. They seem rather diminutive in size, because incomputable longevity has pushed them so far back into her head. Her smile is a prelude to speech.

She inquires why "pale-face runs Injun with big moon?" From which I infer that she is making a significant allusion to my nocturnal wandering at such an unusual hour. And then she wants to know why I am not at home and in bed with my wife! Her manner is decidedly blunt. I may very justly accuse her of imperturbable audacity—for she quizzingly insinuates that every white man in St. Paul ought to have a wife of his own!!

Again, entirely unconscious of being at home and in bed and asleep, I seem lingering in the identical state of existence while here previous to my first dream. But my feelings are precisely what they were immediately after this marvelous old creature revealed herself to me with that sarcastic allusion to my fear of "Injun squaw!"

An idea opportunely occurs to me that she might greatly expedite the pedestrian labor which I imagine is yet to be performed. Will she guide me back to town? But first, what is her Indian name?

"Haugh! Me go anywhere! Big knife got *kosh-popee!* Old Betz's name, *Hah-zah-ee-yun-kee-win*" (one who gathers huckleberries while running!)

I ask her what she means by *kosh-popee*, and she signifies "ten cents!" She evidently presumes that I have "plenty ten cents"—which denominated numeral may be the limit of her arithmetical education. For kosh-popee, she is willing to escort me anywhere. Cheap enough! If she would contract on such terms, I might employ her as a guide for daylight excursions among the thousand lakes, the great prairies and the romantic hills. At that proposition, she gives her uncombed head and tangled hair a quick negative shake, to say:

"Injun nowhere when pale-face want him! Old squaw be way over there, fore sun come back in morning. Can't find old Betz sometime!"

I imagine not, if she is in the habit of gathering huckleberries while on a run. But see! she points toward the west, as if intending to go far that way before sunrise.

I now inquire what brought her here at this time of night. Not berries, at this season of the year?

When I have spoken, she squats down at the edge of that curious pile of round blue stones, with her head between her hands, and immediately begins rocking to and fro. What moans and lamentations! She is repeating the performances at which I at first found her.

All this seems very much at variance with the character she bears by reputation. Is it possible that people judge too harshly when they speak of her as an old dragon of the female gender? From her conduct, she is evidently mourning the loss of something that was once near and dear to her—and that impression is quickly confirmed when I hear her sorrowfully cry:

"*Me choonkshee! Me choonkshee!*"—which in the Dacota language means, "My child! My child!"

Then the despised old Indian squaw has been a mother; and her weary heart is even now full of grief for the loss of a beloved child. I listen to her words; which, though uttered in her native tongue, are very beautiful in meaning.

"Alas, alas! me choonkshee! me choonkshee! Thou art gone from my sight forever! The Great *Wakan* came to my humble teepee in his anger and stole thee away! It was a dark night; and when the full moon rose, thy spirit had fled! The brightness of the moon was like the sunshine of the day; yet when thou wert taken from my sight, I saw nothing but desolation around! Alas! me choonkshee, my first-born child, who lived here in my heart, which is now old and sad! My voice is hoarse with that wailing song which I have sung so many moons for the bitter loss of thee! I have no joy, no comfort, no hope of to-morrow! The pale-face has lost no child—and if he has lost many children, he does not mourn for them all as I do for thee! He can swallow his grief; but poor old squaw's heart must bleed till she dies! Alas, me choonkshee! Without thee life is cheerless to me now! My eyes are dim from weeping! I have been wandering from the lakes to the rivers, from the bluffs to the gorges in the hills, from the forest to the prairies—ever wandering without a warm teepee or home of my own! But I shall continue to wander on, on, on until I fall into the great boiling lake over which I must pass before I can touch thee! Alas, I loved thee so much, and thou didst love me so dearly in return! My people laugh at my grief, and say thou wert only a female child! Hadst thou been a boy, a strong young brave, panting to scalp thine enemies, my heart could not have loved thee more! Long grief for a daughter the Sioux mother is taught to despise—and yet I cannot relinquish my sorrow for thee! Thou wert my light, my life and my all! My limbs are shrunken from age and constant travel; but whenever the full moon rises up from beyond the ancient cavern of *Wakan-tebee*, where lie the bones of the illustrious *Naudowessies*, thy great warrior forefathers, here I shall place another round blue stone brought from beneath the singing waters of *Minneinceopa*, in which, like the young elks, thou didst so fondly love to play! Hither I have brought a stone at every full moon since angry *Wakan* took thee away—for the moon was rising full at the very moment I saw thy warm lips turn to clay! Many moons have come and gone since that sad hour, and many stones are now piled up here! Thy bones—the bones of my first-born child—are carefully hid away in the rock, down beneath this pile of stones, and the ugly wolves cannot gnaw them with their sharp teeth! Alas, me choonkshee! I cannot eat when I think of thee! I have brought thee ofttimes many choice things! In the spring, young ducks; in the summer, sweet berries! Sugar I have begged and stolen from the white man's store to gladden thy pretty tongue! Ribbons of red and yellow, and green and blue, and handkerchiefs of beautiful design, I have pilfered from the white woman's grand teepee! All these things I have gathered together for thee! But the Chippeway dogs come by stealth and tear them from thy grave! All thy playmates have died long ago! The wild crows have eaten the parched corn I placed here! Many snows have covered thee o'er! The keen frosts of many winters have hardened the earth, and howling storms of wind and rain have swept across the hill with doleful requiems to make thy resting-place dreary and wild! But no grass nor flowers shall mock thy decay! While I live this mound shall be sacred to thee; and, like my heart, sleep in sadness that is forever! Alas, me choonkshee! I am weary of life, and long to come and lie with thee here!"

At this juncture, I succeed in silencing her lamentation by the offer of a ten-cent currency stamp with an articulation of the word, "Kosh-popee!"

"Kosh-popee!" she echoes in response. And reaching out one of her horny claws to clutch the money, with the other she endeavors to wipe the tears out of her eyes.

What a sudden change in her manner has been produced by the acquisition of kosh-popee! One would imagine to see the complete transition of her mind from the bitterest grief to emphatic manifestations of joy, that kosh-popee was the surest balm for the sorrows of a savage breast.

Rising to her feet, she quickly adjusts her blanket and slings back her coarse matted hair, with a vehement grunt, in prelude to a declaration of willingness to do anything or to go anywhere. I take advantage of her obliging humor and suggest how she might at once guide me through the uncertain path to the public highway.

"Injun no go round! White man too much fraid him fall. Injun go down *there!*"

She points into the frightful gorge over which I sat so long in ignorance of my perilous position! She can not mean that a safe descent is practicable through the yawning abyss? It is nearly five hundred feet above the river! And yet she insists that I must follow. I assure her that I am very much obliged for the invitation, but at the same time respectfully decline to break my neck.

Smiling at my trepidation, she further astonishes me by promptly offering to carry me down upon her back! The proposition is so very absurd that I try to laugh. But I seldom can laugh in a dream. If I do, it is sure to wake me up. I fancy myself upon her shoulders, while she is climbing down the almost perpendicular precipice at our feet; but the picture is too awkward and thrilling for my contemplation; and I ask her if she is not afraid of death. She shrugs her shoulder and seems to think the question too trifling for serious consideration.

Where does she expect to go when she dies? Her answer is a prolonged grunt. Has she any *idea of God?* Oh, yes—*many!* She reveres everything incomprehensible, which, in the language of her people, is called *wakan*—signifying "sacred." She believes that a spirit inhabits every natural object, from the little pebbles strewn along the margins of the lake and the banks of the river, to the twinkling stars and fixed planets in the sky. She believes that articles owned by a man is *wakan* after his death, but not so with those left by a woman. If she sees any one with the toothache, she recommends an appeal to the spirit of a worm or of a woodpecker concealed within the tooth. A cough comes from the machinations of the sacred men through goose-down or buffalo-hair. It is sinful to run a sharp instrument into a piece of meat, and equally wicked to cut a stick of wood taken from the fire. To smoke a pipe with a black stem would bring evil upon a woman; and ill fortune would lie in the path of a man wearing a woman's moccasins. And to throw gunpowder in the fire would be a great crime!

Moonlight View of an Ancient Naudowessie Burial Place, formerly on the verge of that Great Bluff above the Cavern of Wakan-tebee, and overlooking the Mississippi River, near the site of St. Paul.

I find many strange beliefs in the old creature's heart and head. Instead of only one soul, she imagines that she has *four!* When she dies (if she ever should die), one of her souls will go with some article which she has worn, until a friend can throw it into the Chippeway country; one will remain with her body to guard it from injury; one will enter the form of a child or of a dog; and one will go into the happy land where only good spirits dwell!

She has no fear of punishment hereafter for her sins, nor does she expect future reward for the good acts of her life!

That happy land, where the good spirits dwell, is somewhere across a wide lake of boiling water! An old squaw, like herself, is sitting in the sand upon the other side, steadying the end of a slender pole, along which the souls have to climb in order to reach the celestial shore! Warriors with scars from wounds in battle can easily walk the slender pole. Papooses with blue veins are carried across by the breeze. Many slip off the pole in trying to pass over, and they sink into the boiling water to be heard of no more.

She does not esteem an honest person any better than a thief and a liar! But if a woman commits suicide, she will be compelled to drag a pole fastened to her feet—and in her wanderings through the happy land, if the pole should break down the growing corn, the spirits may beat her with heavy bludgeons.

When her parents lost a child, the father went and killed a Chippeway! When her mother died, he went and killed two enemies! And when her father expired, their friends came and wrapped the corpse in his best clothes. Then one of them harangued the spirits, while another enumerated all his virtues. Smearing their faces with a black pigment, they uttered loud lamentations, and cut and lacerated their bodies with their finger-nails and with sharp-edged fragments of stone.

Instead of putting the corpse into the ground, they laid it upon a high scaffold, with the scalps of enemies, and food and other articles, which his spirit was fond of while in the body. When the flesh had dried up or fallen from the skeleton, then it was deposited in the earth, and stakes driven around the spot, to protect it from wolves. She is very communicative, and reveals much that I never knew before. She has lived so many moons that she stopped counting a long time ago.

Did she ever *love?*

A long sigh implies more than words can tell! She was once a maiden. To see her now, that would seem almost impossible. The son of a Chippeway chief loved her when she was young, and she loved him in return. But she belonged to the Sioux, who were eternally at war with the Chippeways. There was a temporary peace, and her lover would soon take her to his teepee. He was covering one with choice skins, and when it was completed they would be very happy.

Then a band of Sioux killed a Chippeway mother and her child! That was the signal for another war. The Chippeways surprised the village of Shakopee, where she lived when a girl. Her lover was among the infuriated invaders, and she and he met in the conflict. He raised his hatchet, but paused an instant to gaze at her upturned face, while she begged for her life and implored him to make her his captive!

No! he had sworn to kill every man, woman and child among the Sioux! She must die! And, without regarding her cries for mercy, he seized her long, black hair and ruthlessly gashed her forehead in execution of his savage purpose. Another instant, and she would fall a bleeding corpse beneath the feet of the warriors who were yelling in delirious fury around them! Closing her eyes in despair, she sank upon her knees to die! But she was permitted to live. The strong arm of a young Sioux saved her. With a heavy, sharp-edged stone he dashed out the brains of her merciless lover, and then quickly tore the scalp from his head!

When the battle was over, and the invading Chippeways were driven back into their own country, her preserver brought the scalp that he had torn from her lover's head. It was all reeking with gore, and he held it up so that she could see. Then he told her that he wanted a wife. If she would accept him for her master, and ever after be his slave, she might have the trophy to decorate their teepee!

She did not shudder at the ghastly scalp, nor did she recoil from his wooing embrace.

Sioux maidens never were anything more than savages of the feminine gender. This always has been my opinion—and when I hear her enthusiastically talk of scalps and love, I feel satisfied with my previous impression. All those uncivilized maidens of the forest and the prairie, described as angelic heroines divine, by overly sentimental writers who compose epic legend, are after all merely creatures of imagination to delight credulously dreamy minds!

Doubtless this antiquated squaw was quite as lovely as the fairest of her tribe, when in the bloom of youth; and yet she tells me she reached forth her hand and took that ghastly scalp without a pang of grief or a thrill of horror! And I presume that her eyes were accustomed to seeing fresh scalps dripping with blood, and her ears might have often heard the night-winds rattling through a string of them all dried with time, as they swung upon a rawhide thong near the door of her father's teepee!

She accepted her preserver's offer of marriage. The nuptial ceremony was in accordance with the simple custom of her tribe. Together with their friends, they sat down upon the grassy hill-side, and presently arose united by the formal compact which they deemed binding for life.

It was her first-born child whose remains now lie buried among the rocks beneath that great pile of round blue stones. And now she begins to rock herself again, and to moan, "Me choonkshee! me choonkshee!"

I administer more kosh-popee, and she receives it with repeated grunts and a prodigious grin. Kosh-popee is an elixir—a charm! For ten cents, she will forget all her sorrows. But one other balm has more efficacy with her than money. She loves *minne-wakan*, or whisky, better than anything else!

There is one beautiful superstition in her half-savage breast. She believes that a mother's spirit is always with an absent child when it thinks of her, and that a pain in her heart signifies the agony or the misfortune of a child who is far away!

She is now impatient to depart, and significantly points down into the gorge, as if to inquire whether I am ready.

No—not down there! I perceive a less precipitous ravine further along, and perhaps we can prudently risk that. She pretends to know every inch of the rocks all the way down to the base of the bluff.

But can I trust her? Possibly I can! Yet it is a question of doubt in my own mind. I have been told that she is an inveterate liar!

The moonlight discloses something like a safe footing; and I'll venture down with her. She instructs me how to lean upon her left shoulder, while she goes before.

There are certain clefts and knobs where I can place my feet. They are all visible to her eyes, and she will point them out as we climb down!

Nevertheless, I do not begin the descent entirely free from suspicion of possible disaster. She laughs at my fear, and tells me to "look much big," and follow!

Down we go! Two or three hundred feet without any mishap, and I begin to felicitate myself on a safe performance of the perilous undertaking, when a projecting knob which she is standing upon, suddenly snaps off! Fortunately for me, I instinctively hug the rock and release all further claim upon her shoulder!

A moment or so she totters on a precarious balance in the air, and then plunges down among the broken rocks—shouting out to me as she goes:

"Old Injun squaw no care much for one big fall!"

My footing is also giving way! I feel it going now! A dizziness comes over me; and down, down I tumble, headlong to—— Hah, I awake!

Some one is knocking at my chamber door. Who's there?

The voice of the chambermaid replies: "Dinner's ready. Are you going to sleep all day?"

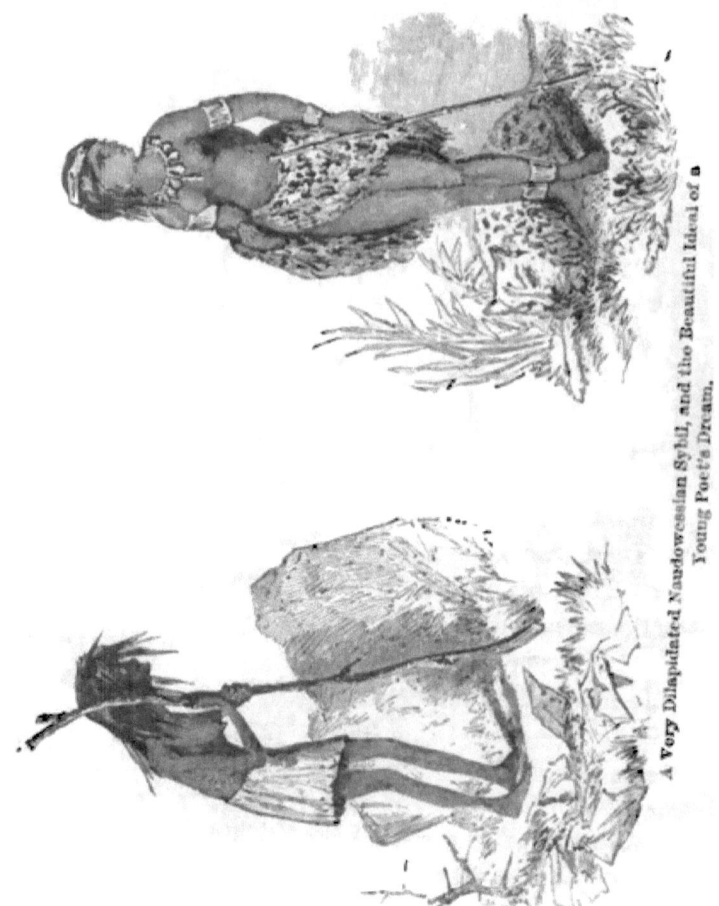

A Very Dilapidated Naudowessian Sybil, and the Beautiful Ideal of a Young Poet's Dream.

CHAPTER VIII.

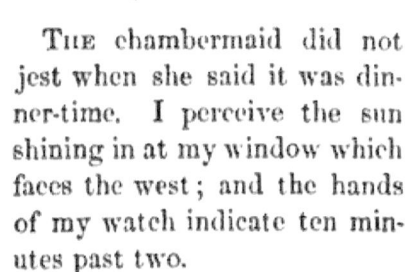

The chambermaid did not jest when she said it was dinner-time. I perceive the sun shining in at my window which faces the west; and the hands of my watch indicate ten minutes past two.

Having fasted since yesterday afternoon, my appetite craves immediate attention. Twenty minutes is the time I usually devote to toilet performances for the day, but upon this occasion, the entire programme concludes somewhat sooner.

"Dinner from one to three!" I mentally repeat, while hurrying to get down stairs. And entering the dining-room, "Luke" produces that indispensable cup of tea, which I would not exchange for the best bottle of wine in the cellar.

But Brigadier General Festivus, with those extremely elaborate shoulder-straps, sitting in the opposite chair, sipping his champagne, eyes me compassionately and proposes that I shall join him. I respectfully decline, and at the same time wonder why he persists in soaking three slices of roasted venison with a quart of effervescent grape-juice and alcohol, when his object in visiting Minnesota was to recuperate his health. How absurd it is, while complaining of ill-health and incurring any amount of trouble and expense for recovery, to deliberately and persistently exasperate the functions of life. Now, this distinguished military gentleman has been told that he is *consumptive;* and his "family physician" recommends a gentle stimulant, a generous diet—*and a trip to St Paul!* What he wants the stimulant for, I can not even guess.

How wise some "family physicians" are, and how many patients they fail to cure! I wonder if the General innocently imagines that his quart bottle of champagne is merely a gentle stimulative? And I think that gorging three large slices of venison, with an extraordinary quantity of vegetables, and a perfect load of dessert, may be estimated as unmistakable symptoms of omnivorous inclination. If such a diet is requisite to eradicate the germs of consumption, it would be entirely too expensive for people of ordinary means who are obliged to eat at some of the hotels kept on the "European plan," in New York City. But here at the *International*, an inveterate glutton may devour all he wants without extra cost. Wine is extra everywhere in the United States.

And General Festivus really has an ugly cough, which seems to worry his wife, who suspects nothing amiss in the wine. Fortunately, she is not inclined to be consumptive herself, and therefore eats very moderately and avoids the sparkling liquid of the bottle.

But now she sniffs the delicious odor of my second cup

of tea, and inquires of Luke if she can have some, too.
Certainly she can. Whereupon she does not hesitate to
express her delight by bestowing upon my humble self
a sweet little smile. The General has a charming wife!

But I have eaten all I require, and bow myself from
the table, while the General is pouring out the last of
his champagne, and Mrs. F. sips her third cup of tea.
She'll feel happier than her husband an hour hence!

Meanwhile I shall go and smoke; and quietly resume
the discursive retrospection which occurred in my protracted reverie last night over there on top of the great
bluff beneath that lonely pine.

I left the long Ox-cart train, and the male and female
equestrians in motion, with their flag flying, at early
dawn on the second day of their journey, and might
review a great many pleasant and several irksome inci-
dents which they encountered before arriving at Mendota—but shall reserve all that for similar scenes in a
subsequent chapter. At present I shall follow a couple
of canoes that were launched near the mouth of the
Minnesota River, the next morning after the unique
caravan came to its destination.

Each of the canoes was managed by an Indian squaw;
and one of those squaws was no less a personage than
Old Betz, the antediluvian female about whom I had
such a singular dream last night. In her canoe sat
Madame Zorah, and Leonore and Major Levasseur.
The other contained Tashae and Florinda, and jealous
Kaskadino.

After paddling up near the ferry at Fort Snelling, to
look at that quaint fortification, they softly glided
down the stream; and in an hour or so, the whole party
landed upon the spot where the depot of the *St. Paul
and Pacific Railway* stands at the present time. They

came down to visit "Carver's Cave," or the Cavern of *Wakan Tebee*, which Major Levasseur had heard much about, but never seen.

But Old Betz insisted that they should first explore the settlement of "Pig's Eye." And, without any permission on the part of her passengers, she put them ashore. The squaws pulled their canoes out of the water, and with the excursionists walked up hill.

Old Betz had already attached herself to Leonore, whom she pretended to like because of a very great resemblance (?) to her own daughter, who died a great many moons ago—and I presume the same one, according to my dream, who was buried beneath the curious mound of round blue stones upon the bluff. Leonore was not displeased with the affectionate declarations of the old squaw, but on the contrary she really evinced her gratitude by presenting the crone with a little fancy reticule, which her dear mother had made for her and taught her to carry at her waist, in accordance with a Parisian fashion then out of date.

Old Betz, jubilant with delight, was more eager than ever to become the sole proprietress of every article that Leonore had upon her person. However, as Tashae's longing eyes were continually upon the lovely girl, he witnessed the squaw's greed of acquisition, and at once put a veto upon any further bounty.

"Oh, let the poor creature have this little bit of ribbon," persisted Leonore, completely fascinated with the deceitful crawling and the affectionate grimaces of her insatiate patron.

"Augh!" grunted Kaskadino. "Give Injun squaw little, and she want *all!*"

What Kaskadino said was true. But Old Betz made a sign to him in response, that signified how much she would like to have her hard, stiff fingers about his throat. And a frown from Florinda, in testimony of her disapprobation of the half-breed's ill-natured insinuation, not only gratified the old squaw's feelings, but at once established a bond of friendship between them.

It is said that Indians never entertain a sincere friendship for pale-faced companions; but that assertion is not established by facts, when the latter sympathize with the former in the accomplishment of their revenge. And in the instance here cited, Old Betz was quickly ready to hazard her own life for Florinda, if such service should be required. Kaskadino saw it all, and scornfully turned away with his characteristic grunt.

Tashae and Madame were ahead, and Levasseur and Leonore followed them, leaving Kaskadino, Florinda, and the two squaws together in the rear.

Standing near the path was a shanty where whisky could be had, and Kaskadino dropped in to get a dram. Florinda looked to see whither he was going, when suddenly she beheld something which caused her to stop short and stare into the shanty! She appeared greatly astonished at what she saw, and held her breath in wonder and doubt.

Old Betz misinterpreted her emotion, and kindly inquired if she was thirsting for *minne-wakan*. Florinda made no reply, but kept her eyes bent upon some object inside the whisky-shanty, until Kaskadino emerged with a grunt of contempt and proceeded to ascend the hill. By that time Florinda was ready to speak; and, pointing within the shanty, she asked:

"Who is that man?"

Imitating the "boo hoo" of swine, Old Betz jocularly closed one of her fiery black optics with the pressure of her thumb.

A First-class Hotel during the Reign of "Pig's Eye," and before the christening of St. Paul.

"No, no!" pettishly exclaimed Florinda. "The man there behind the bar. The slender man with light hair. Who is he?"

"Boo-hoo!" repeated Old Betz, with a chuckling attempt at laughter and two or three sharp and decisive nods by way of an emphasizing assurance that what she endeavored to explain was really true.

"Bah!" snarled Florinda. "I allude to the man with a defective eye!"

"Augh! Squaw mean one-eye, too!"

But Florinda could not understand Old Betz's answer; and, after a moment's thought, she motioned for her to "go on."

The whisky-shanty was seldom empty; but just at that moment the customers were all absent, leaving the proprietor entirely alone—and Florinda slowly but resolutely walked in, with her eyes fixed searchingly upon his face. Raising his head, their gaze met.

The man was seriously startled; but, quickly recovering his natural placidity of demeanor, he tried to say in a careless voice:

"Well, ma'am, what can I do for you? I can fill a bottle for you. My jugs are all gone."

"You do not know me, then?" sneered Florinda, while advancing close to him, and thrusting her face very close to his.

"Look again, sir! The sight of your good eye was sharp enough when you held——"

"Yes; I believe I do know you now!" quickly interrupted the man. There was a slight tremor in his voice—and doubtlessly a thrill of emotion, perceptible only to himself. "But I thought you were dead!" he added, with stammering articulation. "They told me——"

"No matter what they told you," interposed Florinda. "You see me here now! And, considering the circumstances, I am resolved that you shall loan me a little money. I presume you understand what that means!"

"I don't think I can—no how. Money is awful skerse in this here part of the country."

"Then I shall denounce you! I need not suggest what the result will be."

The man was frightened pale at her words, and in a husky voice meekly replied:

"Believe me. I don't lie any more. I'm awful poor! *He's* rich, and always got plenty! Ask *him!*"

"*He* is dead! I need aid from some other source now. It is very fortunate that I have discovered your hiding-place just at this time. Come, the money!"

"Hah! He is *dead*, hey! Then I don't care a cent! I can snap my finger in your face! Ha, ha! *He's dead*, and nobody'll believe *you!*"

And the man did snap his fingers. He was highly elated at the death of some one. "Go—go!" he continued, with a suddenly assumed dignity that was entirely unnatural to him. "I want to be free! You clear out! You're nothing to me, no how—and you can't harm me in no way at all now! Go! This is not a nice place for sich ladies as you've been!"

"Not so fast, if you please!" retorted Florinda, with increased determination. "Your memory is still good, I presume; and it is scarcely possible that you have so soon forgotten the existence of ——. Ah! You are changing your expression, and do not look so defiant now. A brave man you are, to quail at the mention of so trifling an object as *that*. I once *told* you that I intended to remind you of it some day when you least expected. I have carried it with me ever since—and can produce it any time!"

"Let me have it, then!" he roughly demanded, and approaching as if he would take it by force.

"I am not a fool!" sneered Florinda, unconsciously pressing one hand against her bosom and involuntarily shielding the object of contention.

"Ah, I see where it is! In your dress!" exclaimed the excited man, fumbling desperately in his pocket. "This knife will open the way! Let me have it, or you die!"

They were already in conflict when the great, horny fingers of Old Betz, who had been listening outside the door, violently grasped the man's hair from behind, and threw him sprawling upon the floor. And then, with the simple ejaculation of "Hugh!" she urged Florinda to go away.

"Not yet," cried Florinda. "I must have three hundred dollars from him before I go a step!" She then slammed to the door and bolted it to prevent intrusion.

"Will that satisfy you?" panted the fallen man, completely vanquished and eager to embrace a sudden gleam of hope. "If I give you all that much money, will you leave this place and never come back here no more, long as you live?"

Florinda thought an instant, and then said: "Give me the money, and I will surely leave on the steamer going down the river to-morrow. But I shall keep *that* to remember you by!"

"Your life may be shorter'n you 'xpect," he muttered—but not quite loud enough for her to hear. Upon regaining his feet, he audibly replied, "You'shl have the money. I can't give it to you now; but meet me there by the square rock, below Mendota, at sundown, and I'll bring you three hundred dollars all in gold—every cent of it—sure's I live!"

Leonore's voice was then heard calling, and Florinda left the shanty, after agreeing to the man's proposition. Old Betz followed; but not until she had obtained a drink of whisky, which she demanded of the crest-fallen proprietor in ratification of the treaty just concluded between him and Florinda. Then shrugging her shoulders, and uttering that inevitable grunt, she joined the party as they were descending the hill. And when they repassed the whisky-shanty, to embark in their canoes, the proprietor hid himself from sight.

And then the excursionists floated down to the edge of Dayton's Bluff, where they once more stepped ashore. They were then near the entrance of the great Cavern which Levasseur desired so much to see. Old Betz seemed perfectly familiar with the interior of the wonderful place. The mouth was about ten feet wide and five feet high; and she led them through into the grand chamber, which extended a considerable distance over a floor of beautiful fine sand, to a lake of transparent water. The Major threw a stone into the lake with all his might, and, from the loud noise it made splashing in the water, he imagined the expanse of distance to be very large. But the darkness deterred them from seeing far.

Near the mouth of the cavern, they could perceive many curious hieroglyphics of ancient origin, some of them almost entirely concealed with growing moss. And the cabalistic designs were inscribed upon walls of a peculiar stone, which might be easily dug out with a small knife. The singular formation was more like pressed sand than solid stone.

Old Betz said that the bones of her ancestors were lying in a mound above the cavern; and she took them around to a path by which they ascended the bluff and there saw the old cemetery of the ancient Naudowessies. She pointed out the resting-place of several great chiefs, and particularly designated the exact spot where the remains of her own father were laid several generations ago. For that information the covetous old guide wanted extra pay. Indeed, she expected additional compensation at every turn. But then a mere trifle at a time would appease her avaricious craving.

It was after sundown some time, and the evening twilight would soon fade in darkness, when the whisky-seller landed from a canoe half a mile below Mendota, and seemed to be waiting for some one. He finally ensconced himself in a sandstone gorge of the bluff, and sat there quietly until an Indian, with painted face and soft step, emerged from concealment in the bushes a short distance up the stream.

The Indian stealthily crept to the spot where the whisky-seller was crouching, and suddenly pounced upon him!

A brief struggle—and then the Indian left his victim to die!

Fort Snelling, from the South-east, as it appeared previous to the Sioux war.

CHAPTER IX.

Perhaps Kaskadino was an unseen listener during the interview between Florinda and Parrant, in the shanty at Pig's Eye landing. And inheriting the stealthy cunning of his aboriginal "ancestoresses," it was quite natural for him to make the most of an available opportunity. Therefore, while the whisky-seller was ambushed in anticipation of success in some design upon Florinda, the *half* red-skin pounced upon him to get possession of his gold. Rascal and rogue both struggled desperately together. But the assailant was vigorous and strong, and his victim at best rather feeble in muscular strength. The result was fatal to the latter; and the former unintentionally left him for dead!

Kaskadino then concealed the gold under a broken rock, and hastened to wash his face in the river, intending to immediately alarm the camp by an announcement that he had just found the body of a murdered man.

And as Tashae, his rival with Florinda, actually passed that spot a short time before, he would boldly accuse him of the crime. Such an accusation would seem all the more probable when Tashae's knife might be found with the body.

The rascal had stolen Tashae's knife only yesterday, and accidentally lost it in the struggle with Parrant. But there was a witness to the whole transaction. Old Betz had restrained Florinda from a consummation of her rash intention, by proposing to go alone and bring either the gold or the whisky-seller himself into the camp.

Florinda was naturally shrewd; and yet, while the experience of her life had been calculated to sharpen her sagacity, she frequently allowed herself to be outwitted. She might have surpassed Madame Zorah in deceit; but the latter was one of those dauntless women whom we sometimes read of and very seldom meet in the every-day walks of life.

Personal fear never deterred Madame from confronting anything in human form. And her recent acquaintance with the savages and half-breeds of Selkirk Colony had thoroughly familiarized her with rude and treacherous people. Even Leonore, the beautiful flower of sixteen, possessed more real courage than a dozen city damsels all put together. But Leonore was not inordinately brave or daring by nature. And though circumstances were tutoring her to combat with and to resist the harsh realities of life, her manner was graceful, her voice soft, her touch gentle, while her laugh rang in that silvery tone which rouses all the enthusiasm of a susceptible heart.

Old Betz saw Kaskadino surprise Parrant; and after he hid the gold, she stealthily took it away. Hastening back to the camp, she gave the alarm herself, and also declared that she had seen Kaskadino kill a man behind the rocks. But upon leading the excited traders to the place where the supposed murder had been committed, she was made a butt for all manner of sarcasm and verbal abuse, in consequence of no corpse being found. And Kaskadino actually produced several witnesses to prove that he was with them all the evening at a place which they named, on the other side of Mendota. At that time lying was common there. I can not say how it is now.

Kaskadino was completely foiled, and Old Betz also failed in her revenge. What then?

Parrant's body disappeared; but not in his own canoe! The next day, when Kaskadino could not find the gold, he immediately suspected Old Betz of taking what he had stolen. And she gave the entire amount to Florinda, who went away the following evening in company with Levasseur, Madame Zorah and Leonore, on board a St. Louis steamer.

Poor Tashae was left in the lurch. Having brought Florinda down to Mendota at his own expense, purposely to have a pleasant companion in the tedious journey back to Red River, he was perfectly amazed when she suddenly departed on board the steamer, without previously intimating any such intention. He was mad, and Kaskadino wild.

There seemed to be nothing reliable in Florinda's affection, even after the perpetration of crime to appease her jealousy. Perhaps moral philosophers are wrong when they say that the affection of a woman at thirty-five or forty is much stronger than the love of a girl but half that age. And yet many occurrences of peculiarity might be adduced to confirm the plausibility of their theory. Observation has revealed to me a species of infatuated insanity—a spasmodic manifestation of love or affection—sometimes remarkably intense, and generally quite blind, which unmarried females of uncertain age and very sentimental predilection, are more or less subject to. I have also noticed that an incipient paroxysm of their untamed passions may suddenly become a perfect volcano; and then unaccountably and prematurely ripen into an iceberg or a hypochondriac simoom, to finally dissolve in the sea of despair, or vanish on desert air.

However, in all probability, Florinda's past history may not have been any more interesting than that of numerous other adventuresses of the same class. She certainly had a particular object in going to Selkirk Colony, and subsequently made a desperate effort to get a husband. And though deplorably unsuccessful in that attempt, she rashly involved herself with Kaskadino so as to render the safety of a protracted sojourn in the community where he lived somewhat precarious. Under such circumstances, perhaps she acted prudently in seeking a home elsewhere.

And thus the old story of social depravity was repeating itself in connection with the early history of civilization in the vicinity of that beautiful spot where the populous city of St. Paul now stands. I shall not attempt to estimate the quantity of maledictive vituperation generated in the usually obdurate bosom of Tashae, the fur-trader, by the total loss of both Florinda and Leonore. Nor need I dwell upon the subsequent conduct of Kaskadino, which clearly demonstrated his fixed resolution to be revenged on Old Betz, if not on any one else.

Half-breeds are sure to inherit some of the direst passions of the Indian race—but the venerable squaw was full-blooded, and she displayed a greater degree of cunning than Kaskadino ever possessed. She could not be outwitted by any number of Kaskadinos; and consequently he went back to the bosom of his family at Selkirk Colony, a wiser and a far more disagreeable husband and father than he ever was before. Tashae also journeyed home again in a very melancholy humor.

Meanwhile, Parrant, the queer-eyed whisky-retailer, disappeared from the vicinity of *Im-in-i-jas-ka*. And he would never return!

Madame Zorah and Leonore were going each to fill one of those remarkable destinies which are at variance with the course of common events. The future seemed full of promise; but the "boy god" still had plenty of arrows in his quiver, and at least one more innocent would eventually be added to the Golgotha of love!

Major Levasseur, that polished man of the world, who took them from the Colony, could not deny himself the pleasure of possessing Leonore's confiding heart. But her grandma counted on good fortune, and, regardless of past experience, rashly allowed the tempter to approach.

Levasseur was no amateur in the art of wooing. He thoroughly understood the female heart; and erelong the beautiful girl worshiped him more as a god than a man. So handsome, so kind, so noble and so good! How could she help giving him all the pure love she had to bestow? And her grandmother spoke no words of warning until it was too late.

They found a temporary home in St. Louis, where, for a time, Leonore seemed very happy. Levasseur was there, and she asked for nothing more. His caresses banished all else from her mind. They were soon to be

6*

married; and then she would be his wife. To-morrow—not to-day! But Madame said it was dangerous to wait. He offered one excuse for delay, and then another. Marriage there was to be—but what of the marriage-day?

Madame felt ugly and sour, and said something un-unpleasant for Levasseur to hear. They nearly quarreled, and Leonore threw her arms around his neck and kissed him very sweetly, with words of persuasion that he might gratify grandma. Pure, simple girl—she did not then fully comprehend the ultimate necessity of such a ceremony in the light that grandma did! Her education had been very imperfect in many particulars.

He could not refuse her so trifling a favor; and one evening a priest came to marry them.

Madame witnessed the ceremony, and then signed a paper which purported to be executed in evidence of their union.

Some months elapsed, and then Levasseur went away on a journey, waving a kiss for his pretty one to be of good spirits until he returned to caress her again.

They imagined that Levasseur's journey must be a very long one, for he did not return. Days and weeks passed, and still the idol of Leonore's heart remained away! While she sighed and wept, her grandma was absorbed in deep meditation. Madame could not weep. Her tears were exhausted long ago. Yet her brain was alive. Full of thought, one day she sat like a statue, gazing intently upon the floor until the wrinkles in her face seemed to expand with the intensity of emotion. What she was thinking about Leonore did not know. But at length some fixed resolve inspired her to move.

Madame was not yet aware that Levasseur's pedigree went back to the old Marquis Dupontavisse. She unsuspectingly saw the grandson of her deceased noble morganatic husband take her grandchild for a bride! And by that marriage, what a strange confusion of relationship was begun! A genealogist of great perception and skill would be required to elucidate the consanguineous position of Levasseur and Leonore after their matrimonial union!

As if moved by a presentiment of something wrong, Madame felt ill at ease when the brief and simple marriage ceremony was over. A vague comprehension of the technicalities of law suggested that the husband might not be effectually secured, after all. Yet she kept her own thoughts to herself; and when Levasseur did not return, she began to inquire of those who were supposed to know whither he had gone. Her inquiries were useless. And then a suspicion entered her mind. But Leonore must not know what that suspicion was.

Without even the encouragement of a friend's advice, Madame went forth to pursue her inquiries almost every day; and at length she was recognized very oddly by a man in a state of intoxication, who sneeringly exulted in her face.

"Where's your daughter?" he stupidly hiccoughed, with his arm wrapped around an awning-post in the highway. "I say, old lady, why don't you reverence the holy father who made her and the man she loved flesh of one flesh and bone of one bone? Come hither, and receive my blessing. But first, you must confess! And if you've got any loose change, I'll not decline a respectable fee. A priest can't save your wicked soul without remuneration. Ha—hic! No!"

His last articulation terminated with a violent surge, that loosened his arm from the awning-post; and a descending gyration rolled him at her feet. "Here's my

TA-TANKA-NAJIN; or "Standing Buffalo." A Sioux Chief, and friend of "Sweet Corn;" both of whom opposed the Massacre of '62.

card," he muttered, after gaining a comfortable position in the gutter!

Madame snatched the card from his nervous hand, and read "Phineas O'Brien, Attorney at Law"—office in such a street and at a designated number.

"Is this yours?" she emphasized, without noticing the presence of several persons who stopped to witness the deplorable scene.

"I am the son of Michael O'Brien, and I practice law in the State of Missouri. Come and see me day after to-morrow. I shall not go home till morning. Business with the municipal police department may detain me longer than I want to stay. But the majesty of the law must be respected, even by those who live from its frequent violation. I say the law must be respected!"

A policeman came up and accorded with O'Brien's declaration, by hoisting him off to the lock-up, without even a word of explanation.

"You see I'm wanted," jocosely hiccoughed O'Brien, with a parting leer at Madame, who stood transfixed in mental confusion. "They've sent for me now. The case is that of the Municipality *vs.* Phineas O'B. Call day after to-morrow, and we'll see what can be done. The law must be respected!"

Madame returned to Leonore; but said nothing about O'Brien. She was chafing within, yet smiled to cheer her drooping grandchild. And, pretending that she expected to get intelligence from Levasseur in a few days, she waited as patiently as possible until, in accordance with the inebriated lawyer's invitation, she called at his office, and found him in.

Phineas was quite sober by that time, and received Madame with evident confusion. She referred to his awning-post declarations, and exhibited his card. At first he prevaricated just enough to rouse her metal. She eyed him contemptuously, and then said:

"Mr. O'Brien, do not trifle with a desperate woman! Aid me in obtaining justice, and I will not only overlook your complicity with that bad man, but guarantee you a handsome reward!"

Madame looked very resolute, and spoke with an emphasis that he could not misunderstand. Pretending to arrange his papers for a moment or so, he concluded to receive a client in anticipation.

"Bad man!" quoth he, with a severe shrug, and pushing back his chair. "We need not argue that point, while he is so abundantly able to compensate those who serve him. I fear that your reward can not equal his."

"Mr. O'Brien, you are aware of the penalty incurred by personating a priest. And if I tell you that there is a witness ready to identify you, perhaps my proposition will be accepted."

"A witness! That is impossible!"

"Very well! In an hour's time we shall see! Goodby, Mr. O'Brien!"

Madame instantly rose to depart, and Phineas expressed a desire for her not to be in too much of a hurry.

"Will you assist me, then?"

"You forget that I might compromise myself in the undertaking. He is rich, and you are poor. His money can baffle justice itself. And who would believe your story?"

"Mr. O'Brien, open the book before you, and see what the law says in reference to that act of villainy on your part. One witness beside myself, and the evidence of Leonore, who can identify you by that cast in your left eye, will be sufficient to insure your conviction. Where is Levasseur?"

"Gone! He is now entirely out of your reach!"

"I ask whither he has gone."

"To the City of New York. He is there with his wife!"

Madame was unprepared for that announcement of O'Brien; and she struggled to hide the sensation it produced in her brain. After recovering, she inquired how long he had known Levasseur. His reply was an evasive shrug. She then asked when he was married, to whom, and where?

"Major Levasseur married the daughter of a wealthy banker in New Orleans, at least six years ago!"

"How do you know all that?"

"I was a clerk in her father's office at the time of their marriage, and also witnessed the ceremony, in the church of ——."

"What church?" eagerly demanded Madame.

"I do not remember," drawled O'Brien.

"The banker's name? You have not forgotten that!"

"My memory is very poor, and I forget many things."

"Villain! Give me Levasseur's address in New York."

"That is out of my power. I can not acquaint you with what I do not know."

Phineas O'Brien did put on the robes of a priest to marry Major Levasseur and Leonore. There was something between the rich man and the tippling lawyer. A secret divulged might deprive Phineas of the common privileges of a citizen. In St. Louis were many dark-skinned slaves, whose masters could barter them the same as common merchandise without any violation of the laws. And Phineas claimed to be the son of

Michael O'Brien; but his Creole mother was included among the goods and chattels inventoried as part and parcel of the estate of Levasseur's father-in-law, who died in New Orleans soon after the marriage of his only daughter. Michael O'Brien, Phineas' father, was a negro-trader, who made money and spent it, until his temporal existence ended in a pauper's grave.

Phineas was born a slave; but being a likely lad, and very nearly white, he received an education fitting him for the duties of a clerkship in the banking office of his master, where he diligently occupied his leisure hours in studying law. In Phineas, Levasseur found an instrument adapted to his wants; and, after taking the banker's daughter for a wife, he negotiated for the vassal's freedom. Phineas subsequently practiced law in New Orleans and finally established himself in St. Louis, where he did a prosperous business until tippling ruined his expectations.

When Levasseur arrived in St. Louis with his *proteges* from Selkirk Colony, Phineas was quite out at the elbows, and ready for participation in whatever might promise a reward. His services were required. It was not difficult for him to personate a priest. He could adapt himself to almost any emergency when not muddled with strong drink. Money he would have for his deception, and at the same time obey a command. Obedience was necessary for one in his position. He had been freed from bondage as an assessable chattel—but forgery, adroitly executed, was the price of his liberty! From legal bondage he passed into the clutches of the law. Levasseur could explain how the transfer was performed, and who profited most therefrom. Therefore, detection was to be dreaded in accordance with the ill-will of the master. But, debased as was, Phineas O'Brien would have gladly exchanged his present bondage for that which he had been liberated from.

Madame was satisfied that Levasseur had deserted them! And then she went home to Leonore with a heart full of conflicting emotions. And though it might be utterly absurd to expect that the confiding girl would ever realize her pleasant anticipations of being a happy wife, the destroyer of all her future prospects in life should be made to suffer in some way, if possible, for such a cruel wrong! The law seldom reaches the villain who thus despoils the unsuspecting and the pure. Madame knew that; and she put no dependence in the law. She had long since learned that only the rich and the influential can rely upon legal issues. Her wits were trying to fix upon a scheme more reliable than the law.

Revenge is sometimes very sweet to a malevolent heart. Circumstances have ever been the incentives to evil. But Madame was not of a malignant nature. In girlhood none of her playmates were kinder to her than she was to them. Yet that was a long time past; and the circumstances through which she had been living and enduring since then, eventually made quite a different being of her in the autumn of life. Those whom she once loved were false or in the grave. Indeed, the grave held all her best love, save that for Leonore—and she would cheerfully re-endure the bitterest of past trials, if to spare her. All the world to Madame was centred in Leonore!

One "Good Little Injun Boy," elaborately Costumed, and then Postured with some care, expressly "to have his Photograph taken."

CHAPTER X.

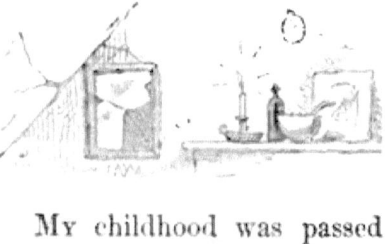

My childhood was passed in a latitude not very remote from the Tropics, and I recollect the month of November there as always connected with associations of inclement weather. How different it is here in St. Paul! During the lapse of that autumnal period of the zodiacal calendar, I am exuberantly enjoying the most delicious atmosphere ever breathed by man!

Indian-Summer occurs after the green foliage has been seared by early frosts, and is then a brief and delightful prelude to the season of inevitable ice and snow. It appears like a dreamy seance of the elements of Nature in sorrow for the smiling summer that is dead and in prayer for a safe transit through the gloomy Hades of the winter to come. It is universally loved and praised by all people who have an opportunity of realizing the enjoyment of its sweet yet mournful smiles. But in no other land on the face of the globe, does it produce anything like the enchantment experienced from it here!

Were I under the influence of opium, or magnetized by that queer stuff sold in fancy drug stores to create dreams of intoxicating bliss, my senses could not realize emotions more delightful than those experienced by me in my pleasant wandering to-day. But while the sun shone intensely bright, and no clouds darkened the sky, a luminous haze gently softened the tranquil light. I was perplexed to understand how the atmosphere could remain so perfectly pure and dry.

Here in Minnesota I perceive none of that irksome inclemency which produces an unpleasant compromise between arid heats and stormy chills so peculiar to more Southern climes, and so intensely disagreeable in all localities contiguous to the sea. Rain seldom falls in November—for when the summer solstice has been attained, the clouds evaporate and become thin, and almost entirely disappear, until they return in December heavily laden with snow. Thus the earth is left clean and dry after the sun recedes from the northern pole, and, remaining in that condition, it forms a hard bed for the snow-flakes in their fall.

To-night—now in the third week of November—I sit writing, with the window of my apartment thrown wide open! And this is what they call Indian-Summer in Minnesota! The gas-light glare within is actually painful to my imagination, while the beautiful moonshine without seems as bright as day!

The bell in a neighboring clock-tower tolls eleven; and it is time that I should lay aside my pen. (I'm sure to hear the bells.) But I must look out through the open casement a moment or two before going to bed.

First I will turn down the gas, so as to enjoy the lovely scene all the better.

The tumult of traffic and the hubbub in the thoroughfares have died away, and, externally seen, the entire city appears to be wrapped in slumber. Now I hear the rumbling wheels of a belated omnibus passing in a distant street, and presently even that sound does not reach my ear. At intervals, a solitary pedestrian is heard "tramping the planks" while homeward bound. And the wakeful dogs are noisy to-night. What they are all barking at, is a difficult conjecture. Possibly at their own shadows, or perhaps at the seemingly prodigious moon. Dogs are very numerous in St. Paul; and sitting here, as I do now, their incessant noise might annoy me, were my kind regard for them less. Let them bark. For while the bells are so saddening, they make me glad! They are the only dumb creatures whom God has imbued with a devoted affection for man! I have had good cause to appreciate their sympathy and devotion, and never pass a respectable individual of that species without desiring to salute him in some friendly way.

I sit at the open window and contemplate the interesting scene until my eyes relinquish external vision, and I gradually lose present consciousness in dreamy retrospection. My mind wanders back through dim and through vivid memories of the past, and fancy recalls two remarkably coincidental events that occurred in the City of New York just twenty years ago, and at this very hour of the night!

But instead of this clear sky and this balmy air, with the moon shining sweetly upon the city in slumber, as it now does here, a cold storm was then raging there. The rain pattered upon the pavements with audible sound, and splashed in the puddles and pools formed where the flagging was low. A mist dim'd the wayside lamps, and the atmosphere above seemed to be smoky and red, as if all illum'd by some distant fire! The green bottles in the druggist's window shed a sickly glare, suggestive of misery and woe. Gusts of wind and rain swept around the corners and moaned among the chimney-tops, while flapping awnings and banging loose window-blinds and rickety doors! It was a cheerless night in the great metropolis. Few people were to be seen in the gloomy streets, and the muffled watchmen hugged their drenched garments about them as they slowly paced their wearisome rounds.

I know of nothing more dismal to a stranger than the silent streets of a large city at midnight during the prevalence of a storm! The lone heart is depressed with a sense of utter desolation, as if walking among colossal tombs! And though thousands of living people are breathing in slumber within the sombre walls so near, a solemnity of feeling calls up imaginary visions of eternity in death.

The scenery of an impenetrable forest, or of a trackless mountain wild, does not inspire such emotions as those arising from a sight of the deserted highways of a sleeping city! Nature in repose may give rise to thoughts sublime, while a contemplation of the works of man, devoid of his presence to infuse them with life, leads the beholder to a melancholy inference of ruin and decay!

The healthy and the prosperous were enjoying all the comfort of life in-doors, little caring for the cold pelting storm that was raging in the outer world. Love nestled in the arms of love, and affection dreamed of the past and of happiness in store for to-morrow. Infants reposed upon their sleeping mothers' breasts, and pleasant smiles played around mothers' lips, revealing the joy they felt to have their sweet darlings there!

Storm-beaten walls concealed the luxury and the happiness—the misery, the want, the sorrow, and the pain experienced within. Palaces yonder, and garrets there—and damp cellars beneath the town! For where so many breathe the same air, the rich and the poor must be very near each other. The greatest and the proudest are but mortals even there! And as time continues to come and go, not all the wealth in the world can keep the ills of human kind from the proud millionaire who scorns the penniless beggar.

And the storm-wind howled among the house-tops while the rain drops continued to fall upon the great city, where lights dimly shone from windows that told of sickness and constant watching, and of prayers for the dawn of day.

Through the casement of a mansion where the affluent are wont to dwell, an unusual light poured out between the elegant lace curtains draping the gold-trimmed screen. Then a carriage dashed around the next street corner, and drew up before the mansion-door. An eminent physician alighted and rang the bell furiously for admission. The door opened and he disappeared within!

Down in the city, another unusual light was seen at a miserable tenement house on a shabby street. From out the dingy attic window in the rear, a feeble ray of light scarcely made a shadow upon the opposite wall. But no carriage, nor even a humble physician, hastened to that wretched abode. The occupants of the attic room were too poor for indulgence in the expense of medical skill.

In the corner of the room stood a cheap cot-bed. An old woman sat beside the cot, anxiously and tenderly nursing a young girl who had just become a mother. Anon the girl-mother fell asleep.

And then the old woman sighed and murmured: "It's all over now! Poor girl! How cruel it was for one like thee! And to think that I am to blame for all thy suffering and thy sorrow! Oh, why did I so play the fool?"

Silently pondering a while, with her eyes fixed upon the bare floor, and mechanically swaying her body, she scowled. "There must be some way for revenge, and I'll try and study it out! He is rich, and we are here in want!"

A slight movement of the sleeping mother silenced the old woman's tongue. But all was well.

"Poor girl—poor girl!" she mused. "If I thought the fate of thy babe would be no better than my own, or thy mother's, or thine, I'd strangle it while asleep, and not let it live to see the light of day. Ah, me! This is a hard world to some! Yes, yes! But what can we do?"

Then the old woman sank into a quiet reverie—again swaying her body, and occasionally breathing a deep sigh, with frequent glances of anxiety toward the girl-mother and her babe, who continued in slumber.

A violent gust of wind startled her, and blew the stuffing out of the broken window-pane. The rain splashed in upon the sleepers' faces, but did not waken them. She quickly reclosed the opening and relapsed into an audible expression of what was passing in her mind.

"If there is any mercy for the poor, we sadly need it now. They may send for me to-morrow, to-night—this very hour! And I must leave her here alone, to go and nurse some rich and happy wife. But that is our only chance. Oh, how cruel it is! Yet we must have money; and the compensation that I shall receive from the rich lady for nursing her, will provide food and shelter for this poor, deserted girl! Better that than starve!"

A loud knocking terminated the old woman's soliloquy, and startled the slumbering girl-mother and her babe!

"Good ebenin! Oney Sancho—dat's all!" said a well-clad and extremely courteous mulatto man, who stood at the door when the old woman opened it with a trembling hand.

"Missus taken suddenly bery ill, an wants de nuss, right way now, dreckley!"

"I was fearful of this," muttered the old woman to herself. And then she said aloud to Sancho: "Wait and show me the way."

"Sartinley! Do dat wid tic'ler pleasure!" replied Sancho, looking round for a chair. But, seeing none, he slowly shook his head with a look of compassion, and glanced inquiringly at the cot.

The old woman hurriedly put on her shawl to accompany Sancho, and whispered to the girl-mother that it would soon be daylight, when probably some of the lodgers on the same floor might look in. She would run back the first moment she could get away!

With kisses and tears she murmured, "God bless you and watch over you until I return!"

Sancho escorted her to his master's mansion. It was the same that the physician entered a little while before. Presenting her to the housekeeper, he said:

"Dis am Madum Zoree!"

Cathedral of St. Boniface, on the Red River of the North.

Madame Zorah was her name! And the girl-mother whom she had just left in the attic without a nurse, was her grand-daughter Leonore.

They had very little money left after arriving in the metropolis, and securing a comfortable lodging. Three rooms, snugly-furnished, made them a tidy home. They did not stop at a boarding-house. Madame entertained an unconquerable aversion for that style of living; and so became housekeeper in a small way.

Meanwhile she sought revenge for Leonore. A wild, mad resolve for a poor old woman in a great, populous city! Yet desperate as it was, a powerful incentive urged her on; and she solemnly vowed that the destroyer should make amends or bitterly rue the wrong.

Major Levasseur's name was not in the published city directory, and she found no one who could give her any information of such a man. Their slender purse was getting more so every day. But Madame persevered in the search until her hope seemed entirely gone.

Down in the world, and nearly buried with despair, she was unable to make a satisfactory return to the agent who called on rent-day for the monthly sum in advance. Poor people in New York are required to pay their rent in that way. Cash down in advance was not particularly objectionable to Madame, while she had the money in her purse. And old as she was, with all the experience of so many sharp vicissitudes, endured with more or less suffering and distress, she hoped that the agent would wait a few days longer. Something might turn up to-morrow. When she found Levasseur, he must make them comfortable, if nothing more. Perhaps he might! But how long would she be finding him?

House agents are not addicted to leniency. And

why? Ask landlords—house owners. Perhaps they can tell! Their code and practice is pay or go. Madame endeavored to explain, and then she implored:

"For Heaven's sake, do show us a little mercy now!"

But the agent never gave himself any concern about the place which she mentioned. His better feelings were dried up before Madame offered her prayers. He had seen beautiful girls turned into the street without a home, and he had shut his ears against the moans of infirm women crouching in corners, hungry and cold! Prayers and entreaties had no more effect upon him than the dissonant sound of the fish-man's horn. His business was to collect money.

Leonore's beauty and Madame's wrinkles were all the same to his eyes. Neither joy nor sorrow met a feeling response from him! A deceitful, cringing smile with the bill, and a sickly obeisance when the money touched his palm, or a half-fiendish grimace when the money was not there!

Madame must move herself, or the merciless agent would call in the constable, who was anxious to come. She did move—into a miserable attic room. But even that could not be accomplished without money; and the no less unfeeling furniture-broker took nearly all they had at his own price. Perhaps not a third of what it should have been.

Intelligence offices! Well, what of them? They are all at best very delusive institutions. The cunning managers generally receive remunerative compensation from both employer and employee, and sometimes make it convenient to swindle one while deceiving the other. Madame had dealt with similar mediums in Paris and also in London, but under different circumstances then. Necessity now drove her to one again. She desired a position as nurse. References would be required, and she had none to give.

"I might accommodate you with everything," suggested the manageress of the institution to which she applied. "I suppose I could do such a favor, if you are willing to pay for it. I have a number of excellent recommendations in my possession. Applicants left them here, and forgot to take them away. You can be trusted, I presume? Should the matter come to light, my reputation would suffer. I am very careful of my reputation. Most of the fashionables rely upon my word in matters of this kind. Say five dollars for an engagement, and ten for testimonials—you understand? Fifteen dollars down!"

The pawnbroker loaned precisely fifteen dollars on a valuable ring that Leonore inherited from her dear mother. It was all they had to pawn—and then, if the intelligence office failed, Madame might well ejaculate, "Heaven help them!" But, luckily, a great lady applied that very day. The lady was not much acquainted in the city, and trustingly sent out her housekeeper to engage a nurse.

Housekeepers are not always sincerely interested in the welfare of those from whom they receive pay to serve. All the better for employees seeking a place. Consequently, the matter was arranged without any questions asked or reference given!

Madame was duly notified that a lady had engaged her. The lady's name was not mentioned, and she did not think to inquire. She was very glad to get the engagement, and it made no difference to her whom the lady might be. Her services would be required at any moment. She must hold herself ready to attend without further warning.

And Sancho, the colored man, did summons her while she sat watching over Leonore, whose babe was not yet an hour old. But when Sancho announced her name to the housekeeper, there was a mutual surprise! If the arrangement at the intelligence office had not been so loosely perfected, an unpleasant meeting might have been avoided!

Very unexpectedly, Madame stood face to face with Florinda, the Canadian adventuress, who exulted in the death of Leonore's dear mother at Selkirk Colony. But Madame did not know all that. She never suspected anything criminal in the conduct of Florinda—and the last she had seen of her was in St. Louis, where they parted, after voyaging together down the Mississippi River.

Madame simply manifested surprise, and really experienced much pleasure in meeting some one in the great metropolis whom she had at least seen before. Florinda was no less surprised; but at the same time exhibited confusion and alarm. She evidently wanted to prevent Madame going up stairs; and her wits were already at work inventing a ruse to get her out of the house entirely. But at that moment the physician's voice was heard impatiently inquiring if the nurse had come!

Madame hastened up stairs into a luxurious chamber, and stood at the bedside of a beautiful lady with a newly-born babe, leaving Florinda speechless in the hall.

"You are the nurse?" said the physician, looking wisely over the top of his heavy gold-framed glasses. "Quiet—very quiet! She is dozing now! You have been tardy! Ahem! This powder will make her sleep again when she wakes. The brown powder—not the white! Allow no one to enter the room until I return in the morning. Much depends upon your experience and attention, as well as upon my skill. She is nervous! Very!"

The physician moved out of the chamber with an air of conscious distinction. His carriage was waiting for him, and he demurely rode away.

Then Madame bent over the unconscious lady and gazed some time upon her beautiful pale face. What a contrast in the position of that great lady and the condition of poor Leonore! Madame felt it all. The easy couch, with its fine linen and its orange-colored silk counterpane. Pillows of goose-down, with deep lace border. A magnificent canopy of blue silk drapery fringed with gold. Costly rosewood elaborately carved, supporting all. Rich velvet carpet, noiseless to the tread. Elegant cabinets, colossal mirrors, and decorative works of art. Pictures—aye, and a large portrait in a massive frame over the mantel. A portrait of whom?

Madame's eyes wandered from one object to another until a sight of the portrait caused her to start with intense wonder and surprise! Her features relaxed, her chin fell, and her eyes gleamed strangely wild! She seemed to be overcome with a dizziness, and, wiping the cold perspiration from her forehead, she appeared older by several years! Choking a moment, she groaned, "Levasseur!"

And, like an evil spirit, Florinda was lurking outside the door, which stood slightly ajar; and a derisive smile relaxed the compression of her lips when she stealthily perceived that Madame already recognized the portrait on the wall!

Landscape, with Indian Camp, near "Red Wood," Minnesota.

CHAPTER XI.

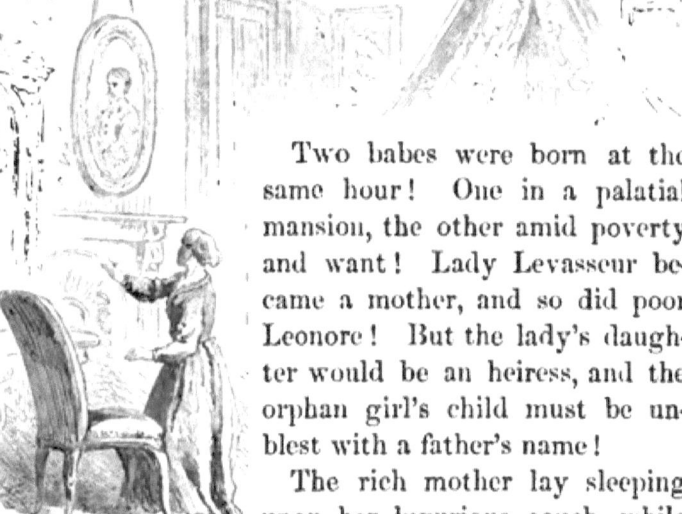

Two babes were born at the same hour! One in a palatial mansion, the other amid poverty and want! Lady Levasseur became a mother, and so did poor Leonore! But the lady's daughter would be an heiress, and the orphan girl's child must be unblest with a father's name!

The rich mother lay sleeping upon her luxurious couch, while Leonore's bed was a miserable cot. And was it any wonder, then, that Madame began to hate Lady Levasseur, the beautiful wife of the man who deceived and deserted her grand-daughter?

She bent over the sleeping wife, and sat for a time absorbed in meditation. A train of thoughts came up in her mind. She had found Major Levasseur at last! But where, and how? Did he love his wife? Was his wife's love for him equal to that of Leonore? Could the elegant lady love as devotedly as the simple girl? Perhaps she did not love him at all. Many rich husbands had wives who returned them no love! It was customary for a lady to marry the wealthiest gentleman she could get. Indeed, husbands were frequently of less importance than their wealth! Any rich man not already married, was a desirable object to catch!

Madame knew all that. She had been only a morganatic bride; but the experience of an eventful life taught her lessons never dreamed of by an unloving or a devoted wife whose marriage was sanctified by holier rites and maintained by law. Mothers educated their daughters for a market. They were instructed how to be attractive, and thoroughly schooled in all the modern arts of flirtation. Maneuvering mammas diligently assisted in conjugating the active verb *catch*, without any consideration whatever for that necessary little conjunction *and*, which joins it to the more important substantive *keep*.

No matter about love! That might not realize diamonds and costly dresses! Love was not reciprocated in every fine mansion! Pretension frequently brought much more luxury than that awarded to the purest love!

Madame believed that love was seldom found among the rich! She never experienced much affection for any one except her daughter, who was dead, and for her darling Leonore. She had seen a great many married people who pretended vastly more than they ever established by their questionable habits of life! Her opinion of society was extremely prejudiced from early association and disappointment in after years. Others have adduced a similar conclusion by even pleasanter evidence than hers!

Madame's heart was very bitter! She hated all the world. All except Leonore, and her babe that was just born. She almost devoured Lady Levasseur's beautiful features as the latter lay wrapt in slumber. How could she destroy that beauty, and wean the Major's love entirely from her—all for Leonore? That babe would be rich, and Leonore's poor! There must be some way to rob her—for the sake of Leonore! She would shrink from nothing that might accomplish Leonore's ascendancy over the wife. A thousand undeveloped thoughts flitted through her half-delirious mind.

If that wife was dead, would Levasseur take Leonore back again to his arms? He might! Well, what then? Madame glanced furtively round the elegant chamber. Her dim eyes gleamed with some sinister intention. She was meditating evil!

All alone! Quiet! Very still! The storm beat against the glass in the window, and a faint moan went up the chimney with the heavy draft from the bright grate-fire! The breathing of mother and babe was audible to her ear, and the ticking of the mantel-clock went regular and clear!

Holding her own breath, she rose as if in a dream! Placing one hand to her forehead to ease a painful throb, she convulsively twirled the other hand and twisted its fingers. Staggering to the marble edge of a costly escritoire, she took up one of the tiny papers of powder left there by the physician before he went away! Opening it, she smiled just a little, and stood a moment to reflect. But gradually raising her eyes, they alighted upon the portrait of Levasseur. His look seemed to divine her thoughts, and she dropped the tiny paper, spilling the white powder upon a satin-covered chair! Still she kept her gaze riveted upon the glowing canvas, as if petrified by his discovery of the wicked design just then in her heart!

Florinda, the housekeeper, was meanwhile hovering near. After disappearing from her first position, she went into the dressing-room by another entrance, and there availed herself of the keyhole in the door communicating with the chamber. She must have been greatly concerned about Madame's unexpected entrance into the Levasseur mansion—else why did she act in that strange way?

The exciting circumstances attending Madame's experience of the night, prevented any inquiries on her part; and thus far she remained totally ignorant of the means by which Florinda gained the position of housekeeper for Levasseur, while she and Leonore had been deserted!

Madame really had no distinct idea of anything except that she was then in Levasseur's house—alone with his wife and her babe who were reposing in luxury, while Leonore and her child lay upon a comfortless cot in the squalid attic, unattended by nurse or friend. She keenly realized the wide contrast! And with bitter contemplation of the extreme difference in their position, she was almost immediately transformed into a fiend! Nearly delirious with the intensity of anger, jealousy and hate that were surging in her heart and whirling in her brain, from the complication of events which had taken place during the last hour, she rashly thought of poison! But casually perceiving the picture against the wall, she was terrified by what seemed to be the living eyes of Levasseur. Their piercing stare went to her heart, and the powder dropped from her hand!

At that instant Florinda softly entered through the communicating door, and with a whispered hush took her by the arm. She was very much bewildered, and mechanically followed Florinda into the dressing-room, where they remained some time whispering together. Florinda proposed that she should resign her engagement before Lady Levasseur awoke. Her compensation should be doubled and tripled, if she went quietly away and did not return! There were good reasons for such a change. The Major would probably come home from Washington the ensuing day, and if he should find Madame installed in his connubial sanctum, a hazardous denouement must be expected.

Florinda argued the case with a great deal of cunning, but instead of inducing Madame to withdraw, she only roused suspicions against herself. And then Madame wanted to know how Florinda came to be there in the position of housekeeper. But that question was not answered quite clearly. And so Madame decided to remain precisely where she was. If Florinda chose to betray her in any way, she comforted herself with the possibility of some severe retaliation!

Leonore's wrongs demanded reparation, and if the lord of the mansion did not acknowledge her claim, his wife should know all. Madame included that desperate alternative in a new resolution instigated by the anxiety of Florinda. Instead of meditating harm to Lady Levasseur, she would be used to circumvent her own husband. His conduct should guide Madame's course of action! If he denied the claim of Leonore—woe betide him then.

Florinda and Madame were becoming enemies. They spoke pleasantly to each other, and both endeavored to conceal the animosity goading them within. But ultimately their mutual deception would not succeed. However, their interview was terminated by Lady Levasseur waking from sleep. And as Madame felt the awkwardness of her position, she asked Florinda for an introduction.

A very unusual scene—but apparently correct. Only a faint smile welcomed Madame. No matter; she had a bold game to play, and resolved not to wince until the stakes were entirely lost. She really had nothing to lose, and everything to gain. In any event, she could not worse her own condition or that of Leonore.

Madame began the duties of nurse, while Florinda went to her own room and wrote a letter to the Major, who intended to return from Washington as soon as he received notice of the event in expectation. Florinda had been instructed to notify him by telegram. In that she was then complete master of the situation.

Levasseur was pushing a negotiation with the Government, and did not wish to leave the capital until he attained the desired ultimatum. Florinda had familiarized herself with his affairs sufficiently to warrant her in taking more liberty than an ordinary housekeeper would dare attempt; and she wrote him a very business-like letter. It ran thus:

"My lady has presented you with a little daughter. But I am sure you will pardon me for not telegraphing immediately when I tell you that, through some unfortunate fatality attending the engagement of her nurse at the intelligence office, old Madame Zorah, Leonore's grandmother, has been sent to wait upon my lady! You are amazed at this announcement; but cannot be any more so than I was when Sancho brought her in. I tried all prudent means to get her out of the house before she even saw my lady, but neither persuasion nor the offer of money had the least influence whatever. Of course she recognized your beautiful portrait over the mantel, and is now in my lady's chamber, impatient to meet you on your return. Therefore, if I may be allowed to offer advice, you had better not precipitate yourself into domestic trouble—at least not while my lady is in such a delicate condition. Remain away for a time, and I will do my best to dispose of the old witch. I might have acted more decisively; but as she evidently suspects me of personal motives, it is best that I should rely mainly upon *finesse*. Write to my lady on receipt of this, and feign a good excuse for your provoking detention. The old thing tells me that Leonore is not in the city; but declines to reveal the girl's retreat. You may depend upon my fidelity at all hazards, and I shall anxiously await your reply." She also added, "Fondly and eternally yours!"

At an early hour in the morning Sancho was dispatched to the General Post Office with the letter, so that it might go out in the first mail.

Madame asked to be excused also at an early hour in the morning. She would not be absent long. But ignorance of the streets somewhat embarrassed her speedy flight to Leonore. However, she was fortunate enough to meet Sancho returning from the Post Office, and he cheerfully escorted her the right way.

Leonore received her grandma with a smile, and their arms were instantly entwined about each other's neck. Baby was doing well; but presently Madame's eyes lighted up with some sudden thought while she affectionately scrutinized its scarcely defined features. She was in a rare humor, and fairly cackled to herself with the new idea in her mind. She did not tell Leonore what made her so jubilant—and it was well for her scheme that she did not.

A poor widow occupying the next attic was employed to nurse Leonore; and with another scene of mutual

Minnehaha Falls, as seen from the Minneapolis side.

kisses and tears, the girl-mother and her grandma separated again.

Madame chuckled as she went out, and then cackled to herself all the way down stairs. She was felicitating herself upon a terrible expiation for Major Levasseur!

"Just the same age—and both girls!" she mused, in the exuberance of her feeling. "No one could tell them apart if they were placed together. Their own mothers would be none the wiser if I should change them! If I should? And why not? *Our* child has as much right to be an heiress as *theirs!* But one of the children can lawfully inherit their father's name and wealth, and—and *that* one shall be *Leonore's!*"

Florinda asked Sancho why he had been absent so long; and in his simple goodness he not only boasted of showing Madame to her squalid home, but sorrowfully added:

"Ah, some us rich folks don't know how orf'l bad off dem ar poor critters am in de low streets and alleys, and down cellar, and way up in de garrets, dar. I seed a lady dat am lub'lee as a angel. She was li'n in Madum Zoree's bed, an I spec she had a little small chile! Old Sancho's heart felt berry sad to seem em dar widout any konweniences ob life!"

And thus Florinda learned that Leonore was in the city—notwithstanding her grandma's assertion to the contrary. But she did not clearly comprehend Sancho's intimation of the unhappy girl's maternal condition. However, she immediately penned another letter to the Major, and then nervously waited for whatever might occur.

Lady Levasseur was rather pleased with her nurse—which might not have been expected, when Madame's coarse face appeared so very masculine. But she endeavored to make a favorable impression by the earnestness of her attention; and the first few days passed without any external sign of the terrible mischief then brewing. There might have been a sudden fluttering in Madame's heart whenever she heard the street-door bell ring in expectation of the Major's return; but only Florinda could even imagine that. Lady Levasseur's future life was not yet darkened by the slightest shadow of impending harm.

More than a week elapsed, and still the Major did not return. Madame wondered why; but prudence forbade inquiry. She knew that Florinda was corresponding with him daily—that Lady Levasseur received letters from him, and employed her housekeeper to write the answers. She was cognizant of that only. Little did she imagine that Florinda was playing a desperate part. Both deeply interested in the consummation of their own plans, they did not anticipate the scheming of each other.

The hour at length arrived for Madame to execute the first act of her revenge. Florinda accepted an invitation to spend the day with a lady in Jersey City who lived there in great style from the proceeds of a remunerative "Clairvoyant" occupation. It was a pleasant afternoon, and Madame suggested that a little fresh air would be extremely beneficial to the baby. Lady Levasseur did not object. Ladies of her position seldom allow maternal solicitude and attention to occupy their minds. They too often leave their tender offspring entirely in charge of hirelings who rarely have any heart in the task.

Lady Levasseur was naturally an affectionate mother. But her whole existence had not yet become identified with that of her babe. And why? Because she was not necessarily actuated by those tender sympathies which are fully developed in mothers whom humbler circumstances compel *to act* and *feel* with all the capacities of body and mind. Therefore, Madame could do whatever she thought best.

Cackling with almost fiendish delight, Madame hurried away to Leonore in the attic room. The widow woman who nursed Leonore was sent off on a long errand. Then telling Leonore that she did not look as well as usual, it was not difficult to make her swallow three of the sleeping powders that were left by the physician after the accouchement of Lady Levasseur. A narcotic dose powerful enough to stupefy any one! But Leonore must sleep very sound. And then Madame cackled again while hastening back to the Levasseur mansion.

The lawful heiress to Major Levasseur's name and wealth was in Madame's arms, and it went out through the massive rosewood door never to return!

Leonore seemed dead to all the world when her grandma brought in Lady Levasseur's child. And then the first act of a drama in real life and sorrow was there performed! Quickly disrobing both infants, Madame clad the nameless progeny of the beautiful orphan in the costly apparel of the baby heiress! She then wrapped the other in the plain clothes and tucked it up in bed!

Both babes were kicking and crowing, and seemed to enjoy the change that might be dooming them to misery in their future lives.

But Madame scowled cruelly upon the little one left at the side of Leonore, while vehemently kissing the other, whom she hugged up to her bosom. Then she hurried back again to the mansion, carrying with her

Leonore's child. She suddenly ceased her cackling at the mansion door—for Dinah, the colored wife of Sancho, answered the bell and grinned a welcoming salutation.

"Young misse kum home gin! Lor bress her nice, swete, preshus sef! An' not bin ride'n in de caridge, need'r. Massa mus' get a bran new wun for 'is lubly darter, right away. Yes, indeed-ee, he mus'! Bress er purty pictur—she's good fur sore eyes!"

Dinah pulled the child's mantle off its face, and that made Madame feel nervous. But she was much more agitated a moment later, when Lady Levasseur kissed it and embraced it as her own.

And then Madame must see Leonore safely out of that deep slumber. It would not take long to run down there. So, pretending to have dropped something at a store where she had not even been, Madame flew back to finish up the attic scene.

Leonore was already awake and staring at the child by her side.

"What now? Have your senses left you, or are you dreaming?" began Madame, in a kind and innocent tone.

"Where is my darling?" gasped Leonore, bewildered and in tears. "This is not mine!"

"How absurd! Why, you silly goose, not to know your own child! Forsooth, here's a model mother! I don't wonder it laughs at you so!"

"Oh, no, grandma—that is not my babe! Take it away!" shuddered Leonore.

"Bah! See its clothes—and that pretty cap made by your own hands. Surely you are not insane! Its mamma disowns it—eh? She does?"

"Oh, dear grandma, there is something wrong! I shudder when I touch its little hands. See, its flesh does not feel like that of my darling! Oh, it is all strange to me! Please—do take it away, and bring back mine!"

Leonore wept aloud. She shrank back and shuddered instead of embracing the child. "Take it away, and return mine!" she continued to cry.

Madame began to feel alarmed. She tried scolding without avail, and then soothing persuasion.

The poor widow returned—and Madame appealed to her.

"She has been dreaming," laughed Madame; "and now she don't know her own babe. Look—she says it is not hers!"

The poor widow was deceived by the likeness; and she also laughed at Leonore's impression. Then they both tried to convince her that she was mistaken. But all to no purpose. She possessed the rare instinctive perception of a mother! And Madame was finally obliged to leave her sobbing in grievous distress!

The little innocent laughed and crowed to see Leonore's face all suffused with tears; and its meaningless smile actually pierced her heart—not with rebuke for her aversion, but like a sting of jealousy from some vague source through its unimpassioned gaze. And when she refused it the nourishment of her breast, the poor widow looked on perfectly amazed.

"I can perceive the image of a beautiful *blonde* lady reflected in its eyes!" Leonore shiveringly cried—"and she scowls at me! Oh, do take it away!"

Fort Abercrombie, on the Red River, near the Route of the "Northern Pacific Railway."

CHAPTER XII.

Aspasia and Cleopatra were both remarkable exemplifications of successful beauty. Since their time, many other women have attained the most exalted position by the influence of personal charms. And without egotism I will suggest a study of this social phenomenon for convincing proof that beauty is the choicest gift of Nature. Such a theory on my part may not elevate me in the esteem of those very spiritual intellects who realize no enjoyment from external things. Yet I am not entirely forgetful of the blessed endowment of mind. Though while the understanding may be improved by education, all the arts known to science will fail to render a physical deformity comely in our sight. A repulsive face and form do not inspire us with emotions of delight. And yet empires have been overturned by the influence of physical attractions pertaining to the fair sex.

The power of reason, embodied in pure morality and

a cultivated intellect, is very often outweighed by external loveliness in women. However, this will not be admitted as a "good result" by those orthodox expounders of the heinousness of sensual emotion, who contend that all personal beauty is only "skin deep." And it can not be denied that the ancient Puritans, with a profane lack of reverence for "God's Image," did their utmost to spoil the personal charms of their daughters by sombre raiment and coerced unemotional restraint. I have heard of one pious New England grandmother who actually caused a portion of her daughter's beautiful front teeth to be extracted, with the avowed purpose of deterring ungodliness that might arise from vanity! And I also remember reading how some of those pious fanatics gratified their insane zeal by burning individuals, with the sincere though absurd belief, that "witches" ought to expire with torture. Thanks to the *printing press* for its diffusion of knowledge, by which nearly all those pious prejudices have been extinguished—I trust forever.

Female beauty, in a corporeal sense, may be defined as a perfectly harmonious blending of the natural functions of life with the external form. When the principal elements of vitality are in a sound state of health, and the general anatomy is developed in graceful outline, may be seen those exquisitely formed limbs, those delicate hands and feet, and that transparent skin, the roseate blush of which is so warming even to an observer's eye. Beauty is the special adornment of woman—and hence she is endowed with an exquisite sense of fondness for whatever pertains to the toilet. With some it becomes a ruling passion, and in exceptional cases moral ruin. The Roman beauties wore masks at home to preserve their complexion. It is said that Diana of Poictiers retained the freshness of youth to a great age by following the advice of Paracelsus. We are told that at sixty her beauty was ravishing to the dullest eyes of men. She bathed in rain-water every morning; and Madame Tallien, who participated in those extravagant luxuries and abandoned excesses revived under the rule of the first Napoleon, actually wallowed in a mash of strawberries and raspberries, after which her form was washed with sponges saturated with milk and costly perfumes.

But while a beautiful form appeals only to our senses, a lovely face, where every other attraction might be wanting, will instantly touch our heart. And accordingly we kiss the eyes or the lips of those whom we love, leaving the cheek, the hand, or the like, to be caressed in token of unimpassioned affection.

Admitting that beauty is so choice a gift to woman, I nevertheless distinctly remember more than one very homely lady whose educational attainments enabled her to be extremely fascinating. And not only the most charming, but by far the most bewitching lady I ever knew, really possessed very little physical attraction. Her charms existed only in the imagination of those whom she fascinated by the adroit exercise of a naturally superior intellectuality, tutored to the highest perfection of mental skill. In plain terms, she was a remarkably accomplished cheat! The appellation is not any harsher than it should be. Her name was quite familiar to the public some years ago—but I presume that it is nearly or quite forgotten now.

When natural beauty of face and form accompanies a bright intellect, all heightened by the artificial attractions and the educational accomplishments of the nineteenth century, we have everything necessary for the perfection of real divinities to enslave the affection of a masculine saint!

For modern appreciation, physical beauty certainly is the choicest gift that Nature can bestow upon a woman. Other attractions she may acquire. A beautiful face is absolutely natural. Art may hide defects—but it can not physically transform!

Lady Levasseur had the double advantage of natural beauty and a polished mind. Her father was a wealthy banker, and she an only daughter. She was in all respects fitted for the wife of a gentleman occupying an exalted position. Alluding to her marriage, the "New Orleans Picayune" closed thus:

"Elegantly robed in white, the belle of the Crescent City blushed and bowed at the hymeneal altar. The ceremony over, the happy couple, attended by the bridal guests, passed down the church aisle for exit at the door where their carriages stood in waiting. A long, white vail concealed the bride's features as they withdrew, but the face of the handsome and noble bridegroom was all radiant with joy."

And Leonore was beautiful, too. Nature smiled tenderly upon her. And though her education had been neglected from circumstances beyond possible control, she nevertheless possessed an innate delicacy equal to that of the most accomplished and refined. The sweet effeminacy of her comparatively unpolished mind and the classic contour of her exquisite form bespoke a superior origin.

Yet there was no complimentary paragraph in either of the St. Louis papers after the same "handsome and noble bridegroom" gave his hand to Leonore.

Did Major Levasseur marry the beautiful and accomplished daughter of the wealthy banker for love? He admired her. Many other gentlemen did that much. She was a city belle, and could have selected a husband from among scores of gentlemen whom she knew. And perhaps either of those admirers would have given her more tender love than what she acquired with the name of Levasseur. But she loved him to idolatry; and it did seem that he ought to have been supremely happy with such a wife.

But the world can not judge between man and wife. It is one thing to say what should be, and quite another to prophesy the result. That indescribable "something" which is a stumbling-block to so many hopes and loves in this misguided world, existed (or did not exist) between Levasseur and his elegant bride. He was not happy, while she thought her happiness complete. She loved him, and he knew it. He said that he loved her, and she believed him. And their acquaintances pronounced them a model pair! And thus their first year of wedded life soon passed away!

But changes continually occur with all things, and everywhere. Nothing can remain the same. Increasing or decreasing is the perpetually inexorable law governing substance, life and feeling! The instant of arrival at maturity is the beginning of decay. Even our love increases until attaining its zenith, and then diminishes every hour. We do not love and *continue* loving precisely the *same!* Either we love more or we love less! All is transitory. What appears stationary and eternal, is changing while we look upon it as fixed forever! Perpetual change leaves nothing to-morrow as it was yesterday.

Levasseur had his wife, and he had her love and her father's money. He bargained for all that, and gave his name and his hand, and promised her his love in exchange. 'Twas a bargain that he coveted, and yet it did not seem to satisfy him. He wanted to be a good husband! At least he thought so. But in the bonds of matrimony, how could he love any one except his wife, without a violation of the sacred ties binding him? Legal statutes, social laws and divine mandates required him to love his wedded wife and only her! How was it possible for him to do that while coveting what he did not possess?

The wealthy banker in New Orleans died! His only daughter became Levasseur's bride in the autumn, and when summer brought its fruits and flowers, they laid him in the grave!

Lady Levasseur was parentless then. Her mother died before she could remember. She was not only an orphan, but had very few relatives whom she knew. Her father and her mother both came from abroad, and neither of them ever said much about their family connections. But her mother's brother, a wealthy bachelor engaged in some foreign trade, was then living in New Orleans.

Yet the elegant lady, with but a solitary consanguineous tie, inherited a large fortune, and bore the name of a noble husband. The domestic slaves of her deceased father's estate thought no other lady could equal their beautiful young mistress; and she regarded them with gratitude and affection in return. Only two of them, Sancho and Dinah. A venerable couple, who first taught her baby-limbs to perform their duties of life, and had ever after striven to anticipate and gratify her expanding wants. She even learned to call Dinah by the endearing name of Mamma, and Sancho by that of Uncle! Her father made no objection to that.

Most Northern parents would have experienced a

dreadful shock to hear their daughter address a colored servant in such terms, while it was considered merely a pleasant kindness among those accustomed to the institution of slavery. Such is the difference between acquired prejudice and spontaneous feeling!

The noble husband of the banker's daughter obtained great riches which she did not trouble herself to count. He made investments and went into disastrous speculations, which lessened the bulk of a vast estate until it became advisable to remove his habitation.

The City of New York is a favorite harbor for deluded adventurers when threatening storms darken the horizon of their chimerical sea; and it seems to be the final resort of many a desperate mortal, where, for a brief period, avenging wrath can be stayed with the possibility of multiplied horrors when the last ray of hope has gone!

Levasseur sold out in New Orleans; and he resolved to sell Sancho and Dinah with everything else. But their mistress shuddered at that suggestion. Sancho, with his head as white as snow; and Dinah, with her hair all frosty, too. Poor old slaves! Part with them? No, no! It was the first time in her life that she resolved to oppose the decree of either father or husband. He said they must be sold, and she declared that they never should be taken from her. She repeated never in a tone emphatic enough for even Levasseur to fully comprehend her meaning.

What tears of gratitude Dinah and Sancho shed! Sell them? She would a thousand times rather set them free. Yet neither Sancho nor Dinah wished for that. They had no use for freedom. How could they leave their dear young mistress, while loving her with the affection of fond parents for a darling child? They would be her slaves forever! The master yielded without much persuasion when he saw their mutual affection.

And then they all found a new home in the great Northern city, where Levasseur purchased a costly mansion to dwell in. And, as a manifestation of kindness toward his loving wife, he caused the deed to be executed in her name. How generous a husband may appear, when, with a small part of the wealth acquired by marriage, he buys a residence in his wife's name! Such magnanimity is characteristic of some rogues who might be named!

The lord and master of the mansion deeded in his wife's name was induced to embark in certain speculations then carried on in the vicinity of the Upper Mississippi River. And thus he was necessarily absent much of his time, on business matters at Washington, and in making journeys to the North-west.

Five of the first settlers of Minnesota, now living in the City of St. Paul, still have some recollection of the handsome Major, whose clever financiering taught them to play sharp or lose. But none of them suspected that he was the grandson of a distinguished French marquis. Yet he could "handle choice corner lots" in embryo cities and incipient towns, with the shrewdest speculator—and doubtless the gentleman from Pennsylvania who "disliked auburn hair," might enjoy a perusal of his subsequent career in life. I am quite positive that the remembrance of a "three-wheeled buggy" would recall a trifling incident to the mind of a Western Judge who knew something of the Major's skill in pugilistic recreation. The Honorable ———, of Springfield, Illinois, paid a wine bill of one hundred and thirteen dollars, in addition to several thousands staked at cards, one night on board a Mississippi steamer while going up to Prairie du Chien. Major Levasseur won that money, and afterward turned it into land, which the Honorable gentleman subsequently bought at a "forced" sale.

Before his trip to Selkirk Colony, Levasseur had made the personal acquaintance of numerous "representative men" from the North-west, who visited Washington for State purposes or to secure their individual aggrandizement by National legislation. Yet, as he never alluded to his wife, it was generally inferred that no matrimonial obligations existed in denial of the privileges which he claimed in ladies' society. And the fair sex seemed to be unanimous in their admiration of him, either as a gallant cavalier or a capital prize in the marriage lottery. He was, in all respects, a popular man. Certainly he was handsome, or the ladies would not have been so eager for an introduction. That his natural gifts had been highly improved by education was plainly evident from the ease with which he infatuated so many almost at the first meeting. Handsome, intelligent, witty, accomplished, refined and rich! What other qualities were required to exalt a man in the estimation of the fair sex? A hereditary title of nobility would have made his individuality a captivating perfection in the eyes of every lady whom he met.

And though Levasseur's acquaintances in this country were ignorant of his royal pedigree, it was surmised by more than one romantically inclined admirer that he might be some prince or duke in disguise. That he persistently declined to reveal his birth, and rank among noblesse, was not any more remarkable than a similar taciturnity maintained by other exiles from France. A political convulsion had then banished many proud grandees, who discreetly assumed untitled names and

A View of St. Paul, taken from the verge of Dayton's Bluff, in 1852, and presenting a very suggestive picture for the contemplation of citizens or strangers who have any interest or even curiosity in relation to the marvelously rapid growth and unprecedented prosperity of that bright new city which is destined to be the great metropolis of a new and populous world of magic origin spread out with enchanting reality beneath the steel-blue sky of Dakota Land. And after viewing this scene, so ascend the high bluff to behold the grand sight now.

remained incognito until the storm passed over. Levasseur also had his own reasons for anything he did.

But his trip to Selkirk Colony proved fatal in more ways than one. He had just devised an entirely original business speculation; and it seemed very probable that his somewhat depleted exchequer might be speedily running over again with the proceeds of a new venture. The fur trade was a very lucrative operation, and in connection therewith he proposed to establish a still more profitable enterprise. His negotiation with the governor of the Colony secured all the advantages he desired for opening one of the grandest schemes ever thought of in that region.

But, alas! he there beheld the lustrous eyes of Leonore, who was destined to enslave his heart! Those exquisite optical orbs should have brought the beautiful orphan happiness instead of blighting the future of so many lives!

The husband who promised to love his beautiful and accomplished wife was instantly fascinated by an artless girl. Her simple beauty so fastened upon his heart that in a moment he resolved to risk every other object in life to make her his own. And had he not been fettered by lawful ties to another, that sweet orphan might have become the solace of his wandering heart. Ah! but that could not be; and so deception must conceal his true position. Thus infatuated beyond redemption, he cautiously and artfully wooed her with the pleasant belief that she was the only being whom he ever purely loved.

I am prepared for a sneer in response to the suggestion of anything like *pure* love in Levasseur's infatuation. Generally it is a popular and professedly sincere principle that love cannot exist without the permission of legal statutes or ecclesiastical sanction. And it is so believed by some who forget that natural laws existed anterior to the enactments of Church or State. Many good Christians never dare think or question beyond clerical rites and secular customs. And it is well for themselves, and others, too, that they never do.

Marriage is a very excellent institution. We all maintain that view of the question. Nevertheless, it frequently causes a vast amount of misery, while no nation can prosper without it. Society would dissolve into barbarism, and moral darkness would soon obscure the light of human reason, were there no laws to preserve virtue and protect the hereditary rights of children. Yet I fearlessly assert that marriage is a precarious lottery, and—not unfrequently a moral fraud! It is open to all manner of deception and even heinous crimes! Ofttimes it is a mask of hypocrisy, beneath which exists a moral leprosy, a cankered heart, or a festered soul!

The despoiler of innocence and the robber of wealth is amenable to the law; and yet if he marries his victim, the law pronounces him a worthy man! In either case, she may not have his love; and therefore robbery and desertion would be preferable to the society of such a man for life. But this is seditious reasoning, and I will not pursue it further than to explain the position of Levasseur, whose villainy in marrying his wife might have been worse than that committed in the deception of Leonore! That he was a villain to deceive and then desert the unsuspecting girl, no one can deny. And he himself admitted the crime.

Then he did not love her, after all?

Oh, yes he did! He loved her more than he did his wife. But circumstances hemmed him in. A discov-cry was accidentally made by those who would not hesitate to expose him in such a way as to ruin him and others, too.

His wife? Not loving her, he scarcely would have trembled in fear that she might discover his perfidy. Possibly he was a coward! His vanity, or as an anonymous writer for a popular magazine would say, "his humanity compelled him to surrender to the dictates of better sense." Whatever the incentive might have been, he deserted Leonore out of regard for his wife.

Was that possible, when he did not love her as much as he loved Leonore?

Yes! Such are the inscrutable workings of human reason when embarrassed by duty and perverted by dangerous passions.

After winning the beautiful orphan's love and deceiving her with a false marriage, how could he crush his own love and hers by abandonment in that cruel way?

Phineas O'Brien had something to do with the enormity of that wrong. Levasseur supplied him with abundant means to make every provision for the comfortable maintenance of Madame and Leonore, until he should return from a pretended voyage to Europe, which an unexpected misfortune in business compelled him to make. He wrote a parting letter for Leonore, and stated plausible reasons for not having time to say farewell in person. The letter also contained assurances of his regret and eventual return, together with a statement that he had made arrangements for their support while he remained away. Phineas was to deliver that letter; but the rascal kept it to put with others that were subsequently written for an explanation why no response had been given to the first.

Phineas retained all the letters and spent all the

money. He forged answers to Levasseur, who thought they came from Madame, and in that way he kept up a bountiful supply of money; until at length Levasseur proposed to reappear in St. Louis and see Leonore himself.

Phineas would be caught in his rascality, if Levasseur did as he suggested. And thereupon he wrote, in apparent haste and surprise, to inform Levasseur that Madame and Leonore had suddenly left the city. Relying upon his vassal, the principal rogue was thus deceived.

And then Levasseur repented. The utter loss of Leonore produced a great revulsion in his feelings; and if she could be found, he resolved to never desert her again. Phineas was instructed to find her at any cost. While trifling with Madame before she and Leonore actually left St. Louis, he had been enriching himself from Levasseur's purse by continued deception, so that, when they did leave, he was frightened, and forthwith drowned unpleasant reflections by a career of inebriety which finally resulted in his death.

There was a brawl among a gang of deck-hands from a steamer, and a pistol discharged, by whom none could tell. In that way Phineas O'Brien was shot. He lingered a few days in great agony, and then, like his father, went to a pauper's grave!

Meanwhile Levasseur was frantically searching for his lost love. And where could Phineas be? The police reports in St. Louis settled that. Phineas had been his base of hope. He was dead, and there seemed no prospect of ever finding the beautiful girl. Yet while the penitent man sought for her in St. Louis, she was in New York. Had he known that, how happy he would have been.

In despair, he went to Washington on business.

While there, Florinda's letter informed him of the events in his mansion at home. She announced the birth of a daughter, and at the same time mentioned the presence of Madame Zorah. And cruel as it was, he scarcely rejoiced at being a father, so delightful was the anticipation of once more clasping the sweet orphan girl in his arms!

And here I must add the assurance that this is not all imagination. It may seem totally unnatural to those who have never lifted the glossy veil of deception which is drawn over the face of actual truth and studiously tucked in at the corners to shut out the inquisitive gaze of even bosom friends, while experience has proven to some that almost precisely similar occurrences stand recorded in memory against the victims of unhappy conjugal alliances. Therefore I shall assert that the untoward state of Major Levasseur's mind was not only an unfortunate reality, but simply one among the multivious eruptions of fidelity in wedded life. And though the portrait be ever so odious a picture, it has had an existence more tangible than that of a villain hero in fiction.

A terrible warning to those who entertain similarly prodigal views regarding the sacred obligations of wedded life. Without any affectedly moralizing intention, I might seriously intimate that connubial apostasy is very rapidly increasing among youthful benedicts and middle-aged fathers in the opulent, if not exalted, spheres of society. It is not only possible, but beyond a doubt, that the pernicious teachings of those itinerant agitators who persistently strive to establish a code of gynecocracy are, more than any other class of demoralizing influences, guilty of propagating the germs of matrimonial inconstancy, aversion, and divorce!

Settlement of Pembina, at the Junction of the Pembina and Red Rivers.

CHAPTER XIII.

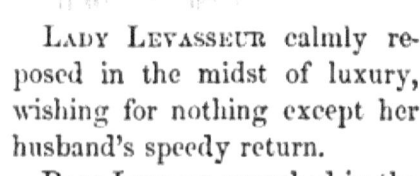

Lady Levasseur calmly reposed in the midst of luxury, wishing for nothing except her husband's speedy return.

Poor Leonore crouched in the miserable attic, weeping for the loss of everything dear to her heart.

Florinda was feverish and cross with artful devices and vague fears.

Madame's wrinkles were getting deeper from wicked designs and pretended smiles.

Levasseur decided upon plans and then shrank from the execution of them. He was really the master of all, but had not the courage to assume command. Possibly his torture was worse than that of his victims. To say the least, he was a wretched man.

In imagination during the day he continually saw Leonore. Her magnificent eyes, all bleared with tears, haunted him everywhere. In his dreams at night her imploring pale face was before him, and he heard her voice piteously beseeching him to return. That fatal love was kindling up again with a delirious passion far surpassing the ardor which impelled him when he whispered those tender words of wooing in her ear.

He asked himself why she left St. Louis? And then his heart beat to think that she might be seeking him. He must see her immediately and have a reconciliation. He would fly to her by the very next train!

In a fit of desperation he paid his hotel bill, and told a porter to carry his baggage to the depot for New York. And he did that while Florinda's letters begged him not to come until matters were arranged. But what did he care for Florinda or her advice? She was a mere cipher in his path to Leonore.

His wife? Ah! what of her? He almost groaned aloud when that thought came up in his wildly excited mind. His beautiful wife, who loved him so dearly, and who had just borne him a child! Oh, he would not think of her then. He must first console Leonore and be soothed by her in return. He could pacify his wife after that! She was doing well enough, and so was her babe!

Something said to him, "Beware!" Pshaw! There was no superstition in him, and he would not listen to imaginary fears.

Leaving an order that all letters for him should be remailed to New York, he hastened to the depot. He was just in time to see the train gliding out on the line of rail, but too late by half a minute for a seat in the cars. The next train went to-morrow; and he must wait until then!

That evening a letter came to tell him of a strange event. It was written by Florinda, and might have averted a fatal calamity had he seen the contents thereof. But the order for remailing his letters was promptly complied with, and the morning train by which he went to New York also carried back the important missive.

Meanwhile, Madame was consummating her dire revenge! Finding that Leonore would not be silenced without the restoration of her child, she resolved to make a confession.

Leonore was horrified—as might have been expected. But for the sake of her own precious darling, she reluctantly coincided with the plan of her resolute grandma. That plan was a wildly rash and a dangerous one.

Leonore's nurse was informed that some very rich lady wanted to adopt the child. Then Madame carried it away. The nurse thought Leonore submitted with but little regret. But what Madame really did with the infant heiress was a secret of her own!

By administering a certain specific absorbent, Madame had already purposely destroyed the mammillary nourishment of Lady Levasseur. Then naturally suggesting the usual substitute in such emergencies, she also said that her daughter had recently become a widow, and that she was obliged to part with her own babe for adoption. Poverty compelled her to give up her child, and the same necessity would induce her to serve Lady Levasseur.

And Madame actually planned to take the poor girl into the very dwelling of her husband, and into the confidential service of his wife! Could Leonore go there and do all that, knowing the truth? Such was Madame's daring. Yet she did not intend that Leonore should know who the lady was.

Levasseur's portrait hung over the mantel—and Leonore would recognize it as quickly as her grandma had done. The picture must be removed. But how?

Madame soon devised a plan for that. She accidentally broke the cord in pretending to dust off the top. The entire structure fell to the floor, and the frame was badly broken. How easy it was to have it taken away by an artisan, so that the damage might be nicely repaired before the master's return.

Leonore remarked that the lady's name was the same as her husband's. Madame explained how that was nothing. She would frequently meet people of the same name, who were in no way related to each other.

If Levasseur had not been too late for the train when he intended to leave Washington, his arrival would have prevented Leonore entering his house to be the nurse of her own child; or had he but received Florinda's letter which was returned on the very train that he went home in, he might have been less precipitous in his action.

Florinda tried to make other arrangements for Lady Levasseur; but Madame scowled and whispered that it would be dangerous to betray her. Florinda understood what she meant, and wisely made no further opposition.

Leonore tremblingly entered the presence of Lady Levasseur!

Seeing so much luxury and so many beautiful things that were new and novel to her, she might have lost herself in admiration, had not maternal feelings been uppermost in her mind. But Lady Levasseur received her kindly, and was greatly pleased to see how she caressed the child.

Where was Florinda at that time? Her presence, if nothing else, would certainly open Leonore's eyes. And really there was not another person in existence who more bitterly wished Leonore harm. Florinda's hate for her was even worse than that which she entertained for her grandma. But Madame's cunning was as marvelous as her daring. In duplicity she could outwit a deeper mind than that of Florinda. And when resolved upon anything, it was sure to be done. Her unrelenting obstinacy would accomplish almost any undertaking. The boldness of her plan in the Levasseur mansion, proved what she was capable of attempting and competent to perform.

And Florinda actually succumbed, with a promise not to reveal herself in person or otherwise. She must assist or contend with great odds against her. Possibly some underplot was putting Madame in a masterly position?

Leonore took the babe in her arms, and almost devoured it with kisses. It was her own, and every feeling within her responded to its smile.

"You seem fond of children," said Lady Levasseur.

"Oh, very!" responded Madame, before Leonore could utter any reply. "She now loves that just as much as if it was her own!"

Leonore trembled and turned her large eyes imploringly upon her grandma.

"And the little darling has already taken quite a fancy to you!" smiled Lady Levasseur.

Madame laughed and said, "You must not be jealous if my grand-daughter should imagine that she is nursing her own child!"

Leonore's heart was in her mouth. Her grandma was cruel to make those allusions. But there was so much pent up in Madame's bosom that she could not keep from saying what she did. Oh, how she exulted! Her old eyes fairly danced while Leonore's heart was fluttering with fearful emotion.

The street-door bell rang one afternoon; not as it usually did, but quick and loud. They all heard it; yet none of them were prepared for the result.

Florinda was in the library, and she instantly recognized a familiar voice in the vestibule.

"Major Levasseur!" she unconsciously exclaimed, turning very pale and bounding from her seat.

The lord of the mansion met her in the hall. She was in time to give him warning and avert the denouement threatening to annihilate even her own hopes of the future. She tried to say something, but her tongue would not move. And she staggered back into the library, while he quickly ascended the stairs.

A kiss for his wife; and a smile of welcome, with an ardent embrace in return!

"Our first-born—it is there!" fondly murmured Lady Levasseur. "Baby, darling, its papa has come!"

The husband and father was almost touching Leonore, who sat like a statue, with the child at her breast. And Madame stood close behind her, apparently pinching her shoulder with pantomimic commands for silence and caution. Poor girl! She was already overcome with the violence of her emotion!

Levasseur turned to see his child, just as it slipped from Leonore's relaxed embrace! Madame caught it in her arms and made an effort to communicate with him! But her warning came too late!

Levasseur was unprepared for meeting Leonore there. Hurriedly entering his own dwelling, and almost in the very arms of his loving wife, they all went headlong into an abyss of ruin!

Leonore gave utterance to a smothered cry. Shivering a moment as if in convulsions, she rose to her feet and gasped, "Oh, my husband!" That was all she said, while falling prostrate and senseless upon the lap of Lady Levasseur. But it was more than enough for the keen perception of a fond wife—and, hurling her to the floor, Lady Levasseur made an effort to speak. She could only clasp her forehead with her hands and pant for breath. The shock was too much for her brain, and reason fled!

And there in that luxurious chamber, which should have been a sanctuary of the purest wedded love and paternal joy, the affrighted destroyer and the exulting instrument of retribution stood face to face over the senseless forms of the deceived orphan and the outraged wife!

Madame's features were distorted with a fiendish scowl as she drew her tall figure to its utmost height and meaningly pointed at the pallid features of Lady Levasseur. But Levasseur did not fly to the assistance of his wife. He thought only of Leonore, whom he gently lifted in his arms, and bore into the dressing-room!

And then Madame smiled. There was triumph and cruelty in her smile. But how coldly she eyed Lady Levasseur, who lay stretched out upon the floor!

Could Levasseur be sane and act in that heartless manner? He was oblivious to all moral reason, but far from being mad. His fraudulent absence from Leonore had not been willful desertion. Phineas O'Brien became demoralized by continued intoxication, and his rascality perverted everything. But Phineas was dead, and no explanation had yet been given!

Levasseur idolized Leonore with all the ardor of a violent passion and a susceptible heart from the moment he first saw her—and prolonged separation had intensified his feelings, until her unexpected disappear-

WAY-AWA-HAN; or "Red Iron." A Defiant Sioux Chief who joined in the Great Massacre.

ance filled him with the wildest apprehension. He knew that he would meet Madame in his wife's chamber if he went home. Florinda told him that she was there. However, he expected to conciliate her immediately, and then fly to Leonore! Madame's sagacity and presence of mind would insure discretion on her part. But he did not know that she had every reason to believe his absence the result of a cruelly premeditated wrong. Nor had he taken into consideration all the circumstances, as he should have done. Consequently, his sudden return was rash and absurd. Such conduct was totally unwarrantable in the judgment of an intelligent man, possessing the perfect knowledge of human nature which he had acquired from social experience.

Levasseur was realizing the dangerous consequences of marriage for money! It has often been asserted that love follows marriage as a matter of course. They say that if a poor girl does really hate the rich man who offers her his hand, she will soon learn to love him! Designing matchmakers talk in that way. I've heard them use such wicked arguments, and afterward seen the happiness of both husband and wife blasted forever by a natural, if not an inevitable, result!

Levasseur's prudence was worn out from the fear of discovery by his wife. He was restlessly impatient for Leonore to repose in his arms. If possible, he wished to atone for that unmanly fraud whereby he first possessed her. He was irritated, and would no longer submit to restraint. But it was not his intention to have severed himself so suddenly and ruthlessly from his loving wife, and that, too, at the very threshold of their child's existence. He relied upon Madame's connivance, for the sake of Leonore. Florinda would do whatever pleased him best! They would all conspire with him against his wife, and thus serve their own interests too!

Pure-hearted and innocent readers will refuse to believe all this. They judge others by themselves—and I sincerely wish there were more of those pure hearts to be met with in my experience of life. In some things ignorance is bliss; and I've many times admitted the folly of trying to be wise. Nevertheless, I can assure the skeptically inclined that moral philosophers easily perceive the inharmonious compulsion of domestic society when coerced by the rigid formality of unnatural laws!

Levasseur was precisely the villain that I represent him. Not a mere ideal monster, created by my imagination to horrify the reader. He was just that "living man among men." And the subsequent unhappiness of his mortal existence abundantly prove that there is no atonement for him this side of the grave!

Carrying Leonore into the dressing-room, he closed the door after him, and sat down with her in his arms. A veil of infatuation hung about him and shut out the entire world. And though he had left his wife lying senseless in the adjoining chamber, he seemed to be totally unconscious of the fact! His entire feeling was centred in Leonore, whom he wildly pressed to his heaving bosom!

"How changed! But more beautiful than before!" he murmured, while gazing upon her pale features, as if abstractedly viewing a picture. And then his eyes began to dance with sudden animation. His heart fluttered, and his cheeks were crimsoned with a warm flush. Hot kisses were lavished upon her insensible lips, and his beard mingled with her dark curls!

The chamber door opened noiselessly, and Madame

entered silently and unobserved. She meant to close the door after her, but it was left slightly ajar. Behind Levasseur, and gloating on the scene, she stood like the incarnate personification of exulting fury. Her dim eyes were strained half out of their sockets, her lean masculine neck was stretched forth eagerly, and her slender fingers lashed her hands! The veins of her neck and face and forehead were swollen and deeply blue, in frightful contrast with the yellow hue of her withered skin! Her lips moved in twitches—yet she did not speak to relieve the volcano of agitation within! But when she saw Levasseur's hot breath warming Leonore's lips, that were almost cold, her wrinkled visage relaxed into a pardoning smile! Then, touching Levasseur's arm, she startled him from his fatal delirium!

"Fool, to bring her here!" he growled, like some wild animal clinging to its prey. "You have ruined all!" he added, as if suddenly humanized to a sense of his real position.

"I brought her here to provide natural nourishment for your child!"

"What! She nurse my wife's child? Remember this is not the time or place for jesting!" He spoke in anger. "She can not supply such nourishment. She is——"

"A mother herself!" interrupted Madame. "A wife and a mother, too!"

In dismay, he gasped, "Where is her husband and child?"

"Her husband is here—holding her in his arms! Her child—no matter where!"

"What do you mean?"

"Just what I say. You are her husband and the father of her child!"

9

She spoke fiercely; and her unusual manner and strange declaration were seriously disconcerting him. But he would not show any fear.

"A man can not have two wives!" he calmly replied.

"Villain! You thought to cheat us with a sham marriage, and you succeeded! But your false priest made a confession to me! You deceived yourself in the ceremony. It was perfectly legal. The existence of a previous wife necessarily subjects you to punishment for the crime of bigamy! I know all!"

"Hush! Here is money! Not another word. If gold will satisfy you, I can make it all right. Serve me, and you shall be rich! Invent some plausible excuse for all this confusion. Deceive my wife if possible! Quick! Decide!"

Madame took the proffered money, and, pondering a moment, finally said:

"First tell me what you intend doing. If the law allows you but one wife, which shall be your choice?"

He kissed Leonore, and declared that she should be nearest to his heart in future!

There was still more change in the expression of Madame's features. And she inquired if he really loved Leonore!

"Yes! Better than my own soul!"

"Then I will serve you! And now remember, Major Levasseur, that we are under a solemn compact which can not be broken! You love her, and will make her your wife, as you pledged yourself to before. But this time swear to me that you will keep your second promise. From this hour, only Leonore is to be your wife, and to share your wealth and position. While you keep that oath, I am your friend. If you fail, I shall find some way to get revenge! Will you swear?"

"You forget that Lady Levasseur is my lawful wife!"

"I forget nothing! There is no alternative! In the sight of Heaven, she is no more your wife than Leonore, whom you taught to love you, and then made her believe that she was married to you by a holy priest with sacred vows. She gave you all her love, and her very soul! You cruelly deserted her; and, still trusting in your return, she has become the mother of your child. She has never lost the hope of a happy reunion; and earnestly prays for you every night before closing her eyes in sleep. You are now together. Beware of separation! I have heard your promise. You give me gold, and talk of making us rich. We accept your offer. But, sleeping or waking, I shall always be near you! And if I discover treachery on your part, woe unto you! Will you swear?"

Major Levasseur raised his arm, and she grasped it tightly as he articulated:

"Yes! I solemnly swear that Leonore shall be my only love to the end of life!"

"Your oath is recorded in the Book of Fate! Violation of it will be *death!*" she said, flinging back his arm, with a laugh in silence to herself!

The chamber door was suddenly thrown open, and Lady Levasseur's form fell into the dressing-room! Reviving from her first swoon, she had crawled there to listen, and thus became a witness to all!

Otter Tail City. A Charming Locality, with room enough to thrive.

CHAPTER XIV.

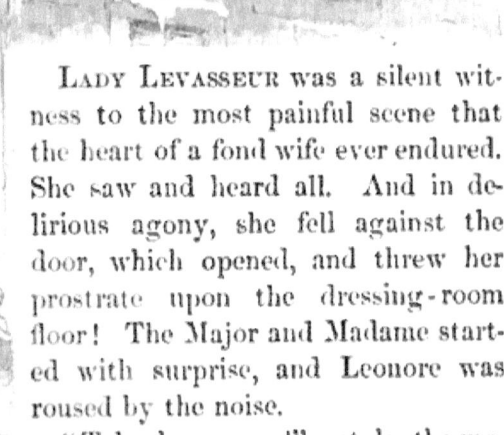

LADY LEVASSEUR was a silent witness to the most painful scene that the heart of a fond wife ever endured. She saw and heard all. And in delirious agony, she fell against the door, which opened, and threw her prostrate upon the dressing-room floor! The Major and Madame started with surprise, and Leonore was roused by the noise.

"Take her away!" petulantly motioned the infatuated man while hugging Leonore all the closer to his bosom!

Madame needed no further prompting. She quickly dragged the insensible form of Lady Levasseur back into the chamber, and slammed to the door, panting with impatient haste!

Leonore's eyes opened, and they rested upon the face of HER husband! Her brain was dizzy from the confusion of the swoon, but she could recognize *him!* There was a vague recollection of *that* wife, and the kisses of greeting, in the scene of the chamber! It seemed like a wild dream! But her husband had come back to her, and she was then lying in his arms! The bliss of that moment was worth years of woe! She had no chidings, nor complaints to offer. His eyes beamed lovingly upon her own, and she saw in them what made him appear a perfect god! Her arms were around his neck, and their kisses mingled in the unison of mutually intoxicating delight! He was all hers! But what a shudder came up with the recollection of that bed-chamber scene! Oh, what did all that mean? She tried to ask, but his warm lips smothered her voice!

Madame looked on in the attitude of a strange statue, her eyes gleaming with delight, while the reconciliation of those two hearts was breaking another heart in the next room!

As usual, Florinda was hovering near. She saw the only chance for herself in pretending sympathy with the deserted wife; and, gently placing her upon a lounge, she soon restored consciousness to her shattered mind.

"O, let me die!!" piteously wept the agonized wife. "He does not love me any more! I am suffocating! My heart is breaking! Lost forever! Only baby is left! All else has gone!"

Lady Levasseur embraced Leonore's child with the belief that it was her own, while her husband caressed its mother in the dressing-room!

As night shrouds the entire world in gloom at the close of day, so there came a dark cloud of mystery around and within the costly mansion of the Levasseurs.

Autumn passed away, and the winter winds blew sharp and cold. The ground was frozen, thick ice covered the rivers, and one night a great snow storm spread its burden of white flakes over the city. Early the next morning, thousands of ragged boys and tattered men, with old shovels and fragments of brooms, were ringing door-bells and begging the privilege of removing the snow from the stoops and sidewalks, for a few shillings in money. Snow storms in a great city are harvests for the unemployed poor who can find utensils and are willing to earn the reward of toil. But alas, for any poor lost canine quadruped who has no home: his diet must be meager until the snow melts to uncover the loose offal and scattered bones!

Up and down the aristocratic avenue, shovels were clattering until noon. The sidewalks and the stoops and areas were brushed off clean. All except one!

A hundred boys and men had been tugging at the bell-knob of a massive rosewood door; but no answer came from within. The shutters were closed, and one little urchin suggested that the inmates might all be dead! Then a policeman tried what he could do. He would make a formal complaint at head-quarters. The law required that residents should promptly remove the snow from the front of their premises within so many hours after its fall. Who could he have fined for neglecting the law? A silver plate upon the rosewood door announced the name of "Levasseur!" The policeman wrote something in a small blank-book, and then walked away.

Days and weeks and months went into the past, and still the rosewood door of the Levasseur mansion did not open from without nor from within. Long neglect permitted an accumulation of rubbish around the colossal stone steps, and cobwebs were stretched across the recesses beyond the reach of the wind and storm. The silver knobs and the plate with the master's name upon it, grew tarnished and red and some naughty boys had been disfiguring the walls with large comic figures in chalk.

The people went up and down every day, wondering at the gloomy walls of the once enlivened mansion. And well they might—for a deserted house standing in silence amid the animated whirl of a populous city, is a suggestive scene to contemplate!

The neighbors began to talk; and some hinted the necessity of an investigation. Where could the Levasseurs all be? No furniture was ever seen to go away.

Mrs. Coe lived with her husband, one Mr. Coe, in the house exactly opposite, at the rear. The domicile of the Coes stood facing another street; but the back yards of the two houses were adjoining. Mrs. Coe's sister was an unhappy old maid. Her dormitory looked out upon the deserted, or rather, as she said, the mysterious dwelling. And, in the singular manner of many other old maids, she was much addicted to malicious suspicion. She seemed to suspect all things, and the "other half" of mankind in particular. But she had more influence with Mrs. Coe than Mr. Coe would ever have. Indeed, the sisters belonged to the "Woman's Rights Society," at that time looming up in the already tainted atmosphere of connubial disputants and dissenters!

Mrs. Coe finally agreed with her venerable maiden sister that something fearful must have happened among the Levasseurs. If the usual appointment of Hibernian damsels had been domesticated in the Levasseur family, perhaps the neighboring Bridgets and Catharines might have learned all the secrets worth knowing, and industriously reported them everywhere.

"Blast them niggers!" chafed the old maid. "They are the closest-mouthed fools I ever saw! Harriet Jane tried half a dozen times last summer to find out what pursuit the gentleman was engaged in, but they snubbed her off by saying, 'Massa tends to his bis'ness and we tends to de chores 'round de house!' I hate niggers! They're so stupid and non-communicative!"

The "blasted niggers," alluded to by Mrs. Coe's venerable maiden sister, were Sancho and Dinah—the faithful and the only servants who waited upon the Levasseurs.

Mrs. Coe's curiosity increased with her sister's, until she insisted that her husband should force an entrance through the back way, and see all about it. Mr. Coe was a very timid man, and he could not undertake such a feat without at least one or two confederates to accompany him. So, rather than forego the luxury of appeasing their inquisitive desire, both Mrs. Coe and her sister convoyed the trembling husband in the dark adventure. The hour of night made it dark; and that idea greatly horrified Mr. Coe.

Wouldn't Mrs. Coe be merciful and relent? No! When her mind was once made up, she never swerved from her purpose. She was ashamed of Mr. Coe for his cowardice. But it afforded her some consolation to believe that all men were cowards, and that they never could do anything brave without the superior nerve of down-trodden women to help them on by intellectual inspiration.

They reached the back area of the Levasseur mansion. The fastening of the kitchen window was moved, and they told Mr. Coe to enter.

Oh, dear! He would deem it an especial and humane favor from Mrs. Coe, if he might be allowed to run away. She could not spare him just then; and with the assistance of her sister she grasped him by the

Children of "Farmer Indians" Winnowing Wheat.

shoulder and the most convenient part of his trowsers, and tumbled him in!

Mr. Coe was so nervous that for a long time the matches would not ignite against the wall; and when one did snap, he fizzled it out trying to light the candle.

Mrs. Coe then took the matches herself, and spitefully shoved him across the floor, where he tumbled over a chair and upset a table, and thereby incurred additional fright from the terrible noise. Mrs. Coe's hands were steady; and she soon had two candles blazing to show them the way.

Mr. Coe fell back in the rear of the reconnoitering advance, momentarily expecting that each shadow would prove to be a frightful spectre. Holding the candles high above their heads, Mrs. Coe and her sister began to explore the entire house. All the kitchen utensils and furniture appeared as if suddenly left while in use. In the drawing-room above a chandelier had fallen, and its broken fragments were strewn over the soft velvet carpet upon the floor. Then they went up stairs, and from one room to another, without seeing a dry skeleton or meeting a white apparition.

Hah! The door of Lady Levasseur's chamber was securely locked within. But the Major's sleeping apartment was more accessible than that of his wife. Nothing short of assistance from a locksmith could make an entrance through the fastened door! So they inspected all the other rooms and recesses, from the cellar to the garret, and found every article remaining as if it had been left but yesterday. Dust covered the furniture, and dampness had soiled the beautiful papering upon the walls.

Their verdict was, unanimously, "Something wrong!"

And they retired with a fixed determination that Mr. Coe should go to the police office early in the morning and have the chamber explored by virtue of the law.

Fire! fire! The old Coes and the little Coes, and nearly all the inhabitants in that quarter of the city, were roused from sleep at the quietest hour of night by the ringing of bells and a tumult of rumbling wheels and tramping feet. The entire neighborhood was in a complete uproar. Fire! fire! tolled the bells; and red-shirted men, dragging engines and hose, bellowed loudly through brazen trumpets as they ran!

"Where is the fire?" Mrs. Coe asked Mr. Coe the same question no less than three or four times in quick succession.

"I declare I don't know, my dear. It is undoubtedly somewhere this side of the Battery!" was his mild and innocent reply.

"Levasseur's!" screamed Mrs. Coe's maiden sister. "Over there. The house is burning down, and we shall never know what a shocking tragedy has been perpetrated in that room!"

It was the first and the only conflagration which to my knowledge ever occurred in that aristocratic quarter of the city. The match of a wicked incendiary must have ignited the element of ruin. Who could solve the mystery?

In the morning naught but charred and smoldering *debris* remained to mark the spot where the Levasseur mansion stood so proudly, and yet so drearily, the day before.

The neighbors each gave an opinion; but none of them could determine, beyond the merest conjecture, why and wherefore such an event should happen. And if any mystery was purposely locked within Lady

Levasseur's luxurious chamber, it would never be revealed.

But a police detective—one of those McJudases who are so numerous at the present time—was then introducing his iniquitous system of fraud for the ostensible purpose of discovering and eradicating (?) crime. McJudas put two of his minions, or more properly imps, upon the supposed trail of an absconding perpetrator of imaginary sins. He was desirous of finding Levasseur. But that seemed to be a much more difficult enterprise than was anticipated when he began. An entire year passed, and not even the astute old thief could unravel the mystery of that gentleman's departure, nor gain the remotest clue to his ultimate destination.

Meanwhile, the people gazed at the pile of smutty bricks, and the fragments of stone among the ashes where the walls formerly stood so high. They gazed awhile, and wondered too. Only a short time, though—for it is said that after the expiration of "nine days," the greatest sight or wonder ever known in New York ceases to attract public attention. I have frequently thought there was some truth in that saying.

The lapse of two winters and one summer turned the ruins of the Levasseur mansion old and brown. The second May came, and then the second June—and, indeed, the second summer. And blades of grass, with tall weeds, were growing out from among the unconsumed ends of timber, the broken bricks, and the shattered blocks of chiseled stone. Yet none could tell why Levasseur did not return!

The simple Method of Crossing Rum River.

CHAPTER XV.

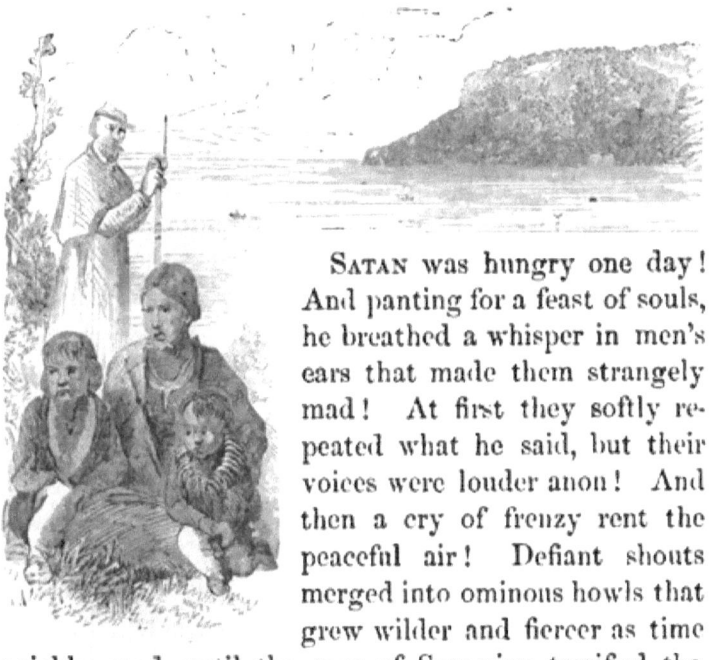

Satan was hungry one day! And panting for a feast of souls, he breathed a whisper in men's ears that made them strangely mad! At first they softly repeated what he said, but their voices were louder anon! And then a cry of frenzy rent the peaceful air! Defiant shouts merged into ominous howls that grew wilder and fiercer as time quickly sped, until the roar of Secession terrified the world!

The "Stars and Stripes" were torn down, and a dismal emblem of the Palmetto-tree was hoisted in their stead!

One morning the sun rose with bright, radiant smiles, and sank to rest in the evening all red and bleared at the sight of human blood!

Millions of hearts were throbbing with rage or fright that night! The bright blaze of Jupiter was dimmed by the ruddy glare of Mars! Languishing Juno was bathed in tears; and the frowns of Jehovah darkened the sky, while the devil laughed in exulting joy!

With the return of to-morrow's dawn, the shrill notes of the fife, followed by the rattling and the measured beating of drums, sent a thrill into the sanctuary of every American home, while long files of martialed men were hurrying from the North and hurrying from the South, to clash in the deadly strife of internecine war!

Consanguineous ties and bonds of love were rent asunder. And there was a great wailing cry of anguish in daylight, with sobbing prayers at night, by fond ones for the safety of those dearest to their hearts. Mothers and wives, fathers and husbands, brothers, sisters, one and all, choked and paled at the demon of war!

Within the lines, and beyond the lines that separated kindred and friends, pent-up souls were shrieking and wailing in despair! Going North and going South! O! anywhere to find the heart's love, with peace in a quiet home!

The booming of cannon gradually approached New Orleans, and *passes* signed by the chieftain in command, sent many citizens safely beyond the reach of harm.

And cruel mortals, in the garb of men and in feminine guise, were lurking everywhere, while "female spies" haunted firesides and public places alike. It was a grand carnival time for the heartless, the abandoned and the vile, when both the North and the South stooped to the siren's guile, and she of "the evil eye" was freely tolerated in almost every camp to ply her arts and betray the lives of men. But I presume that no one will ever write a true history of the wanton spy service during the Southern war!

Those without influence to use might try the potency

of gold. Many did so in New Orleans. And verily the people of that city were doomed to remorseless plunder. First the rebels had their fill, and then the sequel was to come!

One thousand dollars—nay, ten thousand, all in coin—procured the simple order for a lady, her adopted child, and her two slaves to be passed beyond the rebel lines.

Whither would she go? Other ladies had been snugly domiciled in quiet Northern abodes, entirely beyond the dangers of the war, while their masculine connections remained at will or were forcibly held to do the fighting; and ten thousand dollars paid into the pocket of one who wished to lay up a little something for future need, gave her an opportunity to depart. The sum was a large one to pay; but it included the price of her slaves, whom she would not leave behind!

Then there was an intervening space of dark water and uncertain law. Up the river, passing grim batteries along the shore to where the "Stars and Stripes" proclaimed the bondman free! Out of rebeldom, and, with a little white flag, into the Union lines!

Again, what was to pay? Echo repeated—"*to pay?*" And then a joyful reverberation came in response:

"The widow, the orphan and the slave, without money and without price, can find a refuge here!"

And the lady, with her adopted child and her manumitted slaves, sailed on up the Father of Rivers. But they were not happy. Something made them sad!

On up the river, from one steamer to another—and yet they continued on!

The state-rooms all along each side of the main saloon were designated with gilt numerals on knobs of porcelain, while in the ladies' cabin alphabetical letters were used upon the doors.

The cough of a dying consumptive grated upon the ears of Mercy, Eliza, Julia and Jane—four jubilant young ladies who were chattering together in the full vigor of life and hope. But they all paused in awe when they heard that ominous cough. In silence they listened. First it was violent and distressing, and then it continued languidly and dull. It told how rapidly a victim was going to the grave!

"What does that mean?" inquired Jane, pointing at letter c.

"Oh, she's some rebel's wife going to Minnesota!" replied Eliza. "You know father says that the atmosphere up there will cure the consumption. But she'll not live till she reaches Winona. She coughs precisely like poor dear mother used to, awhile before she died! Just listen at her now!"

A hard-visaged man, with a singularly large round head and a thick short beard, sat near the young ladies. He was reading a book; but he heard the consumptive's cough. And whenever the paroxysms were most severe, then his features lighted up with a peculiar smile!

"Do you know that I almost hate that leaden-eyed man?" observed Mercy, shuddering as she spoke. "There is something so wicked and silently malicious— I don't know what to call it—in the sinister expression of his repulsive face! His strange glances are perfectly chilling to me!"

"Hush!" whispered Julia, slightly shocked. "That is Doctor Passion, whose wonderful cures have been advertised so much in the Western papers. All great men have remarkable peculiarities about them. Look at his head! There's a model for the phrenological disciples of Gall and Spurzheim. And his features might have been a perfect study for Lavater, the originator of the science of physiognomy. And then he is very rich! I overheard a conversation about him this morning between father and a strange gentleman, who I believe is a particular friend of his. The stranger said the Doctor had amassed a very large fortune. And he rather hinted that he might soon be a widower. His wife has been an invalid a long time. What a splendid prize he will be for some one, when his wife dies!"

"O, you ought to be ashamed to talk in that way!" remonstrated Mercy. "I'm sure he's a bad man; and with all deference to your respect for the opinions of Gall, or Spurzheim, or Lavater, as you call them, I shall persist in comparing both his head and his face to the worst brute that I can think of. Do you perceive that fiendish grin while the poor lady is coughing herself to death!"

Mercy told the truth when she said that the lady in the state-room was dying. With pale face and attenuated form, and scarcely conscious, she lay there upon the bed! One of her faithful slaves, in sorrow stood near. Her other slave was waiting sadly without. And a beautiful rosy-cheeked girl of fourteen, with long flaxen hair in great wavy, curling tresses, sat by the bed in silence and tears!

Dr. Passion beckoned to the slave waiting without. A venerable negro, with his wool whitened by a long lapse of years, approached respectfully and tried to smile. Poor old man! His features bore a woful contraction of anxiety and grief!

"You serve the sick lady, I believe," said Dr. Passion, holding out a piece of money in one hand and with the other motioning toward the letter c.

"Yes, massa, an I spects to sarve her's long as de Almi'te Creatur spars her life an mine! But I doesn't want no mun'y. I'es wery much bleeg'd, sah! But missus's got plenty fur us all!"

Dr. Passion returned the money to his own pocket, and said, "Hah! From the South, I presume? Very wealthy. And yet she will persist in dying, when by proper treatment a cure would be certain. Now, if you really wish to save your mistress from speedy death, give her my card, and say that I am willing to attend her. Here it is. I am a distinguished physician! Doubtless she has heard of me often before. I have a wonderful reputation from New Orleans to St. Paul. With pride I can say that my name is familiar to the people in every town of any importance the whole length of the river."

"Tanke, sah!" bowed the slave. "Missus 'll be very glad! An' we poor sarvents 'll pray fur you eb'ry time we lies down at night—ef you can only brake up dat orf'l kumsumshin!" And then he softly tapped at letter c.

The card was a tempting bait! How many dying men and women had nibbled at it before? The lady would see Dr. Passion. Perhaps he had been sent to her at the eleventh hour, by Divine interposition, to save her life a little longer for the sake of the fair-haired girl sitting beside her in tears! Her trust was in Providence, and she was willing to go when He called. But the thought of leaving that tender flower in the heartless and deceitful world, without maternal solicitude or care, made her loth to die!

Dr. Passion entered with noiseless step. He gently, kindly, tenderly took her thin, white wrist between his thumb and fingers, with an encouraging, compassionate smile, and a courteous bow.

"Oh, Doctor!" she coughed, and eagerly searched his

face. "Must I die? Do you really think there is no hope for me? They have all given me up. But I have heard a great deal about the air of Minnesota, and thought I would try and get up there if possible. Would you recommend that climate for one in my condition? Ah—pardon me! I had almost forgotten that we are strangers. I should, therefore, advance you a fee. You do think there is some hope—eh, Doctor?"

"Yes—that is—ahem! The air of Minnesota is good. But proper medical treatment—such as I have acquired a world-wide reputation for—is the only thing that can save your life. You are dangerously ill, madam. I am not one of that unprincipled class who delude their dying patients with the false assurance that they are in a fair way to recover, when the last breath is actually leaving their bodies! Nor am I actuated wholly by a pecuniary motive. As a devout Christian, I never forget my obligations to God while serving the sick. But take courage, my dear madam. Permit me to drop this small powder upon your tongue. There! Now your cough will soon be easier. The poor have my attendance free of charge. The affluent may exercise their own generosity. I name no particular sum as a fee. I am more anxious to alleviate suffering than to accumulate money. Ah! You feel easier already. I can easily perceive that!"

The invalid motioned for Sancho to approach. That venerable slave was her secretary and cashier. He drew a huge, well-filled wallet out of his trowsers' pocket, and she took therefrom two bank-bills for Dr. Passion, into whose eyes there came an eager gleam at sight of so much money. But his tongue then quickly articulated what his heart did not feel. And, while pretending to decline the generous fee, his fingers almost perforated the bank bills when they were secure in his hand!

And while Dr. Passion was in state-room c successfully deluding his victim, another individual appeared in the ladies' cabin. A plainly-clad, substantial and fine-looking man of forty years, whose good-natured countenance beamed with an expression of frankness and honesty that is not met with every day. And at his heels came a monstrous great dog, with lolling tongue and wagging tail. His canine majesty recognized the four young ladies, and they saluted him in a familiar way. They each had a pat for his huge, glossy head, while his large hazel eyes glistened with intense delight in response.

The four young ladies called the dog "Goliah," and when addressing his master they said, "Father!"

Samuel Denton, a widower, with his four pretty daughters and his valuable St. Bernard dog, were going to a new home in the North-west. Hitherto he had spent his life as a farmer in a very prosperous section of country in the East, where he was respected by a large circle of friends. In a financial position he was comfortable, but not rich. The death of his wife, whom he dearly loved, left him full of discontent. She was buried in the Quaker Cemetery at Westfield, New Jersey, where a small head-stone with the simple name of "Eliza" still designates her grave!

Farmer Denton was immigrating to Minnesota with the hope that entirely new associations might wean him from his grief.

"Where's the Doctor?" he inquired. "I did not see him go ashore at the landing where we stopped half an hour ago. But, girls, I am glad that none of you noticed him while he hung around here trying to attract your attention. Look out for those fellows. I've no opinion of them, anyhow. I mean those rascals who travel about and advertise impossible miracles to humbug the ignorant and credulous, with all sorts of testimonials purporting to emanate from authentic sources. And I'm convinced that this fellow is in league with another man on the boat. They tried a game that didn't work this morning. The man introduced him to me, at his own request I'm certain, so that I might introduce him to you. Ha, ha! What rogues there are in this world, when we come to find them out! But the Denton girls will not spend their time entertaining Dr. Passion. He's terribly afraid of Goliah. Ha, ha! And I fancy the dog has been looking after him rather sharply. What wonderful judges of character these dogs are! Now, in some cases, I'd trust Goliah's opinion quicker than my own. There is a mutual antipathy between Goliah and Dr. Passion? But where did the scamp go?"

"He is in state-room c," replied Mercy. "He sent his card to the sick lady, by her colored man."

"And she received him? So, so! He will dupe her out of her money, and doubtless terminate her existence before she has a fair chance to test the benefit of Northwestern atmosphere. Ah, if your dear mother had been taken to Minnesota, possibly she would be living now. But I feel it my duty to look after this lady. I presume that she is one of those easy-going, helpless Southern women, who seldom take the trouble to seriously think, and always have a pack of lazy niggers to wait upon them. Just the kind of people for Dr. Passion to bamboozle. They have no proper idea of money, and never count the cost of anything until reduced to starvation. I wouldn't give the plain common-sense

South End of Rock Island, where the Sioux Convicts are imprisoned.

experience of either one of you girls, for all the accomplishments possessed by a hundred of these fine ladies we see with their servants tagging after them wherever they go. But this poor lady claims our compassion. She has my sympathy—there's no mistake about that. And Goliah and I will make it a point to befriend her if we can. Eh, old boy?"

Goliah distinctly understood the words of his master, and gave a sharp glance toward letter c, with an uneasy wriggling motion of his body, and a mute but meaning inquiry up into Farmer Denton's face.

While going about the world, intent upon business or in quest of pleasure, and necessarily keeping an eye open for rogues, with a perpetual suspicion of those who jostle us severely in the great crowd, after mechanically perusing the stereotyped cards that advise us to "Beware of Pickpockets," we are sometimes bitterly prejudiced against individuals at first sight. And in this brief homily, perhaps, the reader will observe an entire omission of that seemingly pedantic pronoun of the "first person and singular number," so repeatedly occurring in almost every other page of the volume. An allusion to which predominant feature may reconcile those who dislike its frequent repetition. In a work of this kind it would be impossible for the writer to succinctly accomplish the task without incurring the sarcasm of prudish *critiques*, who realize the most intense enjoyment from a sneering accusation of *egotism!* But their sneers will not intimidate the perpetrator of the afore-mentioned pronoun, who forthwith recurs to 'the repulsion experienced in our kaleidoscopic *detour* of life, which must account for the intuitive repugnance of Farmer Denton and his daughter Mercy when they contemplated the visage of the great Dr. Passion. And

Goliah's sensibilities were no less acute in the same direction. Most assuredly they and the Doctor were entirely opposite in the attributes of sincerity and truth. For while the designing charlatan told the coughing invalid that he did not belong to the unprincipled class who delude their dying patients with false assurances of recovery, a poor old woman sat in the saloon, then and there depressed by a reminiscence of an event which occurred nearly six months before. The scarlet fever had deprived her son of his hearing. And with a belief in miracles, which the great Dr. Passion was said to perform, she took her son to the hotel where that distinguished personage occupied a *suite* of rooms in grand style. But, as many other patients were already waiting there, some time elapsed before she and her son could approach him. And then he smiled and ran his fat hand through the greasy black hair upon his head while propounding the usual query of—"Well, what troubles you?" That was his habitual expression when a new victim entered his den.

"My poor son is deaf. Heaven will reward you for curing him, I'm sure!"

"Hum!" drawled the Doctor, with a derisive smile. Then he soberly added: "My fee is one hundred dollars. It will cost you that sum to restore the hearing of your son!"

"I havn't that much in the world!" sighed the aged mother.

"What amount can you raise?" the Doctor wished to know.

"Thirty dollars! The saving of a whole year over and above the cost of providing for six children—a penny and a half-dime only at a time!"

"Will no one loan you any more?"

She shook her head and murmured, "I've no friends with money to spare!"

"Then give me the thirty dollars cash down, and I'll see what I can do!" And he held out his fat hand.

Dr. Passion took the poor old woman's money and gave her only a small vial of cistern-water, colored brown. And her boy's ears were still bereft of hearing when she sat in the saloon on board the steamer and saw him enter the state-room where the dying consumptive lay. She wanted to chide him for taking her money and not curing her son; but his cold, leaden eyes made her shiver when she would speak. And so she sat there and cried while no one seemed to care what her sorrows were. At the next landing she went ashore, perhaps to mourn over the affliction of her poor boy, while the great man lingered with the lady who was coughing her life away.

But Farmer Denton became more and more convinced that he had seen Dr. Passion somewhere before. It did not strike him so at first; but an almost forgotten visage gradually shaped itself into a resemblance of the great man's face.

"Let me think!" said he to his daughters. "What criminals have I any personal recollection of? There's Clough, the murderer, who killed his sweetheart because she refused to marry him. But he was hanged for the crime. That must have been when I was a little shaver; for I can just remember running off from school with a larger boy who had a conveyance to go and see the culprit die. The gallows was erected in the centre of a natural sand-basin or circular hollow, a mile or so from the town of Mount Holly, so that everybody could have a full view of the execution. Poor man! They brought him down to the place riding backward in a common cart. And as he passed close by me I could perceive how pale he was. I shall never forget the applauding shout of the multitude when his writhing form dangled up in the air, nor the walloping I got from father when I returned home. Then there was a Mexican named *Mini*. He killed somebody, too, and they sentenced him to death. But he broke jail and fled. They made a great time searching for him; but he was not found. I declare, now that I study upon it, there is a marvelous likeness between Dr. Passion and Mini. Good gracious, girls! I am quite certain that Mini and he are one! If you look closely at him, a small cross, like a scar, is visible on his forehead, almost directly between his eyes. It is a peculiar mark! And just such a one was on Mini's forehead when I saw him in the Doylestown prison thirty years ago! Depend upon it, there is villain stamped in his heart as well as imprinted on his face. And if I'm spared to live long enough, I'll take every pains to ascertain his origin. He's not an American; that's evident in certain physical peculiarities, not visible to a casual observer. I know he speaks our language fluently enough. His accent is rather niggerish; but that comes from association—just as I explained with reference to the force of example! I tell you again, girls, there's some connection between that rascal and the escaped convict Mini!"

During all that time the great Doctor was closeted with the invalid in state-room c. And to think that he should seem reluctant to take her money after defrauding so many poor people everywhere.

But he tucked the bank-bills into his vest-pocket with the air of one who really condescended to accept them, and then cautiously began to propound little questions in no way pertaining to the invalid's health.

He presumed that she was a member of some Christian church, and had already made her peace with God.

"I am a Methodist," said he, with tone and accent unplausibly indicative of sincerity in his pretension. "You are—?"

She interrupted him by expressing a hope that she might find salvation without any violent sectarian adhesion. She had ever been mindful of the future, and, though always attending some church, she claimed membership in none!

Dr. Passion slightly changed the current of his interrogations. Might he know to whom he had the honor of being medical adviser? The wife of some distinguished statesman, no doubt.

Whether a wife or a widow, she simply said that her name was *Levasseur!*

She told him no more. But she really was once the happy wife of Major Levasseur.

And what of her husband, and Madame Zorah, and Leonore? Could she answer all those questions? No! She could not answer one of them.

Poor lady! How weary of life she seemed to be! And how soon she must die! But she thought it was hard to go and leave her darling adopted child.

A Summer Tourists' Encampment, in the Far North-west.

CHAPTER XVI.

When Lady Levasseur awoke the next morning after that terrible discovery of her husband's infatuation with Leonore, she found herself alone with Florinda, Sancho and Dinah. But Florinda was little better than nobody. For after the heart-rending scenes of the chamber, she went about as if dreaming.

Sometime during the night, a carriage came for the Major, and Madame, and Leonore. They were going away. A steamer sailed for Europe the next day at noon, and they hurried on board to cross the sea!

Madame Zorah carried a bundle in her arms. It was Leonore's child that had been taken from the bosom of Lady Levasseur while she soundly slept under the influence of chloroform! Levasseur did not intend to rob his wife even of her child. But a sleeping potion kept the babe quiet until the ship was out of the harbor.

And the father's lip paled and quivered when he beheld what had been done, and calmly reflected upon the unprecedented wrong. The child was his, but he was not its mother; and he declared that it was worse than cruel to tear it from her when nothing else would be left for her to love! The outrage was too bad for contemplation.

Oh, why did they rob the poor mother? Was it not enough to take the husband, and leave the babe in its mother's arms for the comfort and consolation of her frantic heart? Thus he queried while Madame explained that Leonore had been sustaining it with her own life, and that Lady Levasseur was unable to supply the nourishment required of a mother. Nevertheless, he did not consider that a sufficient excuse for taking the child away. And they were careful to keep their fatal secret from him.

Finding herself so utterly deserted and forsaken, Lady Levasseur became wild with grief. But after a few days she settled down into quiet lunacy, and obediently did whatever "Mamma" and "Uncle" told her to. Dinah, her old nurse in her baby days, and her constant companion in youth, had ever been a mother to her; and, as I have already intimated, she grew up into womanhood calling the faithful creature by that name. Sancho, equally as faithful as his wife, had also earned the title that was bestowed upon him.

I trust that my Northern friends will refrain from sneering at this suggestive allusion. I have witnessed many similar attachments between slaves and the children of their masters in the South. And, therefore, the touching manifestation of mutual tenderness presented in the experience of Lady Levasseur and her colored servants, was by no means a rare exception—especially when the companionship and sympathy of a natural mother may not have been known!

Sancho and Dinah concluded that their beloved mistress would be better off in New Orleans, where her mother's brother, her real uncle, might advise and direct them. They asked her to go, and she seemed to be delighted with their proposition. So, leaving Florinda in charge of the mansion, the servants conducted Lady Levasseur back to the familiar scenes of her once happy home.

Arriving there, her mind gradually resumed its natural vigor and tone. But she continued very melancholy, and at times mourned deeply for her child. And when her uncle vowed that he would seek Levasseur and kill him, she persuaded him not to do so. She loved the recreant man too dearly to wish him harm.

Sometimes she murmured to herself, "He will come back by and by! He will return when the mad spell is broken that binds him now! I'll wait for him! He went away at night, and will reappear in the twilight of evening! My spirit shall not leave him! The old love must triumph when his heart grows sad!"

Meanwhile, Florinda had become weary of life. She employed Kaskadino to poison Leonore's dear mother away up in Selkirk Colony; and at last suicide would terminate her own career! I can not say whether it was remorse, or jealousy, or despair that drove her to the act. It was at least one of those strange freaks of human reason, or a loss of reason altogether, that prompted her to lock herself in Lady Levasseur's elegant chamber and there swallow a dose of laudanum. And then, perhaps, she went to sleep upon the luxurious couch, with its rich canopy of blue satin and gold hanging around her. I presume this, inasmuch as the Coes

10*

found the door locked within, and because she was not afterward seen by mortal eyes!

If this theory is correct, and Mrs. Coe and her maiden sister, and Mr. Coe, had been able to unfasten that chamber door when they explored the Levasseur mansion, what a frightful picture would have met their gaze! But by some unaccountable means the mansion and all that it contained went to destruction by fire in a few hours after the Coes were there!

Soon after she had been left alone, a letter was written by Florinda announcing her suicidal intention. That letter was received in New Orleans, but its declarations were not deemed of sufficient meaning to call for investigation until an account of the burning of the mansion reached the uncle of Lady Levasseur. And then the ruins from the conflagration were left smoldering without the personal attention of any one for nearly two years. The property was eventually sold.

Lady Levasseur accompanied her uncle to New York, when he himself consummated the sale; and while in that city she prevailed upon him to accompany her to an asylum for orphan children. She had often heard of such places, but never thought much about them until at that particular time she conceived a great desire to inspect one.

They visited an asylum that was conducted by a religious denomination universally noted for its institutions of charity as a means of promoting the dogmas of its creed. They wisely think that a belief planted in the mind of a child is productive of far more good, and vastly more enduring, than the labored conversion of an adult heathen, or the apostatizing of a sectarian against his voluntary will!

The asylum visited by Lady Levasseur was devoted

entirely to female children, where she saw not less than four hundred little orphans in charge of sober-faced matrons, who tried to look motherly and kind, but whose rigid features were painfully significant of mechanical duty, either as an irksome task of imaginary propitiation or a tedious labor for the subsistence of life.

There was the infant, who had not yet approached the period of dentition, creeping and crowing, or kicking and crying—without a mother!

There was the little toddler, ambitiously struggling to walk from the bed to the chair, with its chirping laugh, or moaning in the agony of bodily pain—without a mother!

There was the three-year old child, eagerly scanning the visage of each stranger, and no doubt wondering what made that little girl look so happy in her pretty dress, when she came to visit them yesterday—*with* a mother!

And there was a long double file of older girls, in brown dresses and check aprons, marching through a large room out into the hall, on their way to dinner; some with sorrowful faces and downcast look, and others smiling and apparently happy—all without mothers!

And in another room there was one sweet little fair-haired child, who shrank behind the nurse's chair and coyly peeped out, imploringly but timidly, with a melancholy yearning in her blue eyes that touched Lady Levasseur's heart more than all the others, and made her sigh, "Poor, dear, sad little orphan!"

And Lady Levasseur must know more of the sorrowful child. The nurse could answer no questions. She really knew nothing beyond the routine of her daily vocation. Fortunately there was one person connected with the institution who evinced an unusual willingness to communicate whatever she could to gratify Lady Levasseur—and that was the registress of the asylum.

The Record described No. 2,791 as a foundling only a few weeks old when it was brought in by a stranger, who picked it up in some by-place. And about its neck hung a string of Job's-tear beads, joined by a small gold locket, upon which was engraved the name of "*Fleurette.*" Lady Levasseur wondered if some fond mother had been robbed of her babe and left as desolate as she was, when her faithless husband and those wicked women took her little innocent away? But what else? She wanted to know all.

The stranger who brought the child said nothing about the locket. Perhaps that escaped her notice by being concealed beneath the child's dress. However, it might be of some service in the future; and the nurse was instructed by the principal to preserve it, and to continually keep it upon the child's neck, so that visitors might see it there.

Lady Levasseur sat down and took the fair-haired orphan upon her lap, and kissed it, and asked if it would like to go and live with her, and be her little daughter.

The child threw its arms around Lady Levasseur's neck, and cried and sobbed, "Oh, yes! Oh, yes!"

But the nurse shook her head in doubt. They did not permit their orphans to be taken away, except upon stringent conditions, and by certain people. Did Lady Levasseur belong to the same church?

"Yes, I do!" replied her uncle. "As to that, I can soon satisfy the principal. If my niece wishes to adopt the child, we can give all the references required."

And thus the little orphan became the adopted child of Lady Levasseur. They called her Fleurette. And from the hour when she first nestled her sunny curls so sweetly upon Lady Levasseur's bosom, the latter began to look more cheerful. She then had something to love! And she tried to fancy that her own darling had come home to her aching heart!

But the blow which Lady Levasseur sustained by the cruel desertion of her husband had nearly broken down her health; and the insidious worm of consumption was gnawing within. Little by little, from day to day, the poison spread. The parched skin, the internal fever, the hectic flush in her cheeks; and then that burning, ominous cough. Paler, weaker, and wasting away, while large sums of money were accepted by physicians who knew they could not kill the insidious worm. Down, gradually, but steadily down—coughing, and coughing on the way!

But the invalid's uncle could not wait for her to die! One night there was a rapping at his chamber door; and old Mortality, clad in that dismal garb of death, softly entered, and silently bade his soul depart and leave his body return again to clay!

Lady Levasseur also inherited the vast wealth of her uncle. But she must soon follow him to the grave. And then where would all her riches go? To her adopted child!

But while life remained, hope could not die. And then she heard of that "bright realm of flowers, of beautiful lakes and winding streams," where invalids do not suffocate with miasmatic breath. The sunny South also had its flowers, its lakes and its streams— all beautiful everywhere. But Nature was too prodigal with her flowers blooming all the year. So much life

Castellated Appearance of Lower Magnesian Limestone Bluffs, bordering on a Small Stream between the Garrard Estate and the Town of Red Wing.

engendered perpetual decay; and though very charming to the eye, there was a poison in the air that toyed even among the aromatic leaves of the fruit-laden orange tree!

Minnesota! The land with lakes and streams of steel-blue water beneath a steel-blue sky!

The land where no malarious vapors ever rise!

The land of hope, where enchantment soon lures the deepest melancholy into cheerful smiles!

The land of promise, where consumptives may rise from their beds, and walk, and laugh in unison with bird-songs of joy heard warbling in the groves!

Lady Levasseur was *en voyage* to Minnesota. Her devoted slaves went with her, and so did Fleurette, her darling adopted child!

But the odious *vampire* would not let her pass! He heard her languidly-breathing cough, and chuckled with a thirsty grin. Assuming human form and Christian guise, with the cold, leaden eyes of Dr. Passion, he gloated in anticipation upon the dying wreck of beauty and tortured love!

Farmer Denton wanted to befriend the weak everywhere. Goliah was ever ready to stand by his master, and did not always wait for his call. He frequently proved that a "dumb animal" may have a slight modicum of reason.

Perhaps I overestimate the sagacity of the canine species, while a majority of my fellow-mortals undervalue the attributes of the noblest creature next to man! Experience will teach the wisest of us to believe what we might otherwise never know—and the knowledge or the wisdom thus acquired will not forsake us very soon!

Goliah did understand the wishes of his master, and

immediately took upon himself the singular task of watching every person and scrutinizing every object that passed in or out of state-room c. He wagged his tail at Dinah and at Sancho, and frisked around Fleurette, while she did not hesitate to put her arms about his immense neck and talk to him as she would to any person whom she loved. Well she might, for his flowing hair was entirely free from odor and soil. A dignified animal, proud and clean!

"O, isn't he nice!" exclaimed Fleurette. In the innocence of her heart, she could not refrain from caressing the noble creature.

How strange it is that while some people have an innate fondness for domestic animals, others will shrink from even the touch of a pretty little kitten. And dogs are quick to perceive who like them. It is also very remarkable and positively true, that the more intelligent breed of dogs can detect the viciousness or the dishonesty of those who shun them! Farmer Denton often said that he invariably suspected any one who manifested a repugnance to his dog, and at the same time he made it a rule to respect those whom his dog did not condemn!

Goliah was evidently shy of Dr. Passion and that friend of his. At least he would not approach them. And, pretending to look in another direction, he furtively eyed them crosswise, while they were no less distant in their maneuvering to avoid him.

As usual in such cases the clerk of the boat firmly remonstrated against Goliah's free entrance to the saloon. Farmer Denton admitted that common dogs were hardly fit to enter the ladies' saloon. But Goliah was an exception. He had been reared with rules of unquestionable propriety; and was accustomed to ladies' society. The ladies admired him! And **Farmer Denton** significantly said:

"You'll find it a plaguy ugly job to get between us, anyhow. That dog is the best friend I've got in the world. I have him with me now, because I'm moving up to Minnesota—and he's just precisely what a man in my situation wants to guarantee safety! There's money in my pocket, and that dog knows it's there. While he is near, no pickpocket is smart enough to rob me. And when I sleep at night, he lies as close as he can get, with one eye open and his prodigious jaws ready to spring like a mammoth steel-trap, should any one come fingering round. You see, sir, that's my dog—and we're in the 'same boat together.' I'll throw in that joke, gratis. Goliah goes in and out with me everywhere. Eh—you see?"

Farmer Denton did make the acquaintance of Lady Levasseur. She was going to Minnesota for her health, and he intended making his future home there. He had some excuse for offering his services on the score of that, if nothing else. And she was glad to meet such an honest-appearing man.

He was not long in speaking his mind about Dr. Passion, and bluntly said:

"Don't take any more of that quack stuff! Throw it all away!" He made a grimace of disgust and contempt. "It won't do you a bit of good. It's only so much white dust from *Montmarte*, with a flavoring of gall, to give it a bitterness for effect—or some other equally inefficacious nonsense, or a slow poison! Try to get out on deck and inhale some of this invigorating atmosphere. We're getting into Minnesota now—and *I* can already perceive a vast change in the air. Come out, do! Here, girls, held her all you can! She's going to throw away them quack powders and take nothing but the rejuvenescence of Minnesota. Now, help her, girls! She'll be stronger to-morrow, and stronger yet the day after. Her cheeks will soon be as rosy as yours. Come, girls, she's not going to lie here any more. Won't it be funny if she's promenading the deck without assistance before we reach St. Paul?"

Dr. Passion was not a witness to that scene. And Lady Levasseur did take courage from the blunt and earnest sympathy of the paternal farmer. His daughters were also kind and attentive to her, and a bond of lasting friendship was being established between her and them. And it did not stop there. The feeling spread. A perfect web of more than ordinarily good feeling reached all around—not forgetting the "colored folks and the dog."

Indeed, the relationship of the invalid and the "colored folks" was somewhat enigmatical to the farmer and his daughters, all of whom entertained the popular prejudices of the community in which they had always lived. He was bitterly opposed to slavery, and yet never imagined that Africans were worthy of such confidence and trust as Lady Levasseur reposed in Sancho. He contended that negroes should have their freedom, the same as white people; but they were at best only miserable creatures, very far beneath the genuine standard of human beings. And for all his concern about their bondage, like a majority of the class with whom his ideas were intimately identified, he did not look to the elevation of their social position. They were good enough for menials, but nothing more. He inherited those prejudices of his father in the same manner that his daughters imbibed them from him, without actual inquiry beyond traditional belief. However, he possessed a generous mind, as well as quick perception, and to his daughters frankly said:

"That old Sancho is the worthiest negro I ever saw. And if it wasn't for his yellow skin and that inevitable wool on the back part of his head, he'd pass for a real gentleman. Why, he's as dignified and self-possessed as a schoolmaster, and not in the least pompous or supercilious, like those black peacocks who live in Jersey. I tell you what it is, girls; there's a great deal in example. That old fellow has been accustomed to what they call society, and he's picked up the mannerisms of well-bred people. We are all imitative beings, ever unconsciously acquiring the tastes and habits of those around us. And the worst of it is, we seem to gather the evil with more avidity than the good. This colored person is an exception to that rule, though; for he appears to have improved upon the inferiority of his race. Ah, but what charming scenery we're passing along the river all this time!" the farmer exclaimed, as a beautiful sunset view appeared to suddenly dissipate his ethical discourse. "Talk about the magnificent Hudson! Why, this is infinitely more sublime! Now, girls, feast your eyes on that!"

But presently "Bob," a sable-skinned individual, acting as steward *ad interim*, tapped the farmer on his shoulder and faintly articulated, "Tea's ready, sah!" That was intended for the sly premonition which dining-saloon *figurantes* habitually give ladies, in advance of the rattling of the bell or banging of the gong. The custom was originally adopted with a twofold object. It enabled ladies to secure eligible places at the table before a general scrambling of the multitude destroyed the formality of conventional etiquette by promiscuous confusion. And it was also a suggestive incentive for the pecuniary remembrance of attention thus bestowed.

"That's the talk!" responded Denton. "Be there instanter!" Then, as "Bob" hurried away, he added, for his daughter's hearing, "Some difference 'twixt these darkies and old Sancho. The latter would not tap a white man on the shoulder in that way. Another instance to illustrate what I told you a while ago—that example is everything. This smart young Ethiop has been reared in the harum-scarum looseness of quick come and go. But we had better take his hint, and get seats near the captain. I like Captain Webb! He's a clever man; and the oldest captain on the Upper Mississippi River.

"By the way; I've already observed that these Western steamboat captains are far more social than those occupying a similar position on the rivers in the East. I once addressed a civil question to the captain of a Sound steamer, and, instead of giving a decent answer, he pushed me to one side and pompously walked on, without so much as a grunt or a smile. And the joke of it was, that I subsequently repaid his incivility with compound interest in the bargain. He happened to be visiting an acquaintance near Westfield. When he got out of the cars, my buggy stood near the station; and some one told him that I was going right past the house where his acquaintance lived, a mile or so from town. He approached me full of smiles then. Of course he didn't recognize me in connection with that little bit of arrogance on the Sound. But I remembered him. 'Would I be so kind as to give him a ride?' he obsequiously inquired. I eyed him with a look of non-comprehension, and uttered no reply. He then repeated the inquiry, additionally remarking:

'The road is so muddy that I shall certainly spoil my apparel if obliged to walk!' I had a great mind to drive off and make no answer at all. But that wouldn't be like me. So I politely gave him a seat in the buggy. When we arrived at his friend's house, I detained him a moment to recall his incivility on the Sound. The circumstance was not forgotten. And he apologized with the most sheepish expression of countenance possible to squeeze out of a living man. And that's the way I repaid him!"

"Bob" assisted them in making a satisfactory evening repast; and then, when the saloon was restored to its normal condition, he and his comrades extemporized a Minstrel Band. First "dey had de oberture," and "den de program ob songs," all terminating with a pleasant cotillon or two for "de ladees and gem'ens" who wished to dance!

The next day about noon they arrived at the levee of St. Paul. Dr. Passion seemed very anxious to land as soon as the plank could be thrown ashore. He stood upon the lower deck where the men bustled around in the hurry and confusion of making fast. And there he received more than one rudely admonishing shove. But perhaps he had engagements to fill. Credulous people might be expecting him at a certain hotel where he was advertised to perform miraculous cures. He was exceedingly impatient, be the cause what it might. But bad luck was in store for him, nevertheless. Somebody did something that pushed somebody else, so that in the surge his foot caught under a rope. A pitch and a stumble, and backward into the river plunged the great medical man! And some cruel jester tantalizingly sang out, in a quizzical tone of voice, "How are you, Hydropathy!"

Romantic Mississippi River Scenery, along the Minnesota shore, near Lake Pepin.

CHAPTER XVII.

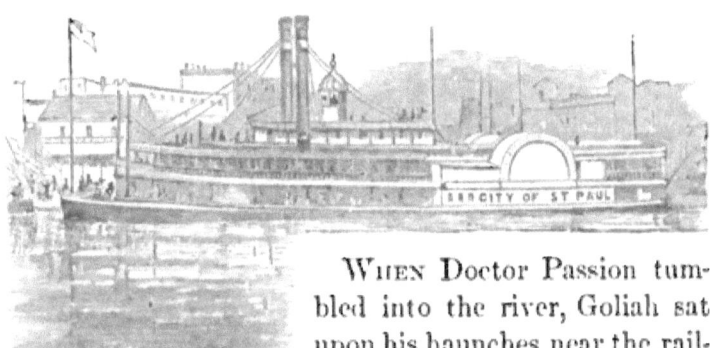

WHEN Doctor Passion tumbled into the river, Goliah sat upon his haunches near the railing above, without appearing to notice what had happened; and a crusty millwright sneeringly cried out to Farmer Denton, "Where's your wonderful dog, now? I say, stranger, guess you've been blowing some. Didn't you tell us all how he'd pull a man out of the water if one accidentally got in?"

"My dog don't consider the life of that fellow worth diving after. He's too sagacious to trouble himself about saving a blasted quack!"

Then a chorus of voices swelled up in ridicule of the farmer and his dog. But the next instant they all heard a feminine shriek as the form of Fleurette was seen falling from the guard-railing of the upper deck. Having rushed out to see what the people meant by the cries of "man overboard!" she lost her balance, in some unaccountable way, during the excitement of the scene, and was also precipitated into the river below.

Goliah heard Fleurette's shriek, and instantly leaped clear over the railing out into the air. With a tremendous splash he struck the water and disappeared for an instant to rise near Fleurette. But he approached her carefully. She saw him coming and endeavored to anticipate his maneuvers. He quickly seized the back of her dress between the shoulders, and tenderly, but firmly, his teeth grasped the top of it in such a skillful manner that he was enabled to keep her head entirely out of the water. And then he swam ashore with her as gently as the pleasant sporting of a swan.

The huzzas of the people on board the boat and the crowd upon the levee were loud and long in applause at the quick rescue of Fleurette, and that, too, while Dr. Passion was borne down with the current to the bow of an "opposition steamer." He would drown for certain if his preservation depended upon Goliah, who was wholly interested in Fleurette.

The bystanders began to gather around; and some gentlemen thought to help Fleurette back on board the boat, after Goliah carried her ashore—but a terrible growl from the jealous animal drove them all back in fright. And then, still clinging to his neck for support, the half-drowned girl was escorted safely up the long plank, to the wonder and amusement of the multitude, and with extreme delight to herself.

"There!" shouted Farmer Denton, amid the clapping of hands and an enthusiastic repetition of vehement huzzas. "There! Now you see! That's what my dog'll do!"

And, indeed, it was not the first time that Goliah had

been a hero! Many exploits of a remarkable nature were connected with his previous history.

The wet garments of Fleurette were exchanged for others, while her canine preserver stretched himself at full length to dry his dripping hair in the sunshine near the outer door of state-room c, where he could hear what was going on within.

A deck hand of the opposition steamer took pity on Dr. Passion, and finally succeeded in getting him on board more dead than alive.

Farmer Denton was considered a good and a humane man by those who knew him well; but when the *vampire* came up out of the river, he could not refrain from muttering,

"I really was in hope that scamp would drown!"

But though Fleurette unintentionally "cut such a splash" by way of announcing her arrival in St. Paul, everybody seemed to be highly delighted at the happy and novel result. Sancho said to Dinah: "I mus say dat ar mon'cerus big dog kin beat ebrey udder animile I'ze seed in my time, all holler." To which Dinah replied: "An eze wuf eze hull wate en bran new goold dollars right out ob de mint!"

If any distinguished personage ever felt "afflictingly bored" by a grand ovation, Goliah certainly experienced the misery of being great. Even those inveterate dog-haters, who exist everywhere, joined in the multiform plaudits bestowed upon him. The deckhands whistled for him to come down among them, and the imps of the culinary sanctum brought out gammon bones, refuse steaks, and surplus chops, to entice him above. And the austere clerk actually snapped his thumb and finger with a patronizing chirp. But the dignified quadruped made no response to any of them.

If his tail wagged at all, it did so only when his acknowledged and more intimate friends gave him their attention. Indeed, he would have preferred much less demonstrative noise on his account.

Busied with Sancho and Dinah in arranging their things for leaving the steamer, Lady Levasseur did not know of the frightful accident to Fleurette, until after it was entirely over; and then, perceiving the attachment between Fleurette and the noble animal, she immediately proposed that his master should sell him to her.

"There ain't enough money in the world to buy that dog!" replied the farmer. "He's none of those common curs. No mongrel in him! Why, bless you, lady, he's a pure St. Bernard; and knows a heap more than some folks who'd like to kick him when he passes them. My wife thought everything of that dog when she was alive, and I value him all the more because she liked him so! And the girls would cry their eyes out if anything should happen to him! He's often saved my property, and he once saved my life! I'd be ever so much delighted to gratify you, for the sake of your daughter; but you don't want to take him from us now, after I've told you all that. We'd feel sadder than ever in our new home, if Goliah wasn't there with us! Ah, we shall be lonely enough without mother! That's Eliza, I mean—my wife that was, and mother to those four daughters of mine. She died with—I beg your pardon for making unpleasant allusions. But mother—I call her mother, you know. We Northern folks have our queer ways—and perhaps you Southerners have some odd customs as well as us. Mother died with the consumption! And I shall always believe that if I had brought her up here, to Minnesota, she would have been alive this day! But you're here now; and depend upon it, you'll recover very soon!"

Sancho and Dinah both murmured something like, "Praise de Lor' fur what dat ar good man wid de big dog am say'n to Missus now!"

"Oh, what a pleasant place!" whispered Fleurette, as they rode up Third street in the vehicle that conveyed them to the Merchants' Hotel. If she was pleased with the short ride up that hill, what would she say when they came to view the grand magnificence of the wide-spread city, with hundreds of costly stores, and stylish residences scattered around in the suburbs, and elegant villas upon the surrounding hills?

The best of friends may be compelled to separate in the uneven course of life; and the parting interview of those two families was not without sincere and emphatically demonstrated regrets. The farmer's new home was beyond St. Paul—nearly a hundred miles from that city. And the following morning, he and his four daughters and Goliah went off by railway cars, that ran some distance partly in the direction which they were going.

Meanwhile, Lady Levasseur had not risen before Dr. Passion called to attend her. Then the card of another distinguished *medicastre* was also brought to her for admission. Indeed, it was apparently probable that the *vampires* actually employed emissaries to watch the arrival of every steamer and report the coming of invalids. And if any wretched consumptive got safely housed without being caught by the "malady detectives," then the auricular sensibility of the professional cormorants who instigated them, was so marvelously acute that they had no difficulty in hearing the least possible symptom of a new cough, breathed or otherwise uttered, in any part of the city. (But such impostors are scarce there now—the citizens having taken measures to greatly *discourage* them.)

But Lady Levasseur was thoroughly impressed with the philosophy of Farmer Denton; and, consequently, none of the *soi disant* Esculapians were successful in their devices of approach.

"Whar on arth, all dem ar doct'rs born, I wund'r?" remarked Dinah to Sancho.

"Bress my stars—de ole gal aint got sperience nuff in dis sinful worle to know ow dat am. You see, honey, in de fust place—dat am in de begin'n—dey wus two speerits. Wun of dem ar speerits wus good, an de udder wus bad. An de bad wun's bin flurish'n all dis time like a 'green bay tree.' An you recumember de beeographee ob dem ar orf'l hungry big fishes what am call'd sherks, an how dey foll'rs art'r a ship on de see, when dey smells sick folks aboard. You does recumember dat quar beeographee ob de fishes! Well, den, my lub; dese yar doct'r chaps is land sherks—an dey is all de time skoot'n or sneek'n round on de sly whar-ebber inwalids trabbel. Dey is wus'n sherks—kase de sherks oney want de ded corpuses, wile de quacks take sick pussun's mun'y wid dar libes, an den leab dar corpuses fur udder folks tu beerry. You see Dinar, ole gal; de mascumline mind ob de starn'r sex'us am abel to par'seeb what ain't all'rs komprehenshunabel to de karnel cents ob lubly wom'n!"

Dinah was proud of Sancho as a man; and, never having listened to the demoralizing precepts of the strong-minded *gynecian* squabblers, who are striving with all their might to instigate a connubial *revolution*, she experienced much pleasure in hearing what she called "de voice ob wis'um." She was all the prouder of Sancho because the blood of his mother's master—a very distinguished statesman—flowed in his own veins. And when he paused for breath, she responded, "Dat am a fac!"

Sancho's comparison of consumption quacks and rapacious fish was better than any I might suggest; and it is quite probable that Dinah's approbation would have been accorded in by a multitude of victims, if they had heard him explain his theory.

The newspapers, next morning, announced the arrival of the celebrated Dr. Passion, who had returned once more after an absence (of I don't know how long), in St. Louis. And there was an accompanying suggestion that invalids would rejoice at his coming. But nothing was said about his aquatic adventure at the levee. Nor did the unamphibious "locals" make any mention of a young lady having been rescued from drowning by a dog. However, the perambulent scribes were excusable for their inubiquity of that day, inasmuch as they had just returned from a rather extended fishing excursion, the convivial hilarity and fatigue of which left their usually multocular faculties of perception in a consequent state of sleepiness. In fact, their visual organs were closed in slumber at the precise moment when Goliah's heroism occurred. But one of them more than atoned for his unavoidable hallucination, by subsequently writing and publishing an epic stanzas in commemoration of the "scenic" event—a copy of which is still among the literary treasures of Fleurette. And, in accordance with the spirit of progress so characteristic of the North-west, that effusive reporter is now the sole proprietor of a flourishing journal in a neighboring town.

Lady Levasseur was very rich. The death of her

uncle left her more than she knew what to do with. Fortunately, the greater part of his wealth and hers was invested in the North; and therefore the rebellion would not impoverish her.

She had a twofold object in leaving New Orleans. A change of air, and escape from the horrors of the war. Many of her Southern acquaintances sneeringly laughed at the idea of going "up the river" two or three thousand miles, almost to the Arctic Pole—as they said—where it was cold enough to freeze the blood in her veins; and that, too, when she had the consumption. And some of them strongly hinted that the inhabitants of the North-west were, for most part, little better than cannibals. The hordes of mud-sills and wild Indians would, in all probability, rob and scalp her before she had been there a week.

Yet she remembered hearing her husband speak of that country and its people. And what he said was not in accordance with the extremely absurd impression of her advisers, who sincerely believed that Paradise existed only in the latitude of orange-blossoms and sugar-cane. She expected to die very soon. But, for the sake of lingering with Fleurette as long as possible, she would go, hoping for some relief.

It might have been that Farmer Denton's encouragement animated her spirits and imbued her with fresh strength. Though, without reducing that theory to argument as a test, it may be recorded that her health began to improve with her advent in St. Paul. At first she rode out in a close carriage only a short distance, and but once a day. The fatigue which seemed intolerable to her when she began riding sensibly diminished in a little while, and in a few weeks' time she voluntarily extended her drives, and repeated them in an open vehicle and on horseback, for the sake of inhaling all the more air.

Then winter came, with its beautiful dry snow, its clear sky and its lovely moonlight nights. Sleigh-bells were merrily ringing up and down the highways, and Lady Levasseur's "turn-out" sped along as gaily as the rest of them. The pallor vanished from her cheeks to admit a roseate glow; her eyes lost their languor in sparkling animation; her colorless lips were ruddy and smooth; her attenuated form resumed its original fullness and beauty; her listless gait was quickened into an elastic step, and the pleasant intimation of a smile upon her countenance disclosed more cheerfulness in her heart. When the blue-birds came back to herald the approach of spring with their twittering song, she and Fleurette were almost daily seen on horseback galloping out on Summit avenue and returning to town by another way. As the buttercups grew, the beautiful mother and her lovely adopted daughter were plucking them like two school children in holiday glee. And with the transition of season from early blossoms to summer flowers, while increasing verdure spread, and productive existence matured into teeming glory, so renewed health and still greater enjoyment were realized by both of them.

Meanwhile, Farmer Denton and his daughters, and Goliah, were quite happy in their new home. Mercy kept up a regular correspondence with Lady Levasseur, or perhaps I should say with Fleurette, who was extremely delighted to act as secretary for her adopted mother. And it was arranged that Lady Levasseur and Fleurette, and Sancho and Dinah, should go and spend a few weeks at the farm, where Mr. Denton had put everything in the very best shape, on purpose, he said, to make it pleasant for them when they came, as expected, during the second week in August, which was then near at hand.

But, alas for human expectations! *The Sioux Warwhoop* suddenly rent the peaceful air that was laden with prosperity and alive with buoyant hopes. The appalling alarm came like a thunderbolt, with howling demons and death! The Indians had been reduced to a state of starvation in consequence of not receiving their *Annuity Money* when they needed it most. And numbers of them actually died in want of food while waiting for the tardy movements of Government officials somewhere!

The Indian is required to bring in his wife and all his children, if he expects to draw anything for them.

"White man can't trust Injun—for he lies!" He would say that he had twenty papooses in his teepee beyond the lake or the river, when he did not really have so much as a teepee or even a squaw! Therefore he must bring his family to the Agency to draw their pay. The agent can then count their noses, without question or doubt.

"Injun can't trust white man—for he lies, too!" And some do say that it was a bad pale-face who first taught the aborigines to lie. But I am one of those who believe that the art of lying has been known to every nation and tribe of men from innocent Adam down to the wily politicians of the present day.

In our "Indian affairs" there has been not only a great deal of lying, but an enormous amount of cheating—all of which stands recorded upon the white man's page of the "treaty" ledger. It has been a continual repetition of "the turkey and the crow," in which game the domestic fowl invariably falls to the white man's lot. The Indian is sure to get the crow; or, as it might accidentally happen—nothing at all! "Fair play" is too precious for the aborigine.

Our indulgent "Uncle Samuel"—the red man's *Great Father*—is cheated by his agents to the tune of millions, over and above what has been stipulated for by his copper-colored children, while they do not receive half their just dues. And yet the *Public* seem not to know what *becomes* of the money. Nevertheless, I might here describe several "lots, tracts and parcels" of very valuable property now in the possession of those who have enriched themselves at the expense of honor and humanity as men, by defrauding the Government and robbing the poor Indian!

Who instigated the great Indian massacre of August, 1862? *Is* there a man now living in luxury who indirectly or directly sacrificed the lives of several thousand fellow beings, and destroyed millions of property, to amass a fortune for himself? *If* such a man is living, how does he feel? He may reside in a fine house, and have about him all the creature-comforts of life! But possibly remorse is deepening the lines of reflection in his face! And, though he can feast on savory viands and drink costly champagne—in his slumber, at times, there must be a chaos of bleeding victims and incarnate fiends!

Well might Bishop Whipple, in his "Appeal for the Red Man," tell the President of the United States that there was something wrong in the administration of Government affairs on the North-western *frontier*. I say frontier, because there will continue to be a "sanguinary line of demarkation" between the limits of our purchased lands and the territory of the aborigine so long as he has a single acre left to dispose of and the "har-

A View of Crow Wing, when First Settled, in 1839.

pies of favored position" are permitted to enrich themselves by an organized system of robbery, both disgraceful to the nation and shamefully instigative of every crime against the laws of God! For, not content with "arithmetical frauds," those who have the opportunity by right (or by wrong) to honorably represent the Government and faithfully serve the savage, ingeniously and deliberately compel the industrious and virtuous to liquidate the obligations of the indolent and depraved. School money is squandered and other appropriations misapplied to aggrandize individual gains. The reverend Bishop accuses white men of teaching the Sioux and the Chippeways that adultery is no sin and theft no crime! He even intimates that some go so far as to rob the Sioux of their cash by selling them the poison which I have described in a preceding chapter, purposely to destroy their lives, and then forge certificates whereby they are empowered to draw and criminally appropriate annuity money in the name of the dead! And he further declares that every dollar which the Government or the Indian is thus defrauded of must inevitably be atoned for by ten times as much in the cost of war or indemnities for future outrages arising therefrom. Among other conclusive arguments in his appeal, is a suggestive allusion to the significant clause in an advertisement for "Indian supplies" during the autumn of the great massacre, which required two hundred and fifty dozen scalping and butcher knives! But such matters are too interminable for me to effectually dispose of in a volume like this.

Just as Lady Levasseur was about to start for Denton Farm, a horseman came dashing into St. Paul with news of the massacre then begun! In an hour's time every person in the city was aghast! Another horseman came—and then a man on foot. More followed, increasing in numbers—and each with a narrative of fresh horrors from Redwood Ferry, New Ulm, Fort Ridgely, and elsewhere! Such horrors as were never heard of before—and I dare not record the worst of them here. The details would be unfit for type!

A wife and mother had her head split open while she was making bread, and the fiend who did it also roasted her child in the ready heated oven! Other children were nailed to doors, and knives and tomahawks pitched at them until they expired with fright and pain! Mothers were disemboweled, and whole families burned alive! Eyes were gouged out, and tongues torn from their roots. In some instances every member of a victim's body was torn from its place! There was no mercy for infancy or age, and no heed to prayers or tears!

Naked savages, disfigured with paint, and yelling in merriment or howling with fury, murdered and plundered the settlers, and destroyed whatever property and produce they could reach! The old Inquisition never devised such heinous methods of excruciating torture! Each savage vied with his comrades to add a new element of atrocity in the sacrifice of the next victim! Mothers and daughters were taken into captivity worse than death—unless their resistance terminated their lives upon the spot! The fields were strewn with cattle and other domestic animals, their limbs broken or their bodies gashed, bellowing, shrieking, and writhing in terrible agony! Pieces were cut out of living animals and men! Parts of the body chopped off, or a limb torn asunder, and the sufferer driven out upon the prairies, or into corners and holes, to die a lingering death! Pools of blood and destruction everywhere!

The alarm spread and the panic grew. Settlers fled from their homes; and one man sold his farm which cost him six thousand dollars, for only sixty-two dollars and a quarter—just enough to carry his family down to Fort Snelling! Hundreds and, I presume, thousands of men, women and children arrived in St. Paul without a penny in their pockets and famishing for food! Some were but partly clad, and many were mutilated with serious wounds. The houses and the streets were swarming with the impoverished fugitives, who had lost everything that they so recently possessed!

St. Paul became an immense refuge hospital! Some of the citizens were so much alarmed about their own safety, while the foe was at least a hundred miles away, that they foolishly sold valuable property at any price which the more courageous would give!

Lady Levasseur's purse was quickly emptied in her contributions to the panic-stricken and famished refugees. But she could refill it at will. The bankers were all ready to advance her any amount in cash; and doubtless these allusions will be appreciated by many a Minnesotian whose heart is full of gratitude when memory calls up the past! Surely they have not forgotten "The Lady of the Angel Heart!" as they called her then!

"Had any one seen Farmer Denton?"

Lady Levasseur repeated that question again and again every day. She felt concerned about him. His new home was near the scene of carnage, and she feared that his interesting daughters were among the captives and himself among the slain!

"No, ma'am!" was the inevitably cold response from every one in turn. It seemed cold to her ear, because she was so deeply interested in the good, honest man and his motherless girls.

"And Goliah, too?" interposed Fleurette, when they were surmising the probable fate of the Dentons. "Perhaps he has been butchered by those uncivilized and savage men."

Then Sancho conceived an idea. He said, "Some dese yar brave men mought go an fine massa Denton, an his dart'rs. Speck dey'd fotch em in mi-tee quick time, ef missus wus to gib um lots ob mun'y!"

But, though Lady Levasseur did act upon Sancho's suggestion, no one seemed willing to venture among the Indians, either for humanity sake, or pecuniary reward!

Fleurette said that if she were only a man, she would make some personal effort to find Mr. Denton and the girls—and Goliah, too.

Lady Levasseur continued to furnish means for the relief of the impoverished fugitives who were almost hourly arriving in St. Paul. And, while dispensing pecuniary aid with a liberal hand, she eagerly and persistently inquired for Farmer Denton and his daughters; but could get no intelligence of them. Finally another party arrived from the vicinity of New Ulm, and Sancho was dispatched to make inquiry again. The old negro soon returned as fast as his legs could perambulate, and breathlessly exclaiming:

"Massa Denton dart'rs am kum. Dey'll be yar at de otel right away bime'by dreckly, soon's dey kan!"

And in a few minutes, sure enough, Mercy, Eliza, Julia and Jane were in the hotel apartments of Lady Levasseur! A confusion of words and kisses, in the mutual gladness of greeting—and:

"Where's your father?"

For a moment there was no answer. And then, amid sobs and tears, only Jane could reply:

"The Indians have killed him! O, dear! They suddenly sprang up out of the grass, and murdered him while he was reading to us from the Bible. And they hurried us off before we could realize what had happened!"

"Oh, that's terrible news!" sighed Lady Levasseur. "Your father was too good a man to die thus! Poor, dear girls! Alas, you have no father or mother left to guide and to love you now! But I will be your mother. Come to my arms. And may God assist me in what I do?'

Fleurette wanted to ask one little question; but her emotion choked the words back. Presently she murmured: "Where is Goliah?"

Mercy replied, with a fresh flood of tears, that Goliah flew at the savages to save their father. She thought he killed one of them; and then the others chopped him to pieces with their tomahawks and knives!

"It was perfectly heart-rending!" sobbed Eliza. "Neighbor Lawrence's house was already in flames; and the Indians instantly dragged us away. But we could hear Goliah piteously howling and crying in the agony of death! And then we also saw our own house and the out-buildings all on fire!"

"Oh, what shall we do, now that dear father is dead?" cried Julia, weeping aloud!

THE ESTLICK FAMILY. (The Father was killed during the Great Massacre; and while the Mother was a captive among the Indians, her eldest Boy heroically preserved the life of his Baby-Brother.)

CHAPTER XVIII.

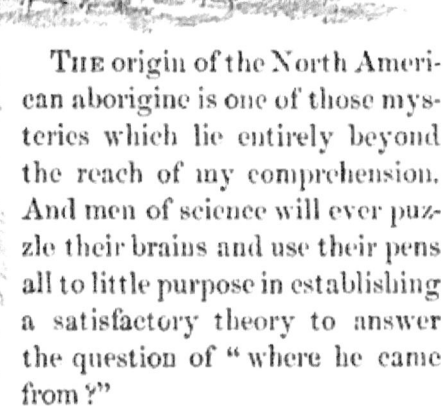

The origin of the North American aborigine is one of those mysteries which lie entirely beyond the reach of my comprehension. And men of science will ever puzzle their brains and use their pens all to little purpose in establishing a satisfactory theory to answer the question of "where he came from?"

The Asiatic tribes of Guebres and Tibetians, the Japanese and the Chinese, have worshiped the sun as their greatest divinity, the same as our Indians. Here in Minnesota, the *Kitchi-manitou* of the Chippeways and the *Taka-wakan* of the Sioux, signify both the Great Spirit and the Sun. But I have not distinctly ascertained whether they look up at the orb of day as only an emblem of their Deity, or the Godhead itself.

If their traditions are reliable, in the absence of any tangible record of genealogy, then they may be considered at least antediluvian, if not pre-Adamite in origin. This I adduce from the persistent declaration of those venerable chiefs who believe that "when a far-off part of the world was depopulated by a great flood, their race were all spared; that while the wicked inhabitants of another land perished entirely, they beheld the sun rise every morning from the surface of those waters in which the unrighteous were destroyed forever." And inasmuch as we are informed by Holy Writ that God gave Noah only three sons to repopulate Europe, Asia and Africa, I am pardonable for presuming that America was *not* totally submerged in the execution of Divine wrath! But I do not intend to follow up this theme in the present connection.

Both the Chippeways and the Sioux are extremely insubordinate by nature, or at least in accordance with popular custom. They are fond of living in a manner and at the place most agreeable to their individual tastes. And in the matter of authority, they seem to acknowledge none! Their chiefs are so only in name— and impeachment by unceremonious acclamation has been known. But generally those dignitaries retain their title and position unto the end of their lives, whether impeached or not. The policy of Tah-o-ah-ta-doo-ta, at the inauguration of the great massacre of '62, may be referred to as a deplorable example of the limited power exercised by a noted chief.

The father of a family is absolute monarch in his own teepee, unless more than one family occupy the same lodge; and then the oldest man is ruler over all. Sons have neither love nor respect for their fathers, and fathers manifest very little affection for their children. They sometimes hold councils, but such a mess of hierarchy seldom terminates in any definite organization or satisfactory understanding. As their property generally consists of only what the squaws can carry from one encampment to another, the enactment of a defined code of protective or distributive laws would be entirely useless. Public officers are not required when each man is permitted to be his own executioner of the assassin or other criminal who commits any offense against himself or his family. And, strange to say, this method of vengeance is not visited with retaliation. The offender is prepared to die, and usually makes no attempt to resist or escape. In this species of cruelty, an Indian can surpass a Nero, Maximin, or Caligula, when his ferocity is fully aroused; and even his squaw and papooses may be participants with him in every species of physical torture inflicted upon the writhing victim. And victims have been known to purposely exasperate their executioners to greater cruelty still.

Achilles sacrificed prisoners of war to Patrocles, and the Mexicans to their idol deities, just as the Minnesota Indians do to the *manitous* and *wakons* of war. They pay great deference to their infernal gods. And they make no distinction between the sexes, or the very old and the very young. If a male prisoner is spared in battle, they bestow him upon one of their women who may have lost her master in the conflict. But then if he does not suit her fancy, she forthwith sacrifices him to the manes of her departed husband!

Instead of a "wake," with copious potations of whisky, in the Hibernian custom, over the fresh corpse of the dead, an Indian will have a grand howl, and a huge feast of dog meat prepared for the mourners and surviving friends. And then the corpse is retained for ceremonial attentions, in some particulars similar to the ancient practice of the Egyptians, the Greeks, the Romans, the Christians at the time of Tertullian, and also of certain kings, popes and cardinals, and the Arabs and the Chinese of modern times. The corpse is subsequently placed upon a scaffold some eight or ten feet from the ground, where it remains until the flesh has either dried up or fallen from the bones, and then the hideous remains are deposited in the ground, with the face always toward the East, and stakes or stones fixed around the spot to protect it from beasts of prey.

In lacerating their flesh with sharp fragments of stone, to increase the frenzy of their howling grief, they show considerable skill in anatomy, always selecting such parts as are guarded by integuments of strength. And after all, the violent contortions performed by them when death takes away one of their companions, are but a formal demonstration scarcely more absurd than a cortege of empty carriages behind the sable-plumed hearse and blanketed horses carrying a defunct citizen of New York to his little home in a fashionable cemetery.

The marriage ceremony of these untutored people is in some instances similar to that of the ancient Romans. But the affianced squaw does not have the *flammeum* worn by the brides of Rome on their marriage-day. I have had several unsatisfactory descriptions of their nuptial rites, from all of which it is only possible to infer that matrimony among them is simply a compact of utility and convenience, with as little formality as the Greeks practiced in their marriages *per usum*. Here the *patria potestas* would be a dead letter.

Their connubial relationship seems to be quite as prodigal as that of the Saints in Utah, and even more extravagant in the promptings of hospitality. For example, when the first negro appeared among the Sioux he was requested to affiliate with their marriageable young squaws. They believed him to be a devil, but fancied that if they could have his posterity in their midst the other devils would fraternize with them, and in that event a peace might be concluded with the spirits of evil.

Some extremely philogistical Dakotas deem it a justly natural privilege to have as many wives as they please. Also, in accordance with the suggestions of St. Augustin, Diderot and Helvetius, socially inclined husbands mutually accommodate each other by loaning their wives!

Abstemious Bedouins consider one wife sufficient for a family, and occasionally a Dakota entertains the same notion; in which case the unfortunate female is retained as a creature in bondage, with a harder lot than any female domestic ever experienced in ancient Briton.

Where affection does not exist, jealousy will not come; and in such a case, promiscuous cohabitation is attended with very little dissension. I have been told that the Sioux are jealous of their wives; but possibly they may unconsciously appreciate the wise principle of Monsieur de Montespan—which was to feign virtue for the purpose of better pay! Their divorce custom is equally as liberal, and even more convenient, than similar usages permitted by law among civilized nations, with the arbitrary exception of allowing the male savage all the elective rights and privileges of separation.

When a "big Injun" wishes to get rid of his squaw he puts her away with no less compunctions of conscience than that exhibited among the ancients mentioned in this connection in the Bible. But the Justinian code governs a disposition of their children, and consigns them to the care and responsibility of the mother, whose consanguinity is less doubted than that nominally claimed by the ostensible sire!

During their youth, the forms of the women are attractive. But, like summer flowers, they soon fade. In the life of a squaw, evening succeeds morning without any interval of noon! However, she is generally appropriated at an early age by some individual of the opposite sex. But if she and her husband live ever so near her parents, he must not mention their names nor look them in the face. Sometimes the young couple occupy a part of the paternal teepee, and the same etiquette is observable even then. Other couples live in a large teepee, and the husband provides the parents-in-law with food for their smaller abode in the rear. I fancy civilized sons-in-law would demur at arrangements of this kind!

Some prejudices of the Indian mind are inherent. At least it is impossible to trace out their origin. Regarding the degradation of menial employment, there is but one feeling among the women as well as among the men. The war-path and the hunting-ground are the only places where the man deigns to exercise his limbs in the execution of laborious duty. He will scarcely paddle his own canoe, if accompanied by a squaw. And all the drudgery devolves upon her, as a matter of course.

When a party of Dakotas play *shinney*, a favorite game of ball, they expect that their squaws will run and bring it out of the water, the ravine or the rocks up the hill, whither it may chance to fly from the propulsion of a random blow. And the squaws dart after the truant ball with impetuous alacrity and the lightning speed of bounding deer, while their masters impatiently wait their quick return. And although denied any interest in the game, the squaws' concern for the success at issue, is generally as enthusiastic, if not more intense, than that of the players themselves. And without permission to join in the orgies of incantation, or grotesque dances of joy, they are required to contribute the most hideous screams and howls whenever the demon choruses come in.

At home—if it can be said that they have such a place, wandering as they are prone to, every few moons, from one locality to another, either to gratify a naturally roving propensity, or in quest of a greater abundance of game; or, as it not unfrequently occurs, to escape the encroachment of a hostile neighbor, the squaws voluntarily perform all the labor requisite for transportation, boarding and lodging their families. This they do as much for their sons as for the lords of the teepees, because they will not permit the male sex to suffer the degradation of performing domestic chores.

To a civilized woman, the task of cooking, washing, ironing, mending, and cutting firewood for the kitchen, sitting-room and parlor, may seem a prodigious and never-ending toil. But when she makes a definite estimation of the entire routine of the responsibilities and cares of a squalid teepee, their number will dwindle down to a mere trifle in comparison with the household necessities of a well-regulated abode, where industry and frugality dwell.

The teepee of a Dakota is merely a colossal chicken-coop, erected in half an hour by placing several long poles together and wrapping around them a covering of thin pliant bark or well-dried skins, with an opening left at the apex for the smoke to escape, and another at the bottom for a passage-way in and out. Buffalo hides serve for a couch, upon which half a dozen of both sexes can recline for nocturnal repose. In the centre, a slight excavation answers for fire-place and kitchen.

Bed-time has never been definitely agreed upon by them. They are as often sleeping by day as at night—for they rest when they feel like it. But if they sleep in the day-time, they prowl around during the night.

Furniture, such as tables and chairs, are not required; though every young savage of the masculine gender desires a small pocket-mirror for the study of his facial beauty and to facilitate an artistic application of smut or paint when perfecting his toilet on grand occasions.

Indian "fops" are frequently met with. And, totally regardless of all expense, some of them present the most excruciating *tout ensemble* that I ever beheld. But I am provoked when they refuse permission for their sisters to look at themselves in a mirror. The mean scamps tell the juvenile Hiawathas that it is a punishable crime for them to see their own faces. Fancy what a time we should have here in New York, if our fair companions were debarred the convenience and the comfort of mirrors large enough to reflect their entire physiques at a glance!

A single iron pot, or, when that cannot be had, a stout earthen jar, will suffice for all the culinary requirements, and also for personal ablutions or the appurtenances of a laundry. After the filthy little papoose has been washed or sloshed in the pot, a dirty haunch of venison is stuffed into the same utensil and boiled for soup—which will be greedily devoured the moment it comes from the fire.

The Chippeway women are much better looking than the Sioux, and some of them are quite pretty. Their forms are well proportioned, and their flesh quite solid. But their complexion is paler than that of the Sioux, while their mouths and teeth are almost beautiful.

The Chippeway women hate the Sioux more bitterly than the men, because they and their children are made to suffer so much from the revengeful atrocities of the perpetual war between the two nations. They have been known to meet death rather than escape without their offspring. Sometimes the men permit them to dance by themselves—but the two sexes never do so together. As with the Sioux, the woman is too far beneath the man, in his and in her opinion, to be allowed such a privilege.

A contempt for woman, which is so characteristic of all unfeeling men, whether pale-faces or red-skins, must naturally retard civilization, by perpetuating the ferocity of brutal malignity and passion. Indeed, any man, in or out of the Christian faith, who has no sensibility of moral attachment for that being whom God has fitted to participate in his consolations and difficulties, in his smiles and tears, is worse than many brutes devoid of a soul. Whenever there is a gentle feeling in man, he will surely sympathize with the sex whose natural grace and love enable him to live again in the propagation of his race!

If these savages believed in the immortality of the soul, the language of their conscience would not permit them, in the last moments of their life, to exact a promise from their children to kill their enemies, as they have done; and, like them, never forgive those who have injured them in any way. This they frequently do, if they have the opportunity and the power of verbal expression. Nevertheless, a dying Indian expects to go somewhere. And he may require that his faithful

A Very Beautiful Aquatic Scene, between Alexandria and Otter Tail River, which is called "Pelican Lake," from the myriads of that Piscivorous Water-fowl always hovering near.

dog shall accompany him in death. For if he believes in the immortality of his own soul, he also considers his dog equally immortal. Or, having no faithful dog, he may order that his wife shall go with him. And, like the women of Malabar, she is obliged to comply. The dying warrior dwells with enthusiasm upon the past, leaving his survivors to think of the future.

Next to women, dogs are the most unhappy creatures about an Indian teepee. The wretched canines are not only half starved, but worked very hard, chasing game or drawing sledges or trucks, until they eventually end their days in the shape of a "thanksgiving" dinner for the master and his friends. A dog is immolated and quickly smoking on the altar of hospitality when a very distinguished visitor is expected to arrive. But the unhappy quadruped is supposed to be a sacrifice to the manitous or wakans, and the eating of it considered an act of devotion which a guest must not refuse, let his abhorrence of the dish be ever so great.

Every teepee has its dog; and some teepees ten to fifteen. They are generally treated with some manifestations of affection; but canine flesh is a tempting delicacy, from which they can not abstain when their prodigal hospitality or the pangs of hunger demand a sacrifice of the confiding and faithful creatures.

Buffalo hunting is the chief occupation of an Indian when not on the war-path. And if he is well mounted in the chase, his imposing figure as an equestrian would not be a contemptible contrast with the proud statue of Marcus Aurelius or that of the great Numidian king. Himself, his horse, and the game, would form a group worthy of the pencil of Raphael or the chisel of Canova.

Wolves are also measurably dependent upon buffalo flesh for food. But they are not always sufficiently strong to capture an animal. They, therefore, follow the hunters whenever practicable, and, with the aid of their own cunning, avail themselves of any advantage which may arise. Sometimes they join in the general charge upon a great herd; and when the females are occupied in making their own escape, each wolf seizes a calf, and, strangling it, carries the body hence to have a hearty feast.

Sometimes, when very hungry and no hunters are near, the wolves approach five or six of a herd, without appearing to have any design. And, not condescending to be afraid, the buffaloes neither avoid nor attack them until they have singled out their victim, which is invariably a female—that sex being fatter and more delicious than the males. Two of the wolves engage her attention in front by pretending to play with her, while one of the strongest and most active seizes her in the rear; and when she turns to drive him off, those in front fly at her throat and strangle her to death. This is only in keeping with their natural cunning.

But neither the Sioux nor the Chippeway is always rich enough to ride a horse in pursuit of the buffalo. And in that very common extremity he and his comrades not unfrequently play the part of wolves. Knowing that buffaloes are not frightened by the proximity of wolves, they wrap themselves in wolf-skins, and thus disguised it is possible to creep near the grazing animals upon their hands and knees, and silently pierce them with sharp arrows. Guns would be in the way. Arrows can be concealed. And then the arrows make no noise; which enables the stealthy hunters to multiply the number of victims. Each hunter makes his own arrows and puts upon them his private mark, so that when the hunt is over they may determine who were the most expert. They observe the same rule in battle, and thereby the greatest warrior is known.

Many other devices are successful in the destruction of buffaloes. But, as most animals can scent a human being some distance off, the Indian hunters are always careful to approach their game against the wind. They are also cautious about attacking a buffalo while asleep; for it would probably rise and rush upon them. And very often when a male buffalo sees a favorite female companion floundering with wounds, he will endeavor to facilitate her flight by combat; or he may shield her body with his own if she cannot escape, and thus die at her side, like a heroic lover.

An Indian devours like a wolf, and fasts like a camel. And I have heard it surmised that they were akin to the last-mentioned animal, in the faculty of rumination. Possibly there is some truth in that suggestion, inasmuch as they are not at all particular to chew their food while gorging it down. One famished brave was seen to swallow the entire hind-quarter of a deer and the water in which it was boiled, together with half a peck of potatoes and a good-sized loaf of bread. He loosened his belt considerably, and then smoked his pipe—and continued to exist without any sign of overfeeding or even a symptom of indigestion. An Indian with a good appetite, seldom lies down to sleep while anything eatable remains in his teepee. And a guest will insult his host if he refuses to eat all that is placed before him, no matter if it should be a whole buffalo!

But as they depend solely upon the precarious success of hunting, and the wild fruits, vegetables and rice, gathered only in small quantities by the squaws, their diet is regulated according to the chances of the hour. About the only provision made by a man for to-morrow, is girding his waist with a belt which may be tightened to suit an unavoidable depletion of his bowels. The longer he fasts, the tighter he draws his belt. An economical custom, but certainly tantalizing to the organs of digestion. In the spring, they easily gather eggs, and then capture unfledged ducks and geese in the vicinity of the lakes and rivers.

When hard pressed by hunger, it does not matter if the eggs have been partly hatched. And the uncleaned entrails of a duck or a goose, half broiled on coals of fire, are gobbled down with a gusto that may set my readers yerking from imagination. Indeed the dry, osseous remains of animal or fowl are frequently broken into fragments and boiled in water, which, after the process of maceration, may be tolerably nutritious soup.

It is not an unusual sight to see a squaw with a ponderous load of eatables tied up in a filthy blanket and swung upon her back. And, peeping out at the top of the bundle, occasionally may also be seen the black eyes of a papoose, the nether part of whose body is resting among the tobacco and whisky, and the meat and sugar.

The blanket of a man or of a woman is used for every purpose it will serve. A covering at one time, a bed at another; and, with the accumulation of dirt and grease inevitable from six months' or an entire year's general utility, it becomes a textural mass which might tempt the cupidity of a city "soap-fat man," if chance should throw it in his way. I am told that in the maple-sugar season, they actually strain the warm syrup through their blankets when the condition of those articles is sufficiently porous for the operation. The blankets are subsequently worn without washing, or any manifest repugnance by the wearers.

And this inevitable blanket, more than any other article of apparel, is illustrative of the Indian character. While they manage it with a dexterous and graceful simplicity that cannot be imitated by their superiors in refinement, intelligence and skill, its influence will ever prove the most formidable barrier to the approach of civilization. For idle hands, it answers very well. But when mechanical tools, or the implements of agriculture are to be used, only a single pair of hands can not keep the blanket in place and perform the labor of an artisan or a farmer.

The blanket must be abandoned by the red man before he even begins to occupy a promising position in the scale of industry, which is the only reliable evidence of human progress and substantial prosperity. But an Indian deprived of his blanket would be a peacock despoiled of its tail, a horse shorn of its mane, a political candidate without voters, a tree stripped of foliage —in short, a very deplorable object in his own estimation. Where would he put his hands?

I can not refrain from laughing at the imaginary picture of an *ideal* Indian forever divested of his traditional garment. What a woful expression would pervade his usually stolid face! I fancy him surveying the reflection of his figure upon the pellucid surface of the nearest lake or stream; and then I imagine his sepulchral grunt, which would be all the more torturing to him and delightful to me if a live Yankee's tantalizing grin should present itself to his gaze, side by side with the despondency of his own. An aboriginal savage without his blanket would be a fit subject for the practical solicitude of those philanthropic humanitarians who mournfully ejaculate, "Lo, the poor Indian!"

View on the Upper Mississippi River, while standing among countless Mounds of the Ancient Dead.

CHAPTER XIX.

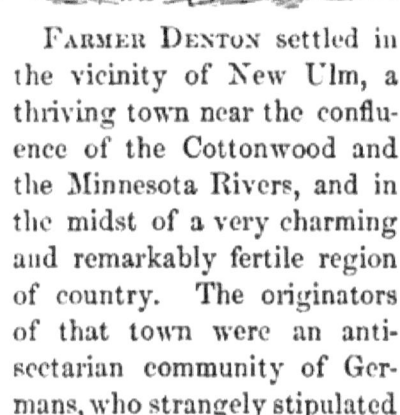

Farmer Denton settled in the vicinity of New Ulm, a thriving town near the confluence of the Cottonwood and the Minnesota Rivers, and in the midst of a very charming and remarkably fertile region of country. The originators of that town were an anti-sectarian community of Germans, who strangely stipulated among themselves and with all new-comers. They bargained and strictly conditioned, in all deeds of property, that no edifice for the propagation of religious creeds should be erected in the place. But they built a hall for public amusements, smoked their pipes, drank their beer, and danced for recreation, while accumulating wealth from industry in the usual way.

Denton Farm was not within the limits of the Teutonic confederation, but their customs and prejudices displeased him. And perhaps he would have sold out and moved into more congenial society before the expiration of another year, had not the savages undertaken to totally exterminate every pale-face in the world. A horde of them unexpectedly attacked New Ulm; and, suddenly slaughtering many of the male inhabitants in and around the town, they set fire to houses, destroyed all the property they could, and made captives of the women.

Farmer Denton was surprised and shot down without a moment's warning. His laborers were also murdered at the same time. But as the Indians have a particular regard for dogs, Goliah might have escaped their tomahawks and knives, if he had not furiously assailed and killed one of them in defense of his master. Nor did they wish to assassinate the farmer's youthful daughters, who might be carried off into captivity as so much available merchandise—but to meet with far less consideration than Oriental slave-dealers show their Circassian beauties.

Yet, fortunately for the girls, one of the three murderers detailed by the gang to march them away in bondage, had stolen a keg full of whisky. Indians will generally surrender to *minne-wakan* when every other spirit might be repelled or assaulted. While "there's whisky in the jug," big Injun is sure to want some. They drank much and often; and then began to quarrel about a choice of their fair captives, who were so terribly frightened that they trudged along as mechanically as a flock of weary and exhausted lambs going to the *abattoir*.

More whisky and fiercer contention, until one of the drunken trio refused to proceed any further. He would return to help murder the *big-knives*, and find a white squaw much more to his liking than either of those four

—and have her all to himself. He snatched a parting dram, and then reeled out of sight.

The whisky-keg was not yet entirely emptied. But the two remaining savages would soon swallow the last drop.

"Oh, how tipsy they are!" whispered Jane. "They'll kill us, after a while!"

"No!" replied Mercy. "When they get a little more we can easily run away!"

Mercy conjectured rightly. Before sundown they both rolled in the dust, with mouthing exhortations for their captives to remain precisely where they stood.

"Now for it!" murmured Eliza, who perfectly coincided with Mercy's suggestion. "They can not pursue us, if they try; and before they recover, we may find safety somewhere."

"We will hasten home!" said Julia.

"Home, sister? We have no home, now!" responded Mercy. "Our only hope is to escape from these beastly wretches. If we return —— But see, yonder come a number of white people, and two wagons, or more!"

Fugitives hurrying away! Would they take with them four orphan girls? Aye, they would—and that too with a hearty good will! But the Indians? Quick! Delay was dangerous just then. Some of the red-skins might be on their trail!

"What have we here?" exclaimed a wagoner, at sight of their drunken captors stretched out upon the ground.

Mercy quickly told her story and explained the whisky-keg; whereupon the man tumbled them over the rocks down into the river, declaring that they should not live to resume their work of destruction.

Then whipping up their horses, the fugitives hurriedly fled. And while so many others were overtaken and murdered in their flight, it seemed like a marvelous chance that Farmer Denton's four daughters and the party who kindly assisted them on the way, should succeed in escaping from the very midst of the massacre, and finally reach St. Paul, without encountering even the sight of another Indian.

The Indian outbreak of August, '62, was terrible, but soon ended! I can not call it a war. It was an universal slaughter and torture of unwarned and defenseless white settlers, and then a speedy armed pursuit of the savages, who were quickly captured, but not killed, as they deserved to have been. Yet humanity and a sense of wisdom actuated General Sibley and the officers and men who joined him in the decisive expedition against the treacherous outlaws; and in less than three months after their first slaughter, the insatiate redskins were either captured, suing for peace, or skulking toward the setting sun.

The Indian captives were treated as prisoners of war; and, after being allowed a fair trial by court-martial, nearly one hundred of them were convicted of the most heinous atrocities. In the list of convicts I have seen the names of Te-he-hdo-ne-cha, the inhospitable; Ta-zoo, the red otter; Wy-a-tah-ta-wa, his people; Hin-han-shoon-ko-yag-ma-ne, the man with an owl's tail; Ma-za-bom-doo, iron blower; Wah-pa-doo-ta, red leaf; Wa-he-hna; Sna-ma-ne, tinkling walker; Rha-in-yan-ka, rattling runner; Do-wan-sa, the singer; and Hap-an, the second son. These, with twenty-seven others, were subsequently hanged, all at the same moment, near Mankato. The execution of many more was deferred for a time. Others were sentenced to imprisonment on Rock Island, in the Mississippi River, opposite the City of Davenport, Iowa. Among the convicts sent thither was a Sioux chief, named Wa-mada-tonka, who, before going, had an interview with his family—a wife and two little sons; and at parting with them he placed around the neck of the youngest a huge necklace of bears' claws, which had been handed down to him through many generations of ancestry, and consequently priceless in its value. The bereaved mother and her sorrowful children, with a soldier near them, may be seen grouped in the foreground of the chapter-head engraving, page 207. The necklace is shown in the picture of the juvenile heir; and *Cap des Sioux*, or "Winona Rock," on the eastern shore of Lake Pepin, is also plainly visible in the distant view.

Thus, some of the "bad Injuns" received punishment, while vast numbers were humanely sent off to a new reservation, in which they can leisurely abide the inevitable extinction of their race with the rapid development of future events.

Old Betz, or Hah-zah-ee-yun-kee-win, that remarkable centenarian female, who "gathers huckleberries while running," counted one among the "good Injuns" included in the decree of their lenient *big-knife* captors, to be sent up the Missouri river; but her son, Ta-o-pee, *a farmer*, who had been true to the whites, was gratified in his request that she might be left with him.

And since then she has been lodging somewhere in the vicinity of Mendota by night, and begging in the City of St. Paul by day. The distance is not less than five miles; and though her age is said to be verging on to two hundred years, a short walk like that is no obstacle to her when she wants a fresh supply of kosh-popee. She is very shrewd in her method of operating while on a collecting-tour. I met her on Third street one fine morning after experiencing that wonderful dream in which she appeared to me over there on the great bluff beneath the solitary pine, where she was mourning for the loss of her first-born child, whose remains lie beneath that curious mound of round blue stones, which she told me she had carried thither from the waters of Minneineeopa. Instantly recognizing her from the memory of that dream, my salutation was, "Ah, Old Betz!"

"Ugh! Hi, hah!" she grunted, with a sharp twinkling of her deeply-sunken black eyes, which glared just precisely as I had seen them in my dream.

I expressed much delight at meeting her, and she grunted and gesticulated in response with an intensely reciprocal feeling. My flowing beard immediately attracted her attention. Probably it was much longer than any other that she had ever seen; and, as if thoroughly experienced in the skill of social deceit, and possessing a perfect knowledge of the weaker points in the vanity of an egotistical man, with her horny claws she gathered up the flowing end of the capilliform appendage of my face, and then coquettishly hugged it to her neck and her cheek, lovingly and admiringly, to conclude with a sentimentally touching appeal for koshpopee. An involuntary shudder caused me to shrink from her first touch, which recalled a vivid recollection of those unpleasant sensations experienced in connection with her grasp during my dream. But curiosity overcame that momentary feeling; and a friend who was with me burst into audible laughter to see how industriously I manipulated her dry old cranium in the pursuit of phrenological knowledge. However, his merriment did not deter me from satisfying myself that I had never before handled such a dry, wooden object permanently attached to the living trunk of a human being. It was not only dry and wooden to the touch, but minutely corrugated and strangely cold. And when I looked into the depth of her weird eyes and saw their cadaveric intensity my hands instinctively recoiled. Perceiving that I shrank, she grinned capaciously enough for me to discern that solitary *cuspidata* pendularity in her upper jaw; and with the most gigantic smirk of tenderness that I ever beheld, she then grunted a repetition of "kosh-popee"—which, I am told, she anxiously reiterates every forty-five seconds when engaged in a *tete-a-tete* with any pale-face who is unfamiliar with her cunning arts.

But as kosh-popee did not immediately appear, she adroitly tried another dodge by declaring that she had known me ever since *she* was "oney so big!" At that moment, the demonstrative position of her hand was evidently intended to define the probable stature of a child not more than three years old. And, calling to mind her centennial longevity, after witnessing the parabolic suggestion of her hand, I inadvertently questioned myself how long I might have been unconsciously living. Where had I been all that time? A question not readily answered. And, as her characteristic restiveness would not admit of her tarrying with me until the narrative of an eventful life was ended, she uttered a petulant grunt, and waddled off on her thin bow-legs which were swathed in dark-blue cloth.

I called her back, and persuasively invited her to oblige us with one of her favorite songs. At that she snorted and grunted as if highly insulted, and would have gone away muttering maledictions upon my head, but for the timely proffer of a ten-cent currency stamp, which elicited an animated and prompt compliance.

A very "good-looking" Sioux, who suffered death in punishment for his cruelties during the Massacre.

"Kosh-popee! Yaw! Me sing! Augh!" And then she proceeded to utter a monotonous "caw-cawing" squall, not very dissimilar to that of a domestic hen in the exuberant season of nest-making and egg-laying, preparatory to the more tedious ordeal of incubation. But she soon subsided into an unhealthy attack of bronchial cadenza, that passed away like the "horse" tone of a debilitated nightmare, conceived from unwisely indulging in too much lobster-salad at a late supper.

Indian songs are spasmodically extemporized bawls or screams, unmellifluously devoid of change in tune. They use a kind of tabor, and something like castanets, with a primitive drum containing seeds or pebbles, for rattling, as an orchestra in their terpsichorean festivals. And an Indian dance is nothing more than an exhibition of violent confusion. A troupe of lunatics might accidentally perform similar antics of body and brain.

Formalities of etiquette are seldom observed by them. Not even a salutation is deemed necessary, except to a particular friend; and then the greeting may be a simple touch of the hand, without the utterance of a word or a look in the face. The *alpha* of a public address is generally the "Great Spirit;" and, if to white men, the *omega* of "whisky and tobacco" inevitably closes the oration.

While traveling, they are guided by the sun in the day-time and by the polar star at night. If the sun or the stars can not be seen, they know that the tips of the blades of grass always point to the south, and that it is less green on the side toward the north. Thus they traverse the prairies. In the forest, they are very well aware that the tree-tops incline to the south, and that there is more moss on the side of the trunk and branches facing the north; and also that the bark is more pliant and smooth on the eastern side than on any other. They measure distances by the number of days required to travel them.

The Dyaks of Borneo are fond of preserving the heads of their enemies whom they kill in war. They retain those ghastly and putrifying trophies to play with as toys, and frequently carry them suspended by a cord from their own necks. The American Indians secure the scalps, the ears, the tongues, and the hearts of their enemies for amusement at home. The Turk, the Tartar, and the Chinese, are satisfied if they can possess even the tail of a horse previously ridden by their foe. A Yankee would "call it square" if he could obtain judgment for pecuniary damage in a civil court of law.

Taken altogether, the Indian is a sublime, horrible, original and grotesque admixture of strange and extraordinary peculiarities. Neither his face, his gestures, nor his attitudes are equaled by any of the celebrated frescoes from the pencil of either Guido Roni, Dominichino, or other Italian masters.

Even the ideal beings that are seen in those hells, purgatories, limbos, paradises, deluges and last judgments, which painters have put on canvas, but faintly approach the remarkable characteristics of the American aborigine. Nor does that extravagant though beautiful production of the Flemish school, called "*Salvator Rosa's Conspiracy of Cataline*," give anything as picturesque or poetical as the visage of a Dakota.

A traveler, whose imagination was more powerful than mine, traced a resemblance between the old chief Wamenitouka and that famous statue of Aristides haranguing the corrupt Athenians, in the Museum at Naples. To his eye, another chief represented the statue of Cato predicting to the Romans that their vices, their luxuries, and their avarice would soon reduce them to slavery. Those chiefs and that traveler are now in their graves.

The uncouth painting of Indian faces and bodies is really hideous. Some of their countenances resemble palettes covered with every variety of color, while others are wholly or in part white or black, and vividly suggestive of millers or chimney-sweeps. Others, still, paint their bodies with winged angels, or horned devils, according to individual taste. They decorate themselves with bones, teeth and claws of wild beasts, tufts of buffalo hair, or the feathers of birds—when they can not procure necklaces of glass beads, ribbons, bracelets, rings and crosses. During the great massacre, they did not wear the apparel which they stole. They tore it into shreds for simple decorations, to give themselves the appearance of ragged demons.

The Chippeway men are physically superior to the Sioux, though their noses are flatter and wider, and their cheek-bones more prominent, with thicker lips and smaller eyes.

An eagle feather in the hair of a Sioux shows that he has killed a Chippeway; and two feathers give him the title of a brave. The color of the feather indicates the grade of his victim. Black, gray or white denotes a man, woman or child. A black band around the waist signifies that the wearer fought hand to hand with his enemy. As in civilized countries, the influence of female smiles will urge men to deeds of valor and honor, or of crime. And as a warrior receives very little favor from the damsels of his tribe until he wears the eagle feather for a plume, it need not be a subject of wonder if he should obtain the coveted talisman by bloodshed and assassination as soon as a favorable chance occurs.

I only wish some of those theorizing humanitarians would visit the unreclaimed territories of the Northwest, and cultivate a personal acquaintance with this noble red man—this gentle savage—this paragon of manhood running wild—this admirable specimen of God's handiwork gone astray! Ah, I fancy that it will require much preaching and practical teaching, with the lapse of interminable time, to regenerate the unadulterated offspring of these aboriginal braves. There is plenty of room for the sanguine theoricians to begin. Perhaps they might succeed in reclaiming one out of a thousand, and then see that one ultimately relapsing into worse barbarism than he was found in before they undertook his redemption. If I may predicate upon the record of unfruitful endeavors in behalf of "ye poor Indian," the reader must pardon the derision which my language conveys. And for an indisputable line of testimony, without enumerating single instances of the obdurate and inaccessible heart of the Indian, I will refer to the great massacre which occurred in a locality where the combined influence of gospel teachings and pecuniary reward had totally failed to win more than a few of them from the moral darkness and physical degradation in which and of which they were born! But I will desist from this useless moralizing, and recur to the drudgery of the woman, who follows her husband, the most abject of all slaves!

Behold the erect form of that Dakota who moves with measured and pompous stride, like the monarch of an empire. He appears to be serenely conscientious while his wife trudges behind him in lieu of baggage-wagon or pack-horse train. He gathers his blanket gracefully around his shoulders, and the eagle's feather majestically waves above his fantastic crown, while the only burden he carries is a red-stone pipe with a very long stem, or a tomahawk and pipe all in one. His wife is ready to sink with exhaustion from all his worldly estate piled upon her back! She follows, weary, panting, groaning—dying! He is a "big Injun"—and scornfully refuses to take compassion on a woman!

In his valuable *History of Minnesota*, Rev. E. D. Neill, of St. Paul, compares Dakota women to the Gibeonite females of old, who were "hewers of wood and drawers of water" for the every-day requirements of life. He has seen a mother on a winter's day, traveling eight or ten miles, with the entire appurtenances of a teepee, camp-kettle, axe, papoose and several small dogs, all piled upon her back. And after arriving at the camping spot and clearing off the snow, she proceeded to cut poles and erect the teepee. She then gathered firewood, brought water, put everything in order, and commenced darning her lord's moccasins before he arrived to abuse her for not providing an abundant supply of minnewakan. Mr. Neill says that in consequence of their ill-treatment, but few happy-faced wives are seen among the Dakota Indians. Also, that suicide is very commonly resorted to by them as the only chance of escape from cruelties which they are unable to endure. The husband of an unfaithful wife may kill her, or cut off her nose!

Exasperated Wives and Daughters, at New Ulm, punishing Indian Captives who murdered their nearest relations and dearest friends, in the Great Massacre.

CHAPTER XX.

GOLIAH was not present when the murderous savages shot down his master; yet only a few seconds elapsed ere he mingled in the terrible scene. As if by instinct, he selected the very one whose rifle sent the fatal ball; and, before any of them could intercept him, his great sharp tushes were clinched at the assassin's throat. A mumbling snarl and howl, as of a wild tiger when venting its blood-thirsty roar, momentarily checked the work of carnage. But the next instant he was chopped to the earth, tearing out the windpipe of his victim in the fall. And though he became a sacrifice, his timely assault thus deterred the savages from mutilating and dismembering the farmer's body even after death. Moreover, the occurrence was an ill-omen in the superstitious minds of the sanguinary Sioux, who believe that some frightful calamity must surely befall the tribe of a man dying from the bite of a dog. Therefore, without effectually silencing Goliah's cries of agony by totally and immediately ending his life, they hastily fired the buildings and precipitately fled, carrying with them the wretch whose throat had been torn open by the revengeful gnashing of the formidable teeth in his ponderous jaws!

The devouring element consumed everything within its reach, and the conflagration was nearly ended when the sombre shades of evening set in. But though the smoldering ruins no longer blazed, a triple pile of glowing embers and coals sent forth a dense volume of smoke that made the dark atmosphere of night seem alive with spectral shadows and quivering glares, while the star-lit sky above was obscured by a dismal pall of red.

Where life and happiness so peacefully and contentedly dwelt only a few hours before, no human voice was now heard, nor did footsteps draw near. The terrified cattle could bellow no more from sheer exhaustion, the fluttering fowls were weary with cackling, and Julia's pet lamb ceased its plaintive cries. And while the surrounding space became hushed in a silence that was awing and strange, many other smoldering fires might be seen with their phantom glares to point out devastated homes, where murdered victims lay or terror-stricken fugitives hid themselves in covert retreats.

The last flickering ray of light from the ruins at Denton Farm was just expiring when a sobbing moan announced that Goliah still lived and breathed. The poor dog gradually revived, and began to scent for his master. Apparently unconscious of the wounds in his own body, he did not cry with the pain which he must have felt, but soon discovered where his master lay, and feebly crawled and whined until he could touch him. Then, with plaintive utterances of anxiety and distress for the condition of his master, he tried to lick his hands and face, while whining more anxiously than before. The loss of blood had so weakened him that his tongue could scarcely move, and yet his caresses were sufficient to rouse his master from the sleep of death!

When morning came, Farmer Denton and Goliah were temporarily concealed a short distance from the farm. And in less than two weeks' time they received a warm reception in the City of St. Paul!

It is unnecessary here to narrate the circumstances of their recovery and escape, as many facts pertaining to somewhat similar adventures, which others experienced in that vicinity about the same time, are included among the "Interlude Notes" of this volume, and voluminously given in the published "Histories of the Sioux War." But the unfortunate farmer heard of his daughters' safety long before he saw them, while they could get no tidings of him until he and Goliah presented themselves in person. And there was a joyous reunion in the parlor of Lady Levasseur when the father and his dog arrived.

"Why, I never had so many kisses since I was born!" he cried, while his four daughters were trying to embrace him all together, and each putting up her lips at the same time. "Now it's Eliza and Mercy—and then Julia and Jane! Two at a time, and all at once! Bless you, girls! My arms are more than full!"

"And here we've been crying our eyes out with the belief that you were dead!" exclaimed Jane. "Oh, pa! I do love you so! And now I shall never disobey you again as long as I live!"

13

"Not until the next time. Yes, your roguish eyes look very much as if you'd been crying them out for me. But come, let's have another kiss. All of you, I mean, you sauce-boxes, you! I never was so happy as now! But—but, girls, we are all beggars now! Do you know that? I have only you left! Everything else is lost!"

"Mr. Denton, you forget!" interrupted Fleurette. "Your daughters are not all that you have left. I can name a very valuable object which you have omitted in summing up your treasures."

"And pray what is that?"

"A splendid dog named Goliah!"

Fleurette had been caressing his canine majesty from the moment he entered the room; and she went on to say: "Oh, what large scars I see upon his head, his back and his limbs! Did the Indians really chop him in all those places with their battle-axes and scalping-knives? Poor dog! How cruel it was to abuse him so!"

"Why, Fleurette, dear; you do not perceive how Mr. Denton's head and face have been cut?" observed Lady Levasseur. "Is his dog of more account than himself?"

"Oh, pardon me, sir!" quickly answered Fleurette. "I do see that, and wish with all my heart that every one of those ugly Indians were driven so far off that they could never find the way back again."

And then they were told all about how Goliah had saved his master's life.

Lady Levasseur felt anxious to assure the unfortunate man that while she had such an abundance to spare, he need not apprehend any inconvenience from want; yet she would avail herself of a more fitting opportunity to tell him so. However, he was not a desponding man in money matters. He had health and strength. Perhaps he could get along in some way. Nevertheless, his situation was extremely embarrassing just then. He had a family and no home. That was a serious reflection! His pecuniary resources were all invested in his farm. What could he expect from that, when the Indians had burned his house and his barns, and destroyed his crops? Winter was coming on; and how would he be able to survive until spring? Lady Levasseur had already exceeded the bounds of magnanimous liberality in behalf of his daughters, and he could not ask nor accept aid from her.

But Lady Levasseur would not listen to any objections while his misfortune claimed her generosity. She did not look upon it as charity. Her home should be his home and the home of the girls, at least until the future enabled him to go forth and prosper again. He must not refuse! She insisted, and Fleurette conspired with the girls to convince him that, under the circumstances, it was right and proper for him to accept.

And then Lady Levasseur removed from the hotel to a stylish residence that was owned by a wealthy citizen, who had been frightened entirely out of the State by the massacre, while it was at least a hundred miles away. The owner's agent wanted to sell; and, though not less than sixteen thousand dollars had been expended on the house and grounds, he would part with all for little more than one-quarter of that sum.

"Good gracious!" ejaculated Farmer Denton, "if the man is satisfied to sell at that price, buy it of him while he is in the humor; and he will come back and offer twenty thousand for it, after these red-skins have been subdued and driven out of sight and hearing. A glorious chance for speculation; and I only wish I had five thousand dollars handy—that's all. I'd be the proprietor of this place before another day rolled over my head, if I could raise the money to pay down!"

Lady Levasseur smiled. She thought a moment, and then bade Sancho bring her something from the escritoire. That colored individual was not only her bookkeeper, secretary and cashier, but really a clever financier. He methodically arranged the writing materials upon the table before his mistress, and then articulated, "Dar am is!"

"Now, Mr. Denton," said Lady Levasseur, after filling up a check for five thousand dollars; "I have drawn it payable to your order; and if you think there is anything to be made in the purchase of this estate, let the deed be executed in your name. It shall be yours, to keep or to sell, as you please. For the present, we can live here all together. Sancho will settle with the market folks, the grocery-man and the butcher, you know! Not a word! When times get straight once more, and you wish to dispose of the place for twenty or thirty thousand, as you say, you can then refund me five. Until that event transpires, consider yourself lord and master of the dwelling in which you live."

"Oh, I'm so glad!" cried Fleurette. "We shall have such a nice time. Won't we, Goliah?"

His dogship coincided by a rapturous vibration of his immense tail. And she was happy in his society; no matter what a great many other beautiful young ladies might think.

In a short time the farmer was gratified with an opportunity of visiting his desolated home. The Indians had been dealt with, but not half severely enough! And the fifteen thousand people who had been driven from their homes, seriously thought of returning. But while the one hundred female captives—wives, mothers and young girls—who had been abused in every way possible, were once more free, the one thousand dead were not all even provided with graves!

The labor of restoration was soon begun. But winter delayed the work, and protracted want embittered the existence of thousands until Government compensation and another harvest season filled the new granaries with reabundance, and gave the needy a generous reward for their patient toil.

Meanwhile, Farmer Denton had time and opportunity for gratifying his curiosity relative to various natural peculiarities of Dakota land. Among other places, he visited St. Cloud, and there enjoyed a great treat, in unexpectedly witnessing the arrival of a train of dog-sledges from Red River. He remembered reading about such conveyances in a book that described the manners and customs of people who inhabited extremely cold countries, where they had long winters of snow, and he had often thought how much he would be delighted to see a team of real Kamtschatka or Esquimaux dogs drawing one of those queer sledges.

He was always pleased with anything he heard about the sagacity of the canine species. And his appreciation of the omnivorous quadruped was practically demonstrated when he spent several hundred dollars to procure Goliah, whom he had brought all the way from the vicinity of Mont Blanc, in Switzerland, the only country where the pure and genuine St. Bernard race is said to happily thrive and multiply. And they are now becoming scarce even there.

A dog train was not seen very often as recently as '62, and the arrival of the one which he was so fortunate as to see while at St. Cloud, proved a novelty to others beside him. It brought down a lot of furs belonging

Tourists enjoying their First View of the Red River of the North.

to the Hudson Bay Company; and he was more than
delighted to learn that its final destination would be
the City of St. Paul. Nothing could please him better.
And although the foot-traveling was then particularly
difficult for a pale-face unaccustomed to such exploits,
he resolved to accompany the train to the end of its
journey.

Therefore he immediately cultivated an acquaintance
with the half-breed drivers, who heartily laughed at his
proposition. He did not particularly admire them for
that. But he soon made them all his friends by a bountiful distribution of tobacco and other cheap "luxuries,"
which speedily opened their black eyes and their willing
hands, if not their turbid hearts.

They suggested a "little rum," but he said "No!" so
flatly that the veto was permanently effectual. Still
they thought he was a perfect barbarian, not to like
"rum of some kind." However, they did not tell
him so.

They asked him "how much he could run!" He did
not presume that such a performance was necessary.

"Ugh! Oie! Dog beat horse—all day!" grunted a
tall, long-haired driver, whose garments presented a
noticeable admixture of the apparel worn by an Italian
bandit, and the furs of a Siberian exile, with a little
French, and some Yankee editions to complete the costume.

"Yes!" interposed a merchant of St. Cloud. "As
they run along at a gait of six or eight miles an hour,
it'll bring the lather out of you like ten thousand, 'fore
you know where you are!"

"Then I'll hire a horse!" blurted out the discomfited
man.

The drivers all gravely shook their heads; at which he

exclaimed with some excitement: "Thunder! I'll *buy* a horse, if they are afraid to trust me here!"

"No, that's not it!" laughed the merchant. "A horse can't travel where them dogs go. He'd break his own neck and your'n too, in less time 'an a cat 'ud lick its ear!"

The countenance of the anxious man fell to an expression of woe. But the captain came to his rescue by offering him "a rope to hold!"

"And what's that, I should like to know?" He looked suspiciously, as if the suggestion of a noose for his neck was intended by the allusion to a rope. The explanation was satisfactory; but it did not comfort him a great deal. It was that he might avail himself of the same assistance allowed the drivers, who generally held on to long ropes attached to the rear end of their respective sledges, whereby they were enabled to run or glide along upon snow-shoes as fast as the dogs traveled, from morning till night.

How could he hang on to a rope, and jump and straddle over all sorts of obstacles, on top of, or amid the uneven snow, at the rate of six to eight miles an hour, from St. Cloud clear down to St. Paul? He couldn't do it, and it was simply ridiculous to make any attempt. But for ten dollars in money, and a pocket-knife, and three plugs of chewing-tobacco, he secured a seat upon a sledge which had been partly unladen at St. Cloud.

"And now prepare to squat!" he jocularly remarked upon seeing the attitude unavoidably necessary in such a small space. And he had no "lean-back," nor even a single "standard" to hold on by. "I've read how Bartlett grumbled about riding on the back of a camel in Arabia," he added; "but I'll bet he had no idea what sort of accommodation he would find on a Red River dog-sled!"

Away they went! And the very first distinct feeling that the enthusiastic adventurer had, was to experience a "cool head" from the loss of his hat, which the next driver whipped up as he ran and laughingly replaced upon his head.

Farmer Denton soon became convinced that the sledge was a frail bark to voyage upon. But they were all precisely alike. Each one consisted of only a single half-inch white-oak board, scarcely twenty inches wide and from ten to twenty feet in length, with the front end curled up similar to the runners of a city-made sleigh, and fastened in that position by buckskin thongs. Cleats or bars, an inch or so square, and perhaps two feet apart, were also fastened to the board by leather strings. In fact, like the "Ox-cart," there was no iron used in their construction. The thongs were drawn through gimlet-holes in the board and wrapped tightly around the bars. And then a long string passed under each end of the cross-bars the entire length of the sledge. To those long strings were tied the ends of the lashings which secured the freight as tightly as a well-corded bed-sacking. The farmer very prudently contrived to wind some of the lashings around a part of his own body in such a manner as to prevent being pitched off heels over head every now and then, as the slender board suddenly bounced up or unexpectedly plunged down, over, around, under and through the uncivilized or at least unmacadamized highway along which the canine quadrupeds appeared to fly. And he could not help comparing the attitude of the drivers, as they bounded after the sledges with the ropes jerking them at random, to some of his own juvenile exploits. For example, when he used to sail across his father's cow-pasture, holding on to old "White-back's" tail, while she did her best to out-gallop time.

There were four dogs to each sledge, "Injun file;" and it was estimated that each team drew about five hundred pounds. The sledge continually undulated to suit the uneven surface of the snow, and the farmer almost fancied that he rode on something actually alive.

When the dogs could not perceive the right "trail," one of the drivers went on ahead with his "snow-shoes," to lead the way. But neither dogs nor drivers ate anything until arriving at St. Paul, where they all made a late supper upon *pemican*. Farmer Denton tried some of that "sweet meat," and he afterward said: "Just take a lot of buffalo meat, or—what is quite as juicy and tender—part of an old starved-to-death bull, from off the salt meadows along Barnegat Bay, on the sea-coast of New Jersey. Dry the flesh in the sun, and then partly cook or scorch it a couple of hours on sticks over a slow fire. Next spread it out upon the ground anywhere, and pound it into pieces the size of oats or barley. Then shovel it into an egg-shaped raw-hide bag, and pour over it all the melted tallow that will soak in!"

That's the way they make *pemican*, according to his report—and he would not make a false assertion.

The dogs are fed only at night, after they have traveled from sixty to ninety miles. Their allowance is the same as that of the drivers, being about a pound and a half for a meal.

Farmer Denton was thoroughly disgusted with the journey, but not with the dogs. They interested him very much; and from what he could ascertain of their pedigree, he inferred that most of them were a "severe" cross between the Esquimaux, the Newfoundland, the wolf, and the common Indian cur. Some of them were extremely bright and cunning, and all remarkably enduring. One half-breed and another, a full-blooded wolf, were trained for leaders. The genuine wolf was highly esteemed by his driver.

I shall here add something in relation to the character of wolves. Experienced hunters tell me that they are not only always hungry, but cannibalish in the extreme. For after feasting upon the carcass of almost any living animal, from man down to a lizard or a frog, they often manifest a keen appetite for the flesh and blood of their own species. And accordingly the stronger devour the weak. If one should accidentally get smeared with blood from the prey which they had just killed, his comrades would also eat him before the feast came to an end. Unlike other *carnivora*, the wolf snaps his prey with lightning rapidity, instead of clenching it and fixedly struggling in the charge of death. And also unlike those predacious animals who seize their prey by stealth, and destroy it at a single bound in the first attack, the wolf is anatomically formed for long chasing, so that the creature pursued by him must eventually succumb in a state of utter exhaustion. I can not say as to his inordinate power of digestion; but when desperately hungry he has been known to thoroughly masticate a rawhide trace and a very hard old water-proof boot. It is generally inferred, from the external aspect of a wolf, that he must be as brave as fierce. But in that facial expression he deceives a stranger; for, notwithstanding his almost vulpine cunning, he is nearly as cowardly and much meaner than a detestable feline thief. And, knowing his cowardice, hunters adroitly preserve the carcass of an animal which they have slain, by simply erecting a pole near the spot, with an old shirt or any fluttering object fastened at the top. The inflated bladder or a strip of the hide of the dead carcass is sometimes used in that way. And sagacious as the rascals are known to be, they have not the courage to approach what the hunters may leave behind them under the protection of such a dreaded ensign. With the same result, travelers may drag a loose rope behind the horse or vehicle which they are riding upon when attacked by a formidable pack of wolves. They always go in packs when on marauding expeditions; which, allowing for occasional slumber, occupy the greater portion of their time during life.

When seriously injured or frightened, a wolf will "play 'possum" so effectually as to often deceive those well acquainted with his artifice in that way. Many rascals have thus eluded their captors, to the no little chagrin of the latter. Nowhere can be witnessed a more terrific scene of confusion than that arising from the excitement among a pack of wolves when they have once secured a buffalo. A frightful, scuffling skirmish straightway ensues, and wildly continues for a moment to the music of furious snarls and growls; while amid a dense cloud of dust, only a frightful chaos of disintegrated hair and a forest of frantically whisking tails are visible to denote the sanguinary process of annihilation so speedily and rapaciously performed.

And yet it has been proven that, when captured quite young, a wolf will not only become tame, but conceive a devoted attachment for its master—in some instances almost surpassing the fidelity of a dog. In certain respects a tamed wolf is more serviceable than even the *canis familiaris;* as clearly illustrated among the teams comprising the train which Farmer Denton accompanied from St. Cloud to St. Paul. Many of those creatures were domesticated wolves, who manifested the most faithful allegiance to their drivers, and obediently submit to the servitude of a nomad existence without any reluctance. But the farmer learned that they were fond of "running off," now and then, to enjoy a playful romp among their wild ancestors, when the latter chance to be prowling about.

Whatever their origin, the sledge-dogs are very unlike the race domesticated in our abodes of civilization. They are generally larger and stronger, and capable of performing the labor of horses and cattle where and when the latter would perish with hunger and cold. They seem particularly adapted for endurance and privation; and in the Northern wilds they are what the camel is in the burning deserts of the torrid zone. In the summer, when the sledge-dogs have no work to perform, their owners sometimes put them out to board with contractors, who feed them on bad fish.

And I will also remark, that the name Esquimaux is a corruption of *weashkimek,* implying "eaters of fish." Thus it seems that there is some traditional origin for the piscivorous propensity of this serviceable breed of quadrupeds. Though it must be remembered that the physical peculiarities of the Red River dog are very different from those used by Dr. Hayes in his explorations of the Polar region.

A dog-hotel or boarding establishment is one of the curiosities of Selkirk Colony, and the rules and regulations for the control of the wretched canines, would serve as a model government in some of our great seminaries of learning. But when the poor animals are not properly attended to, they break loose from the kennel and get up a fishing excursion on their own account. Betaking themselves to the bank of the river, they dart with lightning velocity down upon the fish swimming near the shore, or seize any dead carcass floating on the surface of the stream.

The "Dog Carryall" is similar to the common sledge, but covered with doeskin parchment and ornamented in the usually fantastic conception of an Indian artist, to convey Catholic priests and dignitaries occupying some official position.

That dog-train in the winter of '62 was the last one seen in the City of St. Paul; for since then, the extension of the Pacific Railway does all the freight transportation below St. Cloud.

Farmer Denton says he shall remember his novel ride of seventy-five miles behind four dogs as long as he lives.

And he perfectly agreed with Lady Levasseur in extolling both the winter and the summer climate of Minnesota. Yet, while expressing delight at her permanent convalescence, he would repeatedly deplore his neglect in not bringing his wife to St. Paul before she died. He was every day more convinced from what he heard and saw, that the climate of the North-west would have saved her life.

But though Lady Levasseur escaped death from consumption, and seemed so buoyant and cheerful with the companionship of Fleurette and her newly-acquired and sincere friends, she was very far from being happy; and one day, in conversation with Farmer Denton, she remarked that no amount of wealth could appease the hunger of a blighted heart.

The good, honest man then imagined her grief to be analogous to his own. He had lost a dear wife, and she a beloved husband. Their idols were both in the grave. He did not know all—but he would, anon.

He was only a man; and all men are comparatively the same, when they have bereaved hearts that yearn for sympathy. And admitting that there was such a vast difference in their social castes and pecuniary positions, he felt irresistibly inclined to make a proposition of marriage. He knew that he was inferior to her in refinement, but she had already stooped to an equality with him. She said that her blighted heart was hungry from loss of companionship and sympathy and love—and might not *he* become an acceptable substitute for what death had taken away? Still so beautiful, and so charming in the estimation of all, she could gladden his future by her gentle presence and her sweet smiles.

His head was filled with entirely new ideas, and his heart pleasantly throbbed not very unlike it did when he first learned to love the maiden who became his wife. Time might have cooled the blood in his veins to a less violent heat; but he was imbued with the ardor of old; and, stimulating his courage by a perpetual recollection of having heard it said that a faint heart never won a fair lady, he one evening summoned every incentive for resolution, and said something that startled Lady Levasseur; but not quite so much as her answer astonished him.

"Mr. Denton," said she, "I esteem you very much. You have been extremely kind to me. Both you and your daughters seem near to my heart; and I sincerely trust that the friendship may grow and strengthen to the end of our lives. I am also willing and anxious to prove my regard in all possible ways. But there is an insurmountable obstacle which deters me from ever marrying again. Mr. Denton, I can not be your wife!"

Nevertheless, he might hopefully wait and see.

A Picturesque Spot, far up in Dakota Land, where Lieut. Col. Marshall, now Gov. of Minnesota, and his Men, Captured Little Crow's Fugitive Band of Outlaws.

CHAPTER XXI.

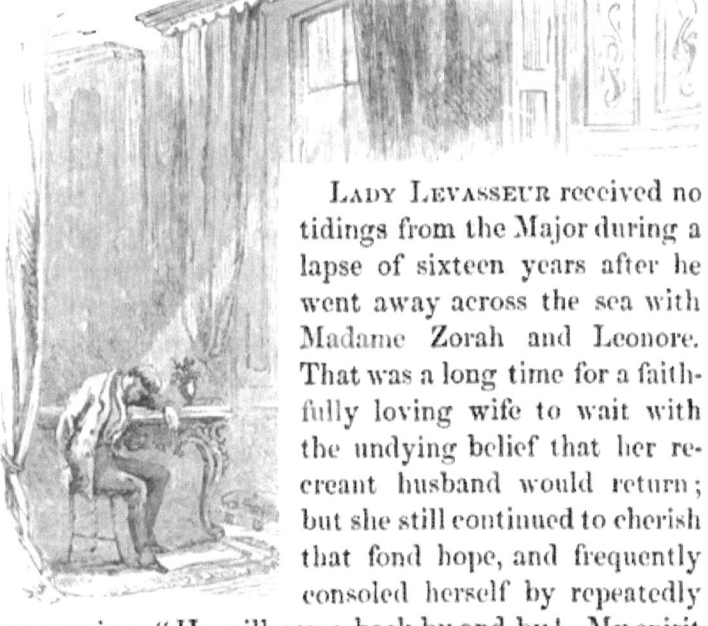

LADY LEVASSEUR received no tidings from the Major during a lapse of sixteen years after he went away across the sea with Madame Zorah and Leonore. That was a long time for a faithfully loving wife to wait with the undying belief that her recreant husband would return; but she still continued to cherish that fond hope, and frequently consoled herself by repeatedly murmuring, "He will come back by and by! My spirit shall not leave him. The old love must triumph when his heart grows sad!"

And did the Major continue to reflect upon the cruelty in robbing his deserted wife of her child? or was he entirely lost to all sense of reflection in the presence of Leonore? Ah, he could not help thinking of the past; but never for a moment suspected that Leonore was holding her own offspring in her arms, while his wife's child had been cast out into the unknown world. That was a terrible reality which would sooner or later startle his very soul. No matter; he was faithfully keeping his oath, so that the future might bring its burden of woe.

And Farmer Denton was not the only man who asked Lady Levasseur to marry. For, if I am truthfully informed, there are many gentlemen now in the City of St. Paul who still have a very vivid recollection of the rich Southern widow, or the beautiful Lady with the "*Angel Heart*," as she was familiarly called by the male and female gossips who courted her society.

Among her most enterprising suitors I shall vaguely mention a certain middle-aged bachelor of the *ton*, whose exchequer had been frightfully depleted by recklessly "handling and carrying choice town lots" in the *furore* of '57, when speculative excitement enriched some and impoverished a great many more. Failing to establish himself as the proprietor of the beautiful mother's hand and fortune, the philoprogenitive masculine cunningly transferred his addresses to the pretty daughter, who was then verging into that adolescent period of existence when extravagantly romantic love-dreams sometimes sweetly prelude a harvest of bitter tears.

At that time Fleurette was popularly designated as the "*Beauty of St. Paul*." And the suggestive sobriquet seemed to be very fitly applied. But the aspiring bachelor was only one among the throng who eagerly sought her smiles with an ardent desire that she might be prevailed upon to wed. Yet, with a single exception, none of them were likely to realize their wishes in that direction. There was but one gentleman who particularly interested Fleurette. And he remains single to this day. Some trifling incident caused a coolness between them, which was not dissipated before an unexpected disclosure in her family relationship effectually turned the current of circumstances controlling the future of her life. Doubtless, that event deterred her from finding a husband in St. Paul.

But where was Major Levasseur, the accomplished and erratic grandson of the proud old Marquis Dupontavisse? In London, in Paris—everywhere that folly and caprice suggested. He did not court repose, but rather sought excitement, and even dissipation, to avoid repentance and shut out remorse, which were frequently suggested by something like a whisper in his ear, that breathed "Beware of impending retribution!" Therefore, his happiness was not without its alloy, while he seemed so merry and gay. And at times, when quiet and all alone, he could not help recurring to the past. He would think of Lady Levasseur, and yearn to see her once more. But there was a dark, broad gulf between them, and a voice of grief came on the wind that swept over the blue waters of the sea, while a frightful spectre of infidelity and wrong rose up with an exulting grin to make him shudder with the reflection that Lady Levasseur's beautiful head could never again be pillowed upon his bosom as it did before Leonore's exquisite form reposed in his arms!

And for some reason he never revealed the thoughts which were passing through his mind when he sat with Leonore's child upon his knee, as he frequently did, gazing almost mournfully into its face. Probably he was thinking of Lady Levasseur, whom he supposed to be its mother, and reproaching himself for having been instrumental in separating it from her in that cruel way. Perhaps he was sorry that they had taught it to call Leonore, mother. He may have experienced deep regret for all that had been done, and secretly devised a plan of future atonement by eventually reuniting mother and child!

Then, too, they named it Irene. And he did not like that!

There was something in the father's heart which neither Leonore nor her discerning grandma could perceive when he insisted that Irene should have an education properly fitting her to be the heiress of wealth and position. And, after receiving instruction at one of the best seminaries of learning for the very young, she was placed in a convent, to remain until her studies were entirely completed, before encountering the great world.

But alas, for her mother, Leonore! She was no longer a timid girl. Launched into the gayeties of a fashionable life with but little restraint, and lured on by flattery and impelled by the promptings of her grandma, she soon became a frivolous coquette. Her beauty attracted the notice and elicited the admiration of the titled and the great, until her love for Levasseur was nearly swallowed up in the fascination of other delights. And Levasseur was quick to mark the change in her heart; for he wanted that all to himself. But his remonstrance came too late. Madame incited her on at the very moment when she should have raised a barrier of restraint.

Then the irritated man put on an air of authority, and said that his will was law. From the indulgent lover and doating husband, he ascended to the imperious lord, whose commands must be obeyed, right or wrong. And, when the first unkind words once were spoken, it was but an easy transition from peace to retaliative discord.

"She shall not tamely submit to harsh coercion!" interposed Madame. "She is your wife, and not your slave—and must be treated with the deference due her position."

Levasseur's ire was then roused beyond endurance. He might have borne resentment from Leonore with subsequent pardon in return. But when the old lady became defiant and urged belligerous opposition to his wish, he could not restrain himself any longer, and peremptorily decided that she should retire into seclusion. He commanded and she might seemingly obey. Nevertheless, he would soon realize the probability of extremes meeting extremes. The sequel proved not only disastrous, but fatally so.

Casting aside her better feelings, Leonore very pliantly coincided with Madame's unwise suggestion of trick and stratagem. And, utterly forgetful of the insecurity of their position, they rashly conspired and plotted to outwit him.

There was also some jealousy at the bottom of Levasseur's displeasure. A young nobleman, whose extravagance had occasioned much scandal in Parisian society, was the principal cause. And when he assumed an arbitrary control of Leonore's freedom, her grandma sought the profligate's interposition. She told him that Levasseur was a perfect tyrant. He had imprisoned Leonore against her will, and that, too, when she was nearly dying to attend the next grand *bal d'opera*. Could the young nobleman devise a scheme for the gratification of Leonore?

Highly elated at the marked preference shown him from one so fair, her unscrupulous admirer arranged his plans. But the Major's valet, an honest sort of man, was not long in discerning his master's position; and, without suspecting any serious result, promptly notified him of the true state of his domestic affairs.

Reluctantly believing what he heard, the aggrieved husband and Leonore were soon closeted alone. He accused her of deceiving him, and also hinted that his forbearance might soon end—and then she would have no home. Thereupon she confessed all, and endeavored to mitigate the offense by charging her grandma with the instigation and encouragement of everything she had done.

"I'll put an end to that!" muttered Levasseur, taking his idol in his arms. "I at last perceive how it is. You and your grandma must separate! I can not permit her to alienate your love from me. We will leave this place and go elsewhere, to begin happiness anew!"

Mutual kisses followed what he said. But, upon raising their eyes, they perceived Madame standing before them, with defiance and mockery in her face.

"I will go, sir!" she sneered. "*We* shall instantly quit the house. But, remember the conditions of your *oath!* Come, child, we will pack up and depart!"

Leonore rose to follow her grandma, and he could scarcely believe his eyes.

"Surely you would not leave me!" hoarsely exclaimed the astonished man.

"If grandma goes, so shall I!"

"And is this the end of my dream?"

"I can not disobey *her!*"

"Ha, ha! Now you see what your unmanly conduct has done!" cackled Madame, with delight at Leonore's prompt decision.

"As your husband, I can compel you to remain!" he proudly said.

Madame cackled much louder when she replied: "Husband! Ha, ha! We deny that now!"

"Silence, woman! Leonore, I am addressing you. Think well before you act!"

"I can not think! Whatever grandma says, I shall do!"

"You hear what she says! You hear, Major Levasseur! She refuses to be your slave!"

"Leonore! Speak!"

Madame motioned to influence her reply, and she tremulously answered: "I shall go!"

"I'll hear no more!" stamped Levasseur. "Go! Both of you leave my sight forever!" His rage was terrible; and he instantly shut himself up in his chamber, to avoid choking Madame, or perpetrating violence in some other way.

And at last Levasseur *was* alone!!

From his window he saw a *voiture* driven down the street, and in that vehicle rode Madame and Leonore!

"Fool! Fool! that I have been! For her I *deserted my wife sixteen years ago*, and *now she has forsaken me!*"

The man of the world bowed his head in agonizing thought. Thus far he had been floating smoothly down the current of time, and lo! a dark abyss of despair was now yawning to receive him. Memory was busy in his brain and in his heart. He went away back to infancy, where a thousand sweet fancies delighted him then. But alas, their melodies were silenced with the lapse of years! The stirring events of early manhood came up vividly in his mind, and before him were two pairs of eyes. One dark and luminous—the other mild and blue! The dark eyes seemed to glare at him with malignant scorn, and those of blue looked mournfully—but oh, so kind!"

A Tourist in Dakota Land is astonished at the eccentric conduct of his Horse, who makes a total immersion while fording a shallow stream.

Courtship, marriage—wife! And he murmured a name which he had not spoken for many years. He repeated that name in a tone of sorrow and with an accent of grief!

The gay world did not hear the groans of that penitent man! The past was all love's delusion, ending in bitter remorse. Daylight vanished and left him alone in the dark. But a veil fell from his mental vision and let in a terrible light!

There he sat, leaning upon the table all night, and in the morning his attitude remained precisely the same! It seemed like the sleep of death!

The sun shone in at the window, and one broad, bright beam rested upon the uncovered head of the sleeping, penitent man, whose soul was then away in another land, dreaming of happiness to come!

The noonday was fair in France, and no morning clouds were in the steel-blue sky of Minnesota. And while the forsaken man slept in Paris, his faithful wife and her adopted daughter were gathering flowers still wet with dew from among the rose-bushes and the vines adorning their residence in the elevated suburbs of St. Paul, five thousand miles away!

It was spring-time; and two little robins, which came close to the arbor sweetly warbling their love-notes in the fragrant air, filled Lady Levasseur's heart with sad memories of the past; for upon entering the house she touched the keys of the organ, and in a moment her own voice and that of Fleurette's joined in an anthem for Heaven to hear! And when the sounds of melody died away, the mother knelt in prayer while the daughter's eyes were moist with tears.

"Oh, ma, why do you so often repeat that prayer?"

"Because I believe that God will answer it by and by!"

But spring and its blossoms soon disappeared for summer to bring forth the fruit, and September had come to ripen the husbandman's products of toil, when one day Sancho was heard anxiously interrogating Dinah.

"My lub," said he, "whar am missus, I shud like tu know? Yars a letter cum fur an ans'r!" And then he thrust his old gray head in at the open window, saying, "Dis am wery 'tickl'r, and mus be 'tended tu now!"

Lady Levasseur broke the seal and read:

"MADAME—I have been sent by Messrs. Crane & Burr, attorneys-at-law, in the City of New York, to confer with you in a matter of deep importance, and take this method of requesting you to name an hour when it would best suit your convenience for me to call in person. Respectfully yours, etc.

HENRY DOWNS."

"Here, Fleurette!" said Lady Levasseur, trembling. "Write! I can not hold the pen! Say that I shall be pleased to have him call immediately."

Mr. Henry Downs soon appeared.

"I was not aware that I had any business with Messrs. Crane & Burr," began Lady Levasseur. "Indeed, I do not remember hearing the name of the firm before—and ——"

"Major Levasseur was a client of theirs," broke in Mr. Downs. "And it is of him that I have been sent to confer!"

"My husband!" she gasped, and reeled in her chair, with the expectation of some fatal news.

"The same!" continued Mr. Downs. "And may I ask if you are familiar with the events of his life since you parted?"

A mournful movement of her head intimated "No!" She could not have spoken if she tried.

"Then, perhaps, it will not be uninteresting for you to know that the Major quarreled with Leonore and her grandmother only a few months ago. Pardon me, if I unintentionally wound your feelings. The difficulty was a serious one, and they both abruptly left him as a final termination to the affair. His daughter—Irene— your child— Perhaps I am too blunt. In our profession, it is necessary to be as plain as possible. Well, your daughter Irene was still at the convent where she had been some years for the purpose of finishing her education, and he removed her the following day, with a suddenly-conceived resolution of bringing her with him to America. The Major's object was to find you if possible, and endeavor to establish the proper feeling and natural relationship between mother and child. He notified his attorneys, Messrs. Crane & Burr, to discover your abode, in anticipation of his intended and speedy arrival. The hostile position of the North and the South rendered it next to impossible for us—I should say impossible for my employers—to ascertain anything definite from correspondents in New Orleans, where you were supposed to be, if still alive. Our inability to accomplish anything did not satisfy the Major. So, placing your daughter under the protection of an old friend of his—in Louisville, I believe—he determined to visit New Orleans in person, and induce you to come North for her sake, and remain here pending a termination of the war. And, without listening to the remonstrance of any one, he hurried off on the hazardous journey. But shortly after he left the Union lines his lifeless body was found among those slain in a skirmish between a detachment of our forces and an independent troop of rangers, or mounted bushwackers, who were plundering and murdering indiscriminately, and totally regardless of the laws of peace or the rules of war."

"Dead!" shrieked Lady Levasseur. She heard no more, until recovering from her emotion—when she murmured, "Then, after all, this is the final answer to my oft-repeated and hopeful prayer! He is dead! And they killed him while he was seeking me! O, why did not God spare him a little longer? But proceed, Mr. Downs. Where is his body? Where is my child?"

"Ma, dear, I am here!" whispered Fleurette, with blanched cheeks and a trembling heart.

"Not you, my darling! My own babe, whom they robbed me of before it could realize a mother's smile. Mr. Downs, where is she now; and what has been done with the remains of her father, Major Levasseur?"

"I have come to tell you that," resumed Mr. Downs. "The captain of the Union skirmishers—a brother of mine, and formerly in the employ of Messrs. Crane & Burr—recognized the body from papers found in the pockets, and also from a watch and a miniature portrait of yourself, which were known to have been in his possession before quitting the camp, a few days previous to his death. In consequence of a serious mutilation of the features there was, at first, some doubt as to their identity. But nearly every article of clothing—even his boots and his hat—were identified by persons who had seen him alive. Here is a ring taken from his finger. Do you recognize it?"

"I do!" she gasped. "It was a gift of mine soon after our marriage! And he has worn it ever since then."

She pressed the ring to her lips with a long, deep sigh.

"And here is the watch, and the miniature, and the other articles! Do you also recognize them?"

"Yes, yes! They are all his! But here is another portrait in the back of the case! I wonder whose it can be? Hah! Take it away! That is not mine! It is *hers!*" and, with a shudder, she dropped the miniature case upon the floor.

"Oh, what a beautiful lady!" cried Fleurette, gathering up the case and gazing at the miniature. "Only see what magnificent black eyes! Ma, do you know who she is?"

Lady Levasseur had never told Fleurette the full particulars of her own sad story.

"Put it away—out of my sight—anywhere!" she groaned, while averting her face.

Fleurette was amazed, but said no more. And yet she felt alarmed.

"Then there is no doubt that the body is Major Levasseur's," observed Mr. Downs. "And we desire that you may choose a place for its final burial. It has been embalmed by some chemical process, and awaits your order. I might say that the captain, my brother, discovered your residence here, in St. Paul, from a rebel prisoner captured on the same day of your husband's death. But how, I am unable, as yet, to explain."

"Bring my husband to St. Paul; and we will bury him in the quiet cemetery beyond the hill there, where I can cultivate summer flowers upon his grave, until God permits me to lie beside him forever! And also bring my child. But I fear that she will not love me, even then. Oh, Mr. Downs, I am at a loss to know what more to say!"

"Cheer up, my lady. Your wishes shall all be gratified so far as we have the power. I will telegraph immediately. And yet, upon reflection, I think it will be better for me to go in person and bring your daughter, if we can find her, with the corpse of your husband. I shall communicate with you in the shortest possible time. Adieu!"

Sancho was a silent witness and a sad-faced auditor of the distressing interview between his mistress and Henry Downs. He had never been denied her confidence in anything proper for him to see and hear. And that privilege not only elicited his appreciation, but imbued him with a profound respect and devoted regard for her. He deemed it a great honor to be her confidant and adviser so far as his humble reason and susceptible heart might serve to lighten her sorrows. So, having conducted the visitor out, and earnestly expressing an audible wish that "de Lor ud bress im fur de good ob de kaus," he repaired to the kitchen where Dinah was impatiently waiting to "hea'yr what de komoshum was all bout!"

"Ah, my lub, sumf'n orf'l is hap'nd. De gem'men's frum Nu'york, and Massa's gwan tu ez long home, whar we mus all fotch up when Proveduns says to kum. An poor Miss Flurey's now kry'n kaze Missuses' own dart'r spects to step in er place."

"She shant do nuffin ob de sort," wept Dinah. "Flurey musn't be shuv'd orph fur no udder dart'rs wen she's all tuck't up so swete in Mussuses' buz'm like dem brite cheerabims wid dar mudder ang'ls in de heavenly sky."

Thus the servants' sympathy already ran in favor of Fleurette, whom their own love had inseparably united with the very existence of Lady Levasseur. And while discussing the matter thoroughly with themselves, they unconsciously resolved to shut their hearts against Irene.

"What ef she am Massa's chile and Missus wus er mudder?" theorized Sancho. "Wont she be like im, an not a tall like er? Didn't e lope wid dem ar wicked wim'n an leab Missuses' harte tu bust? Massa wus a bad man!"

"Hush!" started Dinah. "De speerits ob ded fouks kan hear what de liv'n say bout dem art'r dey's unkonnected frum dar bod'ez. Don't de preach'rs zort us tu pra fur does who am in de kingdumkumdum?"

"Ah, you'z bin read'n sum dem ar books what's written by sectariums who b'liev dar's no udder road but de wun dey am trab'ling demsev's!"

And Farmer Denton was pardonable for frequently saying: "Darkies will be darkies, no matter how white they are!" But in that declaration with Sancho, he somewhat contradicted his arguments in reference to the force of example attending life.

That night the gentle moonbeams calmly watched over the residence of Lady Levasseur; and the rosebushes, the green leaves, and the creeping vines seemed to smile in sweet response, while Fleurette lovingly nestled in her arms, and both were wrapt in slumber.

Ft. Snelling Flag-Tower.

Tourists viewing the South Bend of the Assouri, or "Mouse" River (a branch of the Assiniboine), beyond the Frontier of Dakota Land.

CHAPTER XXII.

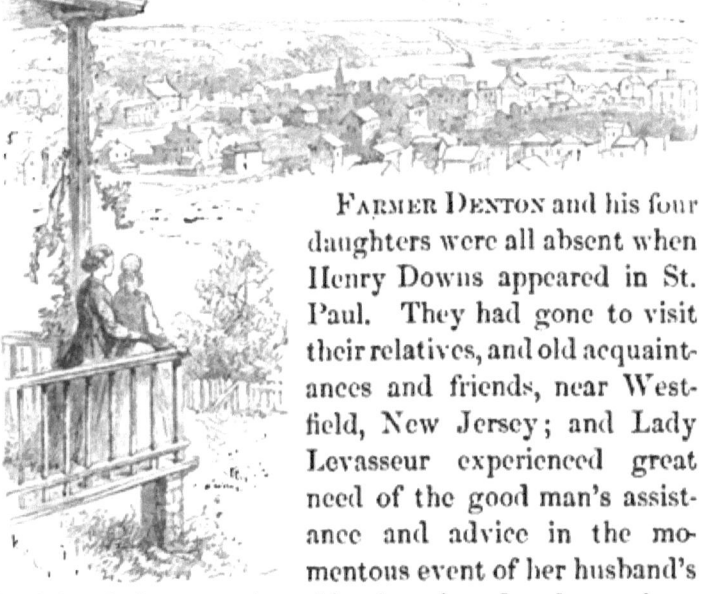

Farmer Denton and his four daughters were all absent when Henry Downs appeared in St. Paul. They had gone to visit their relatives, and old acquaintances and friends, near Westfield, New Jersey; and Lady Levasseur experienced great need of the good man's assistance and advice in the momentous event of her husband's burial and the reception of her long-lost daughter, whom she still continued to think of as a mere child, without actually realizing the fact that during such a prolonged lapse of time, Irene must have matured into a young woman. But the farmer had not yet learned from Lady Levasseur the exact nature of that insurmountable obstacle to her marrying again, which she alluded to when he first asked her to become his wife; and the melancholy denouement about transpiring, would certainly astound him when he and his daughters came home.

However, there was no time to lose; and Sancho was authorized to negotiate for a grave in the cemetery.

"Good gracious!" exclaimed the sexton. "What can Lady Levasseur want with a grave?"

"Massa am kum'n home ded!" replied Sancho. "De rebbels kill'd im when he wus gwine to fotch missus frum Orl'ins! Yeas, dey's kill'n eb'ry boddy now, cept us folks, yar in Sent Paul!"

So the wondering sexton went and dug a grave, while Lady Levasseur was all excitement and expectation. But she found time to review the past and to relive in imagination. She had never ceased to think fondly of her husband; and the recollection of that period of marriage bliss was not any less vivid because of his cruel desertion. The enormity of her wrongs would never dim the bright remembrance that he was once so good and so kind. But all those long years of sorrow, of hope and prayer, had brought her only a dismal coffin, with the sad remnant of life and love. And yet she fervently prayed that God might pardon him as she had done.

Then came intelligence that on a certain day the corpse would arrive, and also an announcement that Irene could not be found. The Major had neglected to leave her address with his attorneys, and perhaps it would take some time to discover where she was; yet they would certainly find her after his remains were put away in the ground.

But the joyful sadness that filled Lady Levasseur's heart was inspired by emotions more tenderly connected with the expected corpse of the father than the recovery of her child. Indeed, all her maternal feelings had blended so sweetly with the filial response of Fleurette, that she really experienced no sincere delight in the promised restoration of Irene. And under the circumstances, after so long a separation from the one which she saw for only a brief period in its infant form, and since Fleurette was so closely and sympathizingly identified with the only sunshine in her heart for so many years, how could she feel otherwise?

There was no room for a new idol in Lady Levasseur's bosom, while occupied entirely with love for Fleurette and in mourning for the death of her husband. And though sixteen years had gone since her head was pillowed in rapture upon his breathing bosom, even the expected corpse, coming back to her despoiled of its life and its soul, would be a melancholy but tangible consolation to her sorrowing heart. It seemed like some precious balm for her blighted love.

"He will soon be here!" she mournfully smiled, while clasping Fleurette in her arms. "And then, at last, I shall be permitted to plant flowers on his grave!"

To-morrow! Only one day more! The sun rose brightly, the hours swiftly sped, and soon the western horizon was ablaze with the gorgeous rays of parting light.

Lady Levasseur and Fleurette stood in the piazza without, peering away through distant space at a point where the faint outlines of hill and water seemed to touch the sky. But they did not see the house-tops and chimneys, nor the church spires in the lower part of the city, spread out beneath them. Nor did they dwell in rapturous contemplation of the magnificent view. Dayton's Bluff to the left, with its grand villas and smiling verdure overlooking the mighty river, and the expanded sand-bar of *la point basse*, upon the other side, were then of equal interest to the anxious watchers in the vine-clad piazza. They were looking out upon the furtherest shimmer of water still bright from ruddy tints in the luminous air.

But the deepening twilight soon began to obscure their vision; and then they stood closer together in silence, with hearts audibly beating, until at length a small speck appeared upon the still bright bosom of the distant river, and, swiftly rounding the great bar opposite the bluff, gradually neared the city. Presently the howling signal of a "white-collar" steamer came up to them on the quiet air over the top of the city, and then went reverberating with loud echoes far away among the great hills along the water's side.

"He comes!" whispered the mother. "Do not withdraw your hand. I must have it here in mine, to give me strength. Oh, my heart is fluttering so! Try to steady me, darling! There! Be near me when he arrives! Close, close as you can get! And do not let me die with emotion!"

"Yes, ma; you may rest upon me! I shall not leave your side! And remember, as you so often tell me, that 'God is always near!'"

Sancho and the undertaker, with a conveyance, were upon the levee when the steamer came in. And there was a long box, which the strong deck hands lifted in silence and with care. Poor Sancho was weeping; but in the darkness none could see his tears.

Another steamer unexpectedly arrived within the hour. Farmer Denton and his daughters came on board of that. And among the passengers were a lady and a gentleman, both strangers in St. Paul.

"Will you accept the hospitality of my house?" said Mr. Denton, addressing the stranger, with whom he appeared to have formed a slight acquaintance on the way. I shall be most happy to entertain you, inasmuch as there is no chance at a hotel. So many tourists and business men are in town just now that the public houses are all more than full. At least I heard so a moment since. We've got as large hotels as you can find in any city of twenty times the size, and several of them at that; but this is the greatest place that I ever read of for tourists in quest of health. You never saw the like! And the fun of it is that they all go away benefited from the climate. Oh, such air! Minnesota beats the world for that! But come with me; and I'll show you the style in which we North-western settlers manage to live! Come, girls, this way! Mind the gang-plank, now, and be very careful that some of you don't tumble into the river, like that rogue, Dr. Passion, did. You remember, eh? I say, my friend; 'tisn't every man who can trot out four such girls as those of mine. That's your wife, I reckon?"

Neither the farmer nor his daughters had as yet seen the strange lady's face. She not only kept her room during the passage up the river, but upon emerging to leave the boat she concealed her features by a thick veil. However, the gentleman gratified their curiosity somewhat by introducing her as his daughter. Yet, still she did not remove her veil. But as they were in the act of going ashore, no great importance was attached to the slight disregard of etiquette; and her father, smiling, added: "My dear sir, under the circumstances, I shall gladly and thankfully accept your hospitable invitation."

Meanwhile, the undertaker and his assistants conveyed their sad burden to the residence of Lady Levasseur. Carefully placing it in the hall, they quietly retired a moment or so before the farmer and his daughters, with the strange guests, drew near.

"Here we are at home once more!" sang Eliza, hurrying on in advance and bounding up the piazza stairs. But there she suddenly paused. And when her companions joined her they were all dumbfounded together.

Through the open door they plainly saw the lamp-lit spectacle in the hall. Lady Levasseur and Fleurette were upon their knees, locked in each other's embrace, near the coffin, and the old slaves also knelt beside them. Even Goliah sat upright in one corner, with downcast eyes, as if he fully comprehended the solemnity of the scene. And while the wondering spectators stood there, speechlessly contemplating what they saw, their amazement was doubly increased by hearing the mournful voice of Lady Levasseur, which broke the stillness of evening in an earnest prayer that touched their hearts with a painful thrill!

"I thank Thee, O Lord, for this favor! Thou hast brought home unto me the last remains of the beloved object of my wedded joy; and now, whenever it is Thy pleasure, I will cheerfully resign myself in the arms of death, and lie down beside him. But, after our long separation in life, do not allow them to part us in the earth. Let our graves be one! And then, O Lord, receive our souls together, entwined with eternal love, unto Thy bosom forever! Amen!"

But the feelings of Sancho and Dinah were not so much absorbed in sorrow at the death of their master as in sympathy for the grief of their beloved mistress. And as Goliah's olfactive sensibility was not long in discovering the proximity of his friends, he unwittingly terminated the impressive ceremony of that simple benediction by a boisterous exuberance of delight which characterizes the canine species. His loud barking salute at once dispelled the silent intensity of the general gloom, and some confusion instantly followed as a matter of course.

Farmer Denton felt himself in an awkward position with his guests. It was an inopportune occasion for hospitality, and he sincerely wished that they were domiciled elsewhere for the time being. But while he was debating in his mind how to act or what to say, the stranger whispered something in his ear.

"You don't tell me so!" started the farmer.

"We shall see!"

A light was ordered in the parlor; the blinds were closed, and Lady Levasseur sat there alone!

"This way!" beckoned the farmer. "You will find her in that room!"

The stranger entered. And closing the door after him, the farmer stood with his hand upon the knob outside, so that he could hear what might transpire within.

First a startling scream, and then a brief silence, followed by a vehement articulation of "Husband!" with another exclamation of "Wife!" in quick response. And when the farmer heard those words, his hand was trembling so that it made the door-knob rattle.

"Are you not dead, when I have your corpse?"

"There has been some mistake, for I am certainly alive!"

Lady Levasseur asked that question, and it was Major Levasseur who gave the answer.

"It is all a dream!" she wildly cried.

"Forgive the past, and let my arms and lips prove that I am real!" he said in reply.

Then there was a long silence of reconciliation, unheard and unseen beyond the walls of the room!

Presently the farmer stood aside, while Fleurette and Irene both passed in.

St. Andrew's Church, at Selkirk Colony.

"Our daughter! Irene, embrace your mother!"

The husband and father paused in dismay! He saw two Irenes staring at each other with evident fright; and the wife and mother beheld two Fleurettes exactly alike, each in a similar attitude of mute surprise!

Irene had thrown off her traveling robe, revealing a simple costume, in color, material and fashion that precisely resembled the dress worn by Fleurette!

"What is the meaning of this?" choked the father. "Irene, speak!"

And the mother, with equal embarrassment, called "Fleurette!"

Irene shrank back to her father, while Fleurette clung to her mother, and the parents themselves were mutely begging each other for an explanation!

The same sunny curls falling upon the shoulders of one also beautified the head of the other. Both lovely brunettes, with sweet blue eyes, and prototypes in feature, in stature, and in symmetry of form!

A light began to dawn upon Fleurette's mind, and she burst into tears! And Irene whispered, "Father, take me away!"

"There is some necromancy in this house!" exclaimed Levasseur. "If there is not, I begin to fear that I am insane. My corpse is in that box, you say, and yet I am standing here! Irene is clasped in my arms, and I see her weeping in yours. I cannot believe what is impossible; but the vision seems real!"

"Oh, ma," sobbingly whispered Fleurette, "you said that I should always be your child. Hold me tightly; please do!"

"Your child?" queried the father, who overheard what she said. "How is that?"

"I adopted her many years ago," replied the mother.

"Adopted! You bewilder me! How can this wonderful resemblance be accounted for?"

Fleurette's origin was briefly explained.

"And now, Irene, embrace your mother!" said the father, drawing them together. But it was a cold and formal pressure, with two mechanical kisses given; and the murmuring of "daughter!" and "mother!" did not seem to come from their hearts.

Oh, how scornfully Irene glanced at Fleurette when explanations had been made, and the general surprise was over. And Fleurette hardly dared to lift her gaze from the floor.

Was it possible that two beings so exactly similar in all outward features could be directly opposite in tastes and feelings? Alas, yes! For, though born alike in every faculty and sense, different associations, examples and precepts in education from infancy until that eventful hour, had been continually molding their hearts to play each an adverse part in after life!

Irene was haughty, selfish and cold; and Fleurette all sympathy and love.

"Henceforth you shall be sisters!" the mother said. "Both so beautiful, and alike!"

"Yes!" responded the father. "Embrace each other now!"

Fleurette had not the courage to face that repelling look; and Irene disdainfully refused to make the first advance. So the moment and the opportunity passed, and their arms were never after extended one to the other.

Levasseur went out and whispered something in the farmer's ear. Then Sancho brought tools to open the long box.

"Hah!" exclaimed Levasseur. "Quick punishment,

indeed! Terrible and sure! In this corpse I recognize one of the villains who plundred me in Tennessee. They not only robbed me of everything valuable, but even stripped off all my apparel and gave me a lot of rags to wear. However, they were soon overtaken by a squadron of Union cavalry, and, in the skirmish, this fellow must have been killed. And being clad in my garments when the victors discovered him dead, it was not strange that they should imagine the body mine. This might have been all the more probable when other prisoners in the hands of the outlaws were unavoidably slaughtered in the fight. Fortunately I had made good my escape before the fatal encounter. Acting upon that belief, the soldiers took charge of the valuables and the body, which were subsequently brought away, as the result proves, while I was journeying hither, after accidentally discovering the abode of her whom I expected to find in New Orleans. Thus the mystery is all solved!"

There was but little sleep that night in the house of the Dentons and the Levasseurs. Such a combination of remarkable and surprising events produced emotions and excitement that would not subside very soon. But the beautiful moonbeams peeped in at the window to smile upon the reunion of hearts, where the forsaken wife was made happy once more. They also played among the rose-bushes outside, suffusing the green leaves with a silvery glow, until finally disappearing from sight beyond the hills. And then the stars came out, laughing like choice spirits whom God had sent to watch over the abode of *lost love found!*

Two weary hearts, with much grief and but little joy in their pilgrimage of life. Years of sorrow for a moment of bliss. And then destiny must be fulfilled.

But the long box was not buried in the grave already dug for Levasseur. It went to an unhallowed excavation in Potter's Field, while the multitude wondered, and gossipers had a great deal to say.

"We must now leave this place!" said Levasseur to his wife. "Town-talk will devour us, if we stay!"

"Anywhere! It's all the same to me, with you!"

And thus Farmer Denton's dream of eventually getting Lady Levasseur for his second wife came to an abrupt end. But he tried to comfort himself with protracted reveries, in which the mutability of human affairs was admitted by him beyond a doubt. He was also convinced that miracles would never cease! And his daughters were quite unanimous in their belief that truth was sometimes stranger than fiction.

But though Farmer Denton could never make Lady Levasseur his wife, he felt very grateful for the extraordinary liberality she had shown him. And there was that elegant residence deeded in his name. She said, "No matter about that," and refused to acquiesce in any settlement of the pecuniary account between them. "It is scarcely probable that I shall need a penny of what you have had from me. If I ever do come to want we can settle it then! When you are tired of living in this fine house, no doubt it will bring a good price. Dispose of it as you deem best. And perhaps you can afford to give an equal share of the money to each of your charming daughters as a marriage-dowry in my name!"

"She's one in a million!" thought the farmer. "And for the life of me I don't understand why it was that her husband should abandon her for another, nor how she could remain faithful to him an entire generation of time! Some women are as queer as anybody, and particularly in matters of love. If all wives were like her, the divorce-law would stand a dead letter so far as their action went! A splendid woman—that she is!"

And it did seem advisable for the Levasseurs to seek a habitation elsewhere. For, even in St. Paul, at that time there existed the usual aggregate of "happy families," who are impelled by a sort of gossiping piety to feast upon the sinfulness of their neighbors. I allude to those exemplary moralists who endeavor to substantiate their own virtue by exposing and denouncing the moral weakness of others. A merciless fraternity, alike devoid of pity and insensible to remorse!

But Major Levasseur would not escape the fearful penalty incurred by his rash violation of Divine law. Go or stay, retribution must overtake him in the end!

They were soon ready to leave St. Paul. But on the morning of their departure, a letter came in haste from the law firm of Crane & Burr, to notify the Major that Leonore and her grandma had just arrived from Paris, with the intention of instituting a civil and also a criminal action against him in the courts of law. No matter; he would return to New York, and there meet the issue.

But he was greatly disappointed when it became evident to him that a proper degree of affection might not be established between Irene and her mother. That worried him. However, Irene's antagonism for Fleurette might be obviated by a removal of the latter—whose claims were certainly less than the former. After a while he could attend to all those matters, and then be happy. But alas, the sequel will show the terrible result from his errors of the past, and then leave him in the depths of remorse, still fruitlessly seeking for one little moment of happiness that can never be found.

Fording the Calumet River, beyond Pembina Mountains, in the Red River Region.

CHAPTER XXIII.

The great Indian massacre of '62 is almost forgotten; and new settlers are pouring into every part of Minnesota. They come from the East and from the South, from Canada and from across the sea. Sturdy laborers, experienced agriculturists, skillful artisans, and business men with money and enterprise, are industriously and successfully developing the wonderful resources of the State. Productive farms, workshops and factories, towns and railways, churches and stores, newspapers and hotels, school-houses and fine residences are multiplying everywhere—while the bright new City of St. Paul goes on increasing in population, wealth and beauty with a marvelous rapidity that is not only astounding and gratifying to its enterprising citizens, but utterly incredible to people in other parts of the world.

And Farmer Denton's prediction was more than fulfilled. That elegant property which he bought for five thousand dollars during the panic caused by the Sioux massacre, did prove a good investment for Lady Levasseur's money. Among the consumptive invalids who visited Minnesota the following year, was a certain very rich gentleman, whose health became restored almost immediately. And he joyfully resolved to live in St. Paul the remainder of his days. With that intention, he accordingly desired to purchase a nice house; and willingly paid "thirty-three thousand seven hundred and fifty dollars" as an inducement for the Dentons to move. The price is specified in the deed that was recorded by the county clerk, and hence I am able to here state the exact sum. But one sour old citizen exclaimed, "What a big sell!"

Then, after deducting five thousand, with interest for the time he had been living there, Farmer Denton divided the balance into four equal parts. And he looked very happy when he said: "Girls, you shall have just seven thousand dollars apiece when you comply with one irrevocable condition!"

"And what is that?" they all eagerly wished to know.

"Each of you must first marry the man you love!"

Four crimson blushes and four ejaculations of "O!" in simultaneous response, brought a loud laugh from their delighted father.

"I see how it is!" he then teased. "You are all going to leave the old man alone, to darn his own stockings and sew on his own shirt-buttons. That's the way with most children in this ungrateful world!"

"Oh, no!" came in a chorus of voices. And four sweet kisses, with sorrowful utterances of, "Father, you should not talk so!" caused his heart to flutter, and almost brought the tears.

And there soon was one marriage. A retired merchant from the East made Julia his wife. And her seven thousand dollars were invested by him in such a way that she is receiving nearly eleven hundred a year interest money, and the chances are that her personal income will soon be a great deal more. She now resides in one of those elegant mansions that have recently been erected in the suburbs of Minneapolis.

Then another marriage created some extra gossip. And Mercy is extremely proud of a handsome husband, who distinguished himself in the Southern war. He was a furious rebel then. But he repented while recuperating his health in the climate of Minnesota, where he found an entirely new world of love in a pair of sparkling hazel eyes, which have since followed him all the way to Florida, where he lives.

The well-pleased father then said, "Whose turn next?" "Mine!" answered Eliza, with an arch roll of her eye. And in due time she did look very pretty as a bride. The bridegroom was either a lawyer or a banker, who said that he intended to retire from business and "tour in foreign lands." But he changed his mind; and she now frequently tells him to "hurry up and go." He laughingly replies: "I hate to leave the atmosphere of Minnesota!"

There has been no other marriage in the Denton family, as yet. Though it is well known that more than one masculine heart is attacked with severe palpitation when Miss Jane happens to be in the same room.

"Ah, she's my only boy!" her father said jestingly one day to a friend, when Jane was by.

"Except Goliah!" was her tart reply.

"That's so! And I hope he'll live until I die!"

Farmer Denton's admiration and respect for his dog

15

was not without the best of reason. Goliah is a splendid fellow. And as the climate of the North-west is so much like that of Switzerland, where his canine ancestors lived, he will probably attain a ripe old age before departing to the place where "all good dogs must go!" Tourists who take any interest in that species of "animal kind," should inquire for Goliah when they visit St. Paul.

I might also mention that although Jane is the youngest of the four Denton sisters, she has a keen eye for business. And the lucky wooer who makes her his wife must be alive and stirring, or she will have him in leading-strings before he is safely through the honeymoon. As an instance of her discrimination in the investment of funds, I may relate that when the stock of the St. Paul and Chicago Railway was put in market, she expressed a desire to have her seven thousand dollars "dowry-money," which had been acquired through the remarkable generosity of Lady Levasseur, all invested in the bonds of that corporation. And it did sound very business-like for a lady to say,

"The stock of that road will eventually pay large dividends, and I want to be counted in!"

Mr. Edmund Rice, the President of the new *air-line* road, will not deny that the first seven one-thousand dollar bonds signed by him, at the St. Nicholas Hotel, in New York City, were subsequently delivered to Miss Jane Denton of St. Paul.

From this I infer that the "musical" young gentleman of her choice may yet be a stockholder in the St. Paul and Chicago Railway, unless she is prematurely proselyted by the "new revolution" doctrine of those monomaniacal *parratonnerres* who emphatically declare that "what's a woman's is her own," including the property of her husband, too. But, at all events, Jane has chosen a good investment for her dowry, and I can not believe that she will ever be inflamed by contact with any of the gynecian firebrands.

Farmer Denton retired from agricultural pursuits after the Indians made such havoc on his farm. He sold his farm the following spring, and engaged in a different occupation, at which he accumulated a great deal of money in a very short time. He is not in any business now. But, being an enthusiastic admirer of horses, he drives a team which is seldom dusted by his neighbors' wheels.

I imagine that he is just now very much concerned in railroad affairs. Perhaps he may also have an interest in the Vermilion Gold Mine. And, judging from the active part he took in a test of machinery for the practical purpose of molding peat, an experimental operation of which I was invited to witness during my visit to St. Paul in the autumn of '67, he must be pecuniarily associated with his friend Sneak and other enterprising citizens, who seriously and enthusiastically contemplate realizing an immense fortune from that monstrous *bed* a short distance beyond the limits of the municipal corporation. But I think that fine residences, built on speculation, suit his ideas better than anything else. In fact, he has done a great deal toward adorning the city, which is so admirably situated for grand and elegant villas that admit of architectural display.

The central part of St. Paul stands upon a beautiful, level plateau, which abruptly terminates in a precipitous bluff, with an elevation of nearly one hundred feet above the water of the river. Upon each side of the bluff there is a gradual slope, affording naturally easy landing for steamers. At one time there was considerable rivalry between the two landings. But recent enterprise has permanently fixed the great centre of transportation at the lower point, where all the railroads will soon be connected in a grand "union depot," adjoining that of the North-western Packet Company. And then passengers and freight, by water or by rail, may be transferred from boats to cars, or from car to car, all in the same building, without the least inconvenience or expense.

The architectural beauty of St. Paul is certainly superior to what I have met with in any other city of its size. This is saying a great deal—but only what all experienced and observing travelers, who have seen it, enthusiastically declare. This peculiar feature of the city may be accounted for in the undeniable fact that a large proportion of its inhabitants are not only possessed of great wealth, but highly educated and socially refined. Some proudly represent distinguished old families in the East, and their establishments here, whether for business utility, or for domestic luxury, are, after all, but the grand result of improvement upon the modes of moneyed policy and opulent taste associated with their recollections of youth. And again, in the popular phrase, others are "self-made" men, who have accumulated abundant riches in the successful pursuit of a legitimate occupation, or from the profits of fortunate speculation and remunerative enterprise in the development of the extraordinary resources of the State. Farmer Denton is one of that class.

And they all seem to be perfectly well aware that the style of architecture in any place is the first interesting subject of consideration on the part of strangers—just as the garments of an unknown individual are taken in judgment for or against him. And, accordingly, I may say that St. Paul (at home) is like a personage of remarkably fine form, clad in elegant and costly apparel of the latest fashion, and possessing a noble countenance, at once proud, dignified, intelligent and kind—with a sparkling eye of hospitality and humor that is ever ready to laugh a fascinating welcome to any respectable visitor knocking for admission.* And there is a loud knocking every day.

But the Denton family are greatly indebted to the patronage of Lady Levasseur for the social position which they now enjoy. Her reputation for "immense wealth" naturally attracted the "exclusives" from their haughty reserve. They were all eager enough to make her acquaintance. Thus the intimate relationship she maintained with the Dentons, compelled *Society* to receive them or ignore her. And as all the "upper ten" gentlemen were intensely anxious to wed the "Beauty of St. Paul"—the popular and very appropriate sobriquet bestowed upon Fleurette—the "Four Sisters" had an excellent opportunity for selecting husbands among those whom she refused.

In this way the good, honest farmer and his amiable daughters were pleasantly elevated to high fortune and social position, which otherwise they might never have attained. I trust that these personal allusions will give no offense to those interested.

And here I shall hint to strangers who are not immediately received into the "best society" of St. Paul, that the multiplicity of "external enjoyments" in and about the city are quite sufficient for the creation of new personal paradises of worldly bliss, in which they may contentedly revel all alone.

There is a rapturous thrill experienced by every one when they first breathe the atmosphere peculiar to the

---

* See "Appendix" for list of eminent and wealthy citizens.

A Spontaneous Strawberry Festival, in Dakota Land.

place. I have felt it myself, and also heard others try to express similar feelings; but am not yet sufficiently versed in the "physical laws of spiritual emotion" to attempt a satisfactory elucidation of the wonderful enchantment pervading that "bright realm of flowers, of beautiful lakes and winding streams, where health and happiness might dwell forever."

The *Society* of St. Paul is really superior to that in a majority of American cities, either large or small. And I have noticed that the proportion of "eminent" and "distinguished" citizens is much larger than in any other community of the same population. Military chieftains, retired merchants, wealthy professionals, and affluent gentlemen of leisure are met at every turn. Intelligence and refinement are predominantly characteristic attainments of the people who constitute the society of the city. All those palatial residences in town, and the numerous suburban villas which dot the great semicircular range of hills overlooking the entire locality, with its magnificent expanse of bluff scenery up and down the river, are conclusively indicative that taste and luxury surround the *elite* "family circles" at home. The countless and elegant equipages, blooded teams, servants in livery, and the stylish *whirl* along the public thoroughfares, are significantly demonstrative of the existing presence of millionaires. And the pretty cottages, all neat and clean, where cheerful wives are heard in songs of content, while their rosy-cheeked children boisterously shout at play, impress strangers with a pleasant conviction that happy firesides are everywhere in the North-west.

When church-bells ring, beauty and fashion answer to the call. The sidewalks are crowded with the lovely and the fair just before and after the hours of worship on a Sabbath-day. And the Opera House, Ingersoll Hall, the *soirees*, the festivals, and the balls, are well patronized, too. *Le beau monde* in St. Paul are harmoniously pious and gay.

Sectarian, beneficial and educational institutions are very numerous. Churches of almost every denomination; Masonic, Odd-Fellow, Good-Templar and Druidical Lodges, fully and efficiently maintained; a historical society, library associations, classical seminaries and excellent common schools; Bible, benevolent, orphan, emigration, hospital and recreative societies; a medical and surgical academy; and, in fact, all and every organization for promoting morality, intelligence, art and worldly happiness, in such a manner as to secure eternal salvation beyond the grave.

River-side View, where the "Iron-Horse" runs, in "Dakota Land."

But as *le demi monde* will ever infest the precincts of wealth, so dissipated prodigals rattle the dice-box, take a hand at cards, fight the tiger at faro, or play keno on the sly, while old men, and striplings, too, may bask in the syren's smile, and riot with alcoholic ruin in their downward career to perdition—even "under the gaslight" of St. Paul.

And yet the dark side of *this* picture is extremely bright in contrast with the criminal records of *other* cities and towns. For, though seemingly incredible, it is positively true that the criminals of Minnesota are comparatively fewer than those of any other State in the Union! A careful comparison of city statistics everywhere shows that the ratio of crime in St. Paul is but one-half of New York and one-fifth of Boston. Thus, actual figures prove that the immorality of puritanical Massachusetts, with all its self-righteous profession and noisy solicitude for the piety of the rest of the world, is five times worse than that of Minnesota! The skeptical or the prejudiced reader can not refute this assertion.

Perhaps the pellucid water, the pure atmosphere, and the steel-blue sky of "Dakota land" have the same powerful influence upon morals as upon health. Farmer Denton is of that opinion. He says: "I wouldn't give Minnesota for all the rest of the world." But he persists in retaining every one of his eccentric notions. He is the same man with his great wealth and newly-acquired social position that he was while toiling on his Jersey farm. And during his first winter in St. Paul, he felt it his duty to reprimand "those plaguy girls" for the "new-fangled" ideas that would get into their heads. He frequently lectured them upon the absurdity of making "such a fuss" about the weather. They fancied that it must be very cold, because it was in Minnesota. And he sharply ridiculed them for "piling on ten thousand unnecessary garments, instead of fighting the cold with spirits and animation!" In that he was right, and soon convinced them by practical illustration. And they are now ridiculing the similar prejudices of those who have not yet realized the truth.

Of late he freely expresses "his own ideas" about the "chance for consumptives" in that region. I had a long talk with him upon the momentous topic; and he then declared, "What's physic for one, might be poison for another. Between the ignorant doctors where they come from and the unprincipled quacks who follow them here, they stand a very slim chance of being cured, or having any money left to bury them when they die. And that isn't all. This climate is intensely dry! Of course it is. Well, then; if it heals an invalid of a 'moist temperament,' it must kill one of a directly opposite peculiarity." I use the farmer's style of speech. He says: "I'm no physician; but I do think there's a little common sense in my head. And when a consumptive asks me if I think he will recover here, I feel of his *skin*, and want to know whether his hands are apt to chap. I don't feel of his pulse. If he says his hands *do chap* easily, I urge him to go home as soon as possible. It's *too dry* for *him* in Minnesota. *He* should take a voyage to sea, and visit some region where there is more moisture in the air. That's what I tell him!"

I fully concurred in his simple illustration of "common sense;" and am much surprised that physicians do not give the subject more attention. Certainly much depends upon the *temperament* of an invalid going thither for relief!

Among other investigations made by that estimable though very eccentric man, was a minute inquiry concerning the singular habits of the wild beaver. Animals of every kind interest him. He went away up near Crow Wing; and Chief Hole-in-the-day there introduced him to a beaver community or town very eligibly situated in the middle of a small but perpetual stream emptying into the Mississippi River. When he returned, his narrative was a marvelous one, indeed. He says:

"They're well worth going to see!"

I had a conversation with him also upon the "beaver subject," as he calls it, and derived the information that they and muskrats are slightly consanguineous. He assured me that their habitations were quite similar in many features. Though the beaver is by far the greater engineer and the more perfect artisan.

A community of beavers will barricade the mouth of a small river with a dyke, displaying quite as much skill as though it had been constructed by human hands. They make that obstruction for the purpose of forming a pond in which to erect their habitations. And they invariably select a stream that is never dry. The most astonishing part of their labor is conveying the large limbs and trunks of trees which are to be laid crosswise or fixed in the bottom of the stream. It is also interesting to see how they procure those pieces of timber. And particularly so when they never use a tree after it has been prostrated by the wind or felled by the axe of man.

Having selected a tree on the bank of a stream, five or six of them cut and saw the trunk with their sharp teeth, while another one stations himself in the middle of the water, and indicates by a peculiar sound or by striking his tail on the surface, which way the top inclines to fall. Thus the cutters and sawyers may avoid being crushed to death. Soon bringing the tree down into the water, they then all unite their strength and skill in navigating the entire object to that particular place where they purpose cutting it into proper lengths. When the stakes are arranged to suit them, they entwine small twigs like basket-work and cement all with mortar, which was prepared by another party while the cutters were bringing down the tree, in accordance with their rule of impartiality in the equal division of labor between them. Under the dyke, when completed, they form a "flood-gate," to be opened in wet weather or shut during a drouth, as necessity requires. Their dwellings are made of wood and mortar, two stories high and double, of a dimension suitable for the families who are to occupy them. The first story is a food magazine, entirely beneath the surface of the water; and the second is divided into dormitories, above the water, giving each family a separate chamber. Numerous avenues are opened under the dwellings for the purpose of going in and out beneath the water, and thus hiding their retreat from the keen-eyed Indians.

Divided into tribes or bands, with separate chiefs, they conform to rules of government that might shame a human being who disregards an obedience to moral law. When the magazines are stocked for winter, no pilfering is allowed; nor is any of the provision to be consumed until the circumstances of season absolutely demand it; and even then, no individual is permitted to take a morsel without the consent, and in the actual presence of, the chief. The store consists of very simple food, such as bark of the common willow and the wild poplar trees. Should bark be scarce, they will also collect the wood, and divide it into distinct parcels with their teeth.

A particular territory is allotted to each tribe; and those who trespass are delivered up to the chief for punishment. For the first offense a simple chastisement is deemed necessary to produce a reform; while an incorrigible thief or miscreant of any kind is doomed to lose his tail—which is the greatest disgrace a beaver can realize! And the miserable convict is henceforth a disfranchized pauper. But in some of those cases of corporeal decimation, the whole tribe of the mutilated culprit will fight in his behalf upon the same ground that "State Rights" people defend themselves from national aggression. And in "war" the victors seize and confiscate with a rapacity almost equaling that of belligerent Christians (?)! The homes of the conquered are ruthlessly taken possession of, and strongly garrisoned for the benefit of young colonies in expectation.

The females produce their whelps with eyes open, and three or four at a time, in the spring, and sustain and instruct them with marked solicitude for nearly a year, when the educated juveniles are compelled to launch out in the "stream" of life, and build homes for themselves contiguous to the parental abode. But if the community is already over populated, the youngsters are advised to join with other "new beginners," and make a new settlement elsewhere. They seldom migrate unless driven hence by the approach of civilization, in which extremity their misfortunes are somewhat identified with the human aborigine.

His Highness, the chief, told Farmer Denton that not unfrequently a bitter feud between two tribes was finally settled by their respective chiefs fighting in the presence of the opposing armies, or by a set combat of three and three. And thus fought the Horatii and Curiatii of antiquity!

Being remarkably virtuous, they live in matrimony, without any laws of divorce, until one of the couple dies. The infidelity of a female is punished with death. In sickness, they express suffering by plaintive sounds not unlike the human voice, and their wants are kindly provided for by sympathizing relations or friends.

But, as in human society, there are some who decline to labor for subsistence. In zoographical terms, those are technically called *Les paresseux*. And they justly merit the appellation of idlers; for they neither "dam nor toil" in any way further than to excavate long tunnels for habitation. It is also a singular fact that the vagabonds are invariably of the male sex, who burrow together as many as possible in the same tunnel. The supposition is that they are mostly vanquished candidates for the possession of admired female favorites, and that their social improvidence and cynical barbarism resulted from mortification and disgust at seeing the success of bitterly-hated rivals. And thus the **contest of** wooing man **is represented in the** amphibious *castor fiber* of the dumb animal species. The Indians say that when the *Les paresseux* have sufficiently recovered their strength in solitude, they voluntarily return to the community from which they seem to be ostracized, and once more endeavor to establish a satisfactory matrimonial alliance. Hunters **easily entrap** the lazy drones, and in that event their sorrows are at an end.

There is a peculiar odoriferous substance secreted by the beaver which emits sufficiently perceptible to be recognized by hunters a long way off. Scholars call it *castoreum*, while trappers designate it by the plainer term of "bark-stone." When used for "bait," it never fails to lure into the **death toil** any unfortunate juvenile who may chance to sniff its odor, which is the most deliciously attractive sensation that their olfactory senses can possibly realize. Yet while young beavers **are thus caught,** the experienced, like old birds, frequently suspect harm, and so shy away, after cautiously springing the trap and averting the danger to any unsuspecting youth or thoughtless simpleton.

But Farmer Denton did not confine his attention entirely to sledge-dogs, beavers, and the like. He was more deeply interested in the welfare of thousands of toiling and struggling men in the East, where he had left them wearing out their miserable existence upon land that would not pay to farm; and that, too, when so many million acres of productive soil in the great North-west still remained waiting for the plow. His letters all reiterated: "Come out here. Don't stay where you are. Instead of working yourself to death to avoid starvation, pack up, or sell out, and take the first train. Get here in time to break up new land, and the first crop will set you crazy with joy!"

And he told only the truth when he repeatedly wrote that the first crop would pay for the land. He also mentioned that the Exemption Law secured a home and a heritage for the poor man's family in case some misfortune left him hopelessly in debt, and named other extraordinary advantages which should induce his correspondents to "Come!"

But as Col. Hewitt, an enterprising lawyer and real estate *financier* of St. Paul, is now sending his "Book of Minnesota" *free* to all applicants by mail, Farmer Denton relies entirely upon that. It contains a *resume* of everything that would interest strangers who contemplate settling in the State.

A Squatter's Claim.

"Minne-Wakan," or "Devil-Lake," near where "Little Crow" was killed.

CHAPTER XXIV.

Summer travelers in Dakota Land are numerically increasing every year. And I do not wonder at it. The only surprise to me is that a few thousand more of those " would-be happy but forever miserable" people who haunt, or rather infest the old worn-out watering places in the East, so pertinaciously every season, do not venture a little further from home, and seek the benefit of relaxation where actual enjoyment can be found. I am well aware that merchants and others who can not leave their business for any length of time, must content themselves with spending only a day or two, now and then, at the nearest place of attraction. But it is none the less criminal, and unmitigatedly ridiculous to domicile their virtuous wives and innocent children at an overcrowded fashionable sea-side resort, or in a dissolutely perturbed spring-house, or even upon an aerially "toploftical" mountain-crag—where all the wedded and celibate "spooney" Toms, Dicks and Harries, and "simpering" Susans, Betsies and Janes are alike desperately endeavoring to flirt themselves into the improper possession of new affinities! And, with seemingly bold assurance, I shall here sarcastically intimate that such family-arrangements are unpardonable in husbands and fathers who have the least particle of connubial or paternal solicitude in them. Also (fully justified by conclusive inferences, adduced from extended observations in the past), I shall unhesitatingly take the liberty of insinuating that the husband who leaves his young wife in such promiscuous and pestiferous society, six days and five nights in the week, while he is away attending to pecuniary affairs, and then consoles himself with merely visiting her from Saturday night to Monday morning, may be a "darling duck" in the lady's estimation, and at the same time appear like a "silly gander" in the opinion of those who flirt with her when he is not there. And yet, how many such arrangements are annually consummated by those who consider it *distingue* to come in contact with the ephemeral butterflies and grasshoppers of *le demi monde!*

I allude to those places of rendezvous only where parasitical Apollyons and their Cytherian decoys sport and flutter so notoriously in the devastation of all that is good and pure; where midnight cards and wine, with paphian smiles and a voluptuous rendition of the lascivious *pas de cancan*, fascinate innocence and prepare souls for hell!

Who says I am too severe? *He* does; and so does *she!* Indeed! Perhaps I ought to apologize. Then, also, perhaps I shall not. No! I have been there, and seen it all. And while some stood in front, timidly gaping at the painted curtain, I looked in behind the scenes. Certainly. Why not? I had the pass-word, and went in free. But how I got out, was quite another thing. Oh, sneer at these lines, in welcome! I admit that I am writing in the same spirit with which a noted reverend gentleman denounced the *Black Crook*. Well, what if I am? He said that the voluptuous beauty of the Parisienne *ballet* might not demoralize his mind, although he cautioned the multitude against venturing too near.

But as it was not my intention to make any considerable portion of this volume read like a criticisingly "moral essay," I will simply add that the better class of visitors are beginning to shun those resorts which have become famous from prodigal extravagance, bought with ill-repute, to quietly rusticate in the sweet retreats of Dakota Land, where the moral atmosphere is not less pure than the health-giving air which the lungs of honesty and virtue love to breathe!

And since the opening of railways in harmonious connection with established lines of passenger steamers on the lakes and rivers, summer travelers in the delightful region of the great North-west will find first-class accommodations on their tour wherever the conveyances are propelled by steam. And, as with the salubrity of the climate there, the scenery is, in many respects, the loveliest upon which the sun ever shone. A steamboat voyage on the Upper Mississippi is now attended with the comfort and luxury of a city hotel while rapturously enjoying the grand and romantic panorama of the strangely castellated bluffs of the mightiest river in all the world! But as any description of the natural sublimity peculiar to the countless points of interest in that voyage alone would fill a huge volume, I can allude to only a few of them here.

Trempeleau Bluff, on the east bank of the river, between the cities of La Crosse and Winona, is a magnificent study. (It has been successfully painted by Mr. Gilbert Munger, a talented young artist from New York, who did it while visiting his brothers, the popular music dealers, on Third street, in St. Paul, when I was unraveling the mystery of that curious mound of round blue stones which had been accumulated by Hah-zah-ee-yun-kee-winn in memory of her first-born child. The painting proved very successful, not only in the estimation of those who were familiar with the original scene, but in the artistic judgment of a Scotch nobleman, who gladly paid a large sum for it while yet in an unfinished condition.)

We will imagine that the soft haze of an October morning is subduing the sunlight, which apparently struggles to come forth in resplendent glory. And there, towering skyward with solemn grandeur, all clad in the richly-variegated colors of autumn, the giant hill is perfectly sublime. Then, creeping down its side, a great phantom shadow is faintly visible, not only upon the surface, but far into the pellucid deep. And the tiny pebbles along the silent shore seem to be kissing each truant ripple as it comes dancing softly and clear before the gentle breeze; while further out in the bosom of the mighty stream, there is a smiling archipelago of clustered islets, where fairies might peacefully dwell in a miniature world all their own. The little archipelago presents a beautiful contrast with the stupendous bluff whose almost perpendicular crest looks down in vivid resemblance of some antique castle long since ruined by time's decay. And as the mellow morning light is quaintly gilding its imaginary walls, a strange fancy inspires the beholder to muse until thought loses all conception in dreams that cannot be defined. I have enjoyed pleasurable musings there.

Trempeleau is decidedly French. And I am told that it signifies "dipping into the sea." But the river pilots translate it "mountain island," from the fact that the lofty eminence has no apparent connection with the general range. It stands entirely alone; and the steamers land at a little village which appears to be doubtfully clinging upon the southern base of the dizzy and almost perpendicular height.

Victoria and Prince Albert Peaks are seen upon the opposite shore, two miles or so below. They are twin bluffs, and the loftiest elevation along the entire river, being about eight hundred feet above the surface of the stream. The apex of one somewhat resembles the English crown—and hence their names.

Driesbach Bluff, also upon the west bank of the river, and scarcely more than eight miles above La Crosse, is so called because it was formerly owned by the once celebrated lion tamer of that name. But why he ever bought it I am at a loss to comprehend. The last time I passed there the sun was sinking to rest behind the monster hill; and I saw strange shadows hovering about that lonely cemetery with its small white headstones pointing out the graves of early settlers who had been buried there. What a singular spot, I mused, for a burial-ground! At an elevation of nearly five hundred feet upon a mountain side, among dwarf oaks, and broken rocks all moss-grown and gray. How desolate and wild! And the weird-cast scene was all the more thrilling from the soft light of parting day.

I leaned upon the guard-railing of the steamer, pensively questioning my own soul whether it would cheerfully leave its poor body of clay in a hill-side grave as dismal as those up there appeared to be. But a voice within me, in sad response, cried out, "No!"

Then I fancied a beautiful night; and tried to imagine how I would feel sitting up there all alone in solemn communion with the dead! Spiritualists say they can talk with the dead. And they endeavor to convince everybody how beautiful their "theory" is, while I can not credit them with entertaining a very sincere belief in all they pretend. But I dreamily thought that an hour or so spent up there, in a calm moonlight night, would seem quite novel, if nothing more. And then, if I could have a magic wand to wave, my first wish would make the moon disappear behind dark clouds, leaving the air totally black. With another movement of my wand I would call up a terrible storm. And there, amid the tombs, with a tempest moaning through the broken rocks and howling amid the tree-tops over my head, I would invoke deafening peals of thunder to echo in response when the lightning flashed an appalling blaze! Then, waving my wand once more, I would command all the storm clouds to vanish, and let the joyful moonlight reappear, so that I might contemplate a million gold and silver ripples quivering and glittering upon the surface of the mighty torrent stream away down below!

The City of Winona is the most important place between La Crosse and St. Paul. It occupies the same spot where the traditional village of *Keora* stood many centuries ago upon Wapashaw Prairie, a beautiful plain, which was dearly loved by the Winnebagoes of olden time. Here it was that the great chief Wapashaw lived and died. Some say he died in exile, in Canada. But I have been shown the spot where his remains, with those of his family, lay buried when white settlers began to build the new town. They found it inclosed by a rude wooden fence, which soon disappeared, in the progress of improvement, to make room for the erection of stores. And by and by the bones were removed in excavating for a cellar, in which a barber has since pursued his tonsorial manipulations without even asking permission from the departed spirits of the illustrious dead.

Gigantic bluffs rise up back of the pretty town, and almost overhang the habitations below; while five beautiful valleys, with each its stream, and bounded on either side by a range of diversified hills stretching away back to the interior of rich agricultural lands, all converge on the plain. The surrounding scenery is very grand from the tower of the colossal and magnificent public seminary—a new edifice, far surpassing any similar building which I have seen in the East. And a palatial temple, costing nearly a quarter of a million dollars, is also in course of erection there, at Winona, for the uses and purposes of the Minnesota Normal School.

Lake Pepin is the choicest portion of the Mississippi River. Father Hennepin called it the "Lake of Tears," because *Aquipaguatin*, the old chief who captured him and his men, wept and compelled his own son to weep with him, all one night near the water's edge, for the purpose of inducing his "court and councilors" to acquiesce in his wish to deprive the reverend prisoner of life. But the tender-hearted old savage spilt all his tears in vain, and the wandering Franciscan lived to narrate his adventures for the edification of the world.

The scenery of Lake Pepin is both lovely and grand. And there are few other localities of equal extent upon the face of the globe which can even remotely compare

Curious Sandstone Concretions, in the North-west.

with it as a pleasant study for the painter or the poet. The lake is formed by an expansion of the river to at least three times its average width for a distance of twenty-five miles, in shape like an amphitheatre, and inclosed by lofty bluffs, which rear their dark outlines in every variety of form, and at intervals seem to be disconnected by elevated valleys or deep ravines. The perspective in all directions is totally unlike any other part of the river, from its source to the Gulf of Mexico. Not a single island is in view. The Indians say that "once upon a time" the bottom of Lake Pepin *fell out*, and that the islands then all went down. Inasmuch as soundings to the depth of four hundred fathoms, or twelve hundred feet, have been made in some places without any result, this tradition would seem true. The water is remarkably clear, and does not appear to have any current. But it is perfectly alive with fish; and among the aqueous novelties there, I might allude to an occasional splash of the ever-restive sturgeon, who is naturally addicted to a peculiar antic of leaping above the surface, and instantly disappearing again, to repeat similar performances in distant places. And when a storm occurs, the whole expanse of element is quite as tumultuous as an angry sea!

The bluffs surrounding the lake are from four to five hundred feet high, and the country recedes from them at about the same level, with the usual undulations of gently rolling land; while numerous streams disgorge here and there. Beside splendid fishing in the lake, an abundance of grouse and other small game may be found in that vicinity; and deer are numerous among the forest hills in winter time.

The village of Frontenac, situated upon an elevated natural esplanade of singular beauty, seems to be nestling at the foot of the western bluff of that mountain-like range called *Point-no-Point*, which rears its bold front ten miles or more along the Minnesota shore of the lake, while the dark outline of *Cap de Sioux*, or "Maiden Rock," is visible nearly opposite, on the Wisconsin side. And those great cliffs appear like two antediluvian monsters of earth in silent anger, perpetually frowning defiance at each other across the beautiful waters which bar their possible meeting in the actual combat of physical strife.

"Maiden Rock" was the scene of a love tragedy which occurred long before the first steam-signal of a roaring *putah-waiah*, or "fire-canoe," disturbed the primeval stillness of the then unexplored caves beneath those bluffs. And that tall promontory will ever be memorable among the Indian legends of Dakota Land, for a physical and historical peculiarity similar to that of Leucadia, where the muse of Mytilene, more learned than beautiful, precipitated herself into death as the most convenient means of curing a passion which the scornful Phaon requited with contempt.

But it was upon the wild shore of Lake Pepin that Oholoaitha, or *Winona*, the "first-born," more beautiful than learned, and quite as desperate as her illustrious example, took a death leap because she was forbidden to love and to be loved by the brave Anikigi. There are many different versions of this romantic tradition. But the most plausible one is that Oholoaitha—a Sioux child of ten years, whose parents lived at the village of Keoxa, in the time of the great chief Wapashaw, situated on the prairie where the City of Winona now stands—was taken captive by a hostile band, and subsequently reared in the teepee of the victorious chief. And upon attaining the irrepressible period of female existence, she fell in love with the chief's son. That was all very proper, for the object of her love had himself been the means of saving her life. Yet, unlike Phaon with Mytilene, Anikigi gallantly and heroically returned Oholoaitha's passion in the spontaneous ardor of a young Dakota brave. And they might have loved happily if their hopes had not been suddenly blasted by the conclusion of peace between their tribes, which made it compulsory that she should be restored to her own people. However, the chief made a formal request of her father that she might remain to marry Anikigi, and thus become his daughter-in-law. But the proposition only resulted in exasperating the revengeful feelings of the paternal old Sioux, who was very anxious to avoid any alliance that might have a tendency to consolidate peace. So he resolutely demanded his daughter back again after her eight years' absence in very pleasant captivity. But Oholoaitha did not return to her father's teepee, nor to his tribe. For, on the very day that he intended sacrificing her by an odious union with one of his own choice, she ascended the bluff and precipitated herself to death among the rocks below. And as the Indians deem suicide an unpardonable crime, the living still curse her memory and attach eternal infamy to her name!

"Winona's Grotto," a cave lined with various colors of sandstone, in strata of an inch or so thick, crumbling easily to the touch, and melting quickly in water, is but half a mile below Maiden Rock.

The Garrard Estate embraces the extent of *Point-no-Point* range, the whole of Marsh Valley, and nearly all the hills and valleys for two or three miles in width between the towns of Red Wing and Lake City. I presume the whole area is not less than ten thousand acres, including the most picturesque and lovely scenery in any part of Dakota Land. Brigadier-General Garrard, and his two brothers, Dr. Garrard and General Garrard, are busily superintending the transformation of the entire estate into an immense ornamental park. They purpose making it the grandest and most delightful summer *resort* on the continent. And, judging from what I have seen already accomplished there by a lavish expenditure of money with "taste and wisdom," it is safe for me to say that their enterprise will be entirely successful. When the valley gradings and the mountain passes are all completed, there will be picturesque driving enough for several days without twice going over the same track or repeating any one view.

An enchanting scene may be enjoyed from *Point Delight*, an inland promontory of immense height, looking over Marsh Valley, and out upon the Lake, for at least twenty miles, to the dimly visible bluffs against the horizon. This is the loveliest landscape that I ever beheld!

The resident Society of Frontenac is that of educated, polished, refined and wealthy people, who offer every inducement for others of the same class to come and join them. Lady McLean, the elegant and accomplished relict of Judge McLean, late of the United States Supreme Court, and also the mother of the Messrs. Garrard, is so delighted with the place that she intends to reside there the remainder of her days. Strangers will find a good new hotel upon the levee. Mr. Kennicott, the landlord, is a hospitable host and a very kind-hearted man.

If happiness can dwell anywhere upon the earth, it may be found in the pretty village of Frontenac. It is quietly breathing in those peaceful abodes upon the beautiful esplanade at the foot of that gray old hill, near where the waters ever flow! I have seen it there in the dewy morning, at noontide, and in the twilight of evening. And I remember once sitting at a chamber-window in the stylish residence of Dr. Garrard, during the midnight hour, when all was hushed and still; and, while gazing out upon the silvery deep with sad and mournful memories of the loved and gone, my listening fancy heard a whispering murmur in the pleasant breeze, which seemed to say:

"Where God is, and they his love doth keep,
Sobs nor sighs shall ne'er disturb their sleep!"

Some marks are still existing in the vicinity of Frontenac to point out the place where an old French fort stood nearly two hundred years ago. And Indian mounds are numerous in the neighborhood of Lake City, where Mr. Lyon, a wealthy New Yorker, is keeping an excellent hotel for the accommodation of tourists and invalids at all seasons of the year. The *Lyon House* is now standing on a spot where the bones of an extinct race have been found in such vast quantities as to induce the belief that, contemporaneous with the antediluvian boyhood of Noah, some vast city covered a large portion of the wide prairie which spreads out far beyond the limits of the present thrifty town. A small steamer plies between Lake City and other landings near, affording pleasure-seekers convenient facility for a delightful trip over to Maiden Rock, the Grotto, the Cave, and any picturesque locality which their fancy may select.

When Le Sueur visited Lake Pepin, nearly one hundred and sixty years ago, he saw numerous caverns of over seventy feet in extent and three or four feet high along the bluffs, in which bears slept during the winter.

The entrances to some of the caverns were entirely closed with saltpetre. In the summer they became the dens of rattlesnakes, who charged their gums with poison in the morning and cast it out at night.

Red Wing is remarkable for the proximity of La Grange, or Barn Bluff, a solitaire eminence, nearly five hundred feet high, the western base of which is only a few rods from the levee in front of the Metropolitan Hotel, kept by Mr. Teele, an obliging host, who endeavors to make his guests feel at home. The grave of old "Red Wing," the noted chief, is on top of the bluff, overlooking an almost endless expanse of land and water, which has already entranced a painter's eye and fired a poet's brain. And, as if to compensate for the entire absence of them in the lake, a "thousand islands" intersperse the river above, forming the most romantically diversified series of scenes. The site of Red Wing, now a large and prosperous town, was occupied only a few years ago by a group of teepees then forming the Indian village of *Remnichah*.

But tourists voyaging upon the Upper Mississippi River must not imagine that all the beautifully undulated scenery of Dakota Land is visible from the deck of a steamer. For many of these great promontories are but the termination or the beginning of long ranges of bluffs, which meander beside tributary streams, in some instances a hundred miles or more from their outlets into the great arterial flood. And in that season when nature is full of bloom, the countless hills and dells are robed in dense foliage, imparting a joyful beauty to the almost inconceivable shapes and attitudes of precipitous heights, rugged cliffs and romantic slopes, which form the kaleidoscopic valleys intersecting the lovely country around.

The mighty river everywhere, except on Lake Pepin, is divided into numerous channels by intervening islands with a marvelously pleasant irregularity, which even the combined efforts of art and nature have nowhere else attained. Thus the eye of a stranger is frequently deceived with the impression that modern horticulturists have been lavishing enormous expense to perfect rural beauty with the utmost profusion of foliage and flowers.

In the Algonquin dialect, *Sepe*, or *Sepin*, signifies "running water;" and hence the name Mississippi. De Soto called it St. Louis; and Count Frontenac honored the then French minister of marine by calling it Colbert. But the great Father of Waters is not only wonderful in magnitude, as seen to the living world, but still more amazing beneath the reach of mortal vision. Or, rather, it is supposed to be, according to a marvelous theory of Dr. Percival, late geologist for the State of Wisconsin. The startling discovery of boiling water, which suddenly spouted out from an artesian well at La Crosse, induced the learned gentleman to conclude that far beneath the bed of the Mississippi there exists another and even more immense stream flowing in the same direction, and whose waters are of much too high a temperature for the ordinary preparation of soft-boiled eggs. This strange theory has been concurred in by "Brick Pomeroy," whose paper is more severely political and widely-circulated than any other journal west of the Allegheny Mountains. And the probability is that he intends to use the boiling water of the artesian well to generate steam for propelling those mammoth printing presses in the basement of that splendid publishing house so recently erected there by him.

Island Scenery of the Upper Mississippi River, viewed from a High Bluff.

CHAPTER XXV.

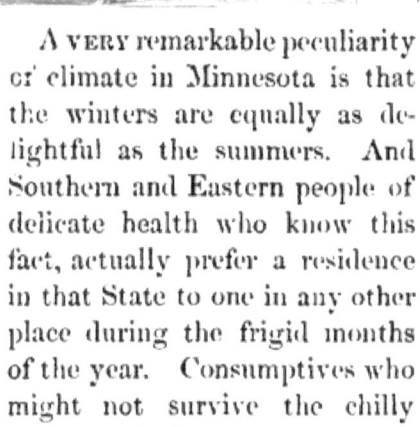

A VERY remarkable peculiarity of climate in Minnesota is that the winters are equally as delightful as the summers. And Southern and Eastern people of delicate health who know this fact, actually prefer a residence in that State to one in any other place during the frigid months of the year. Consumptives who might not survive the chilly weather of "raw" localities, will find the winter atmosphere of the North-west not only pleasant, but marvelously exhilarating. No matter what the thermometer says. For, while freezing very hard, the air is generally so still and dry that smoke from the chimneys will ascend perpendicularly several hundred feet; while at night, a lighted candle may be placed out of doors without perceptibly flaring. Numerous invalids are now in the habit of spending the winter in Minnesota; and since the Chicago, Milwaukee, Minneapolis and St.

Paul Railroad has been completed all the way through, the number will soon be increased to thousands.

Among the natural wonders of Dakota Land are many interesting celestial phenomena. And, as I am such an enthusiastic admirer and demonstrative patron of the canine species, I will first mention the PARHELIA, or "sun dogs." Imagine a scene in St. Paul. His daylight majesty, old King Sol, is rising beyond Dayton's Bluff, in a perfectly transparent atmosphere, and attended on each side by a grand *parhelion*, nearly as large and luminous as himself. Mere words are inadequate to describe the atmospherical display produced by their combined rays shooting horizontally across the perpendicular columns of pure white smoke curling up from a thousand chimneys; but the grand sight may be seen at uncertain times during the winter, in Minnesota. And a similar scene might occur in the evening, when the sun goes down behind the western bluff, opposite Fort Snelling.

Then sometimes *paraselenæ*, or "moon dogs," will rise with her nocturnal divinity, pale Queen Luna, in the same way; but less brightly, and perhaps accompanied by an immense circle of pure white *Lumen boreale*, similar to that strange halo not unfrequently seen around the supposed throne of the chill-demon, whose freezing breath silences the Polar region with a mystic spell, which can not be broken until the end of all time!

Aquatically addicted "pic-nickers" are supremely delighted with the grand "December Steamboat Excursion"—a time-honored celebration which is comfortably and hilariously observed by the *elite* citizens nearly every winter—ice permitting.

The mercury in the thermometer occasionally goes down very low. Sometimes thirty, forty, and even forty-five degrees below zero! And yet the usually clear sky, and the remarkable purity and intense stillness of the atmosphere will so fascinate a stranger that all idea of freezing is entirely dissipated by pleasurable sensations of body and delightful emotions of mind.

I enjoyed a palpable and practical test of this enchanting peculiarity of Minnesota "cold weather," during the winter of '67. It occurred while I was temporarily sojourning at the *Nicollet House*, a splendid hotel in the City of Minneapolis, kept by the Gilson Brothers, who were previously known in connection with the International Hotel and Taylor's Saloon, a magnificent public palace formerly existing on Broadway, in New York, and at the present time occupied as the head-quarters of the "Merchants' Union Express Company," who paid nearly half a million dollars for the building alone.

We were discussing the beauties of the scenery around the marvelously flourishing City of Minneapolis —which is not only a spirited rival to St. Paul, but destined to be part and parcel of the latter when the rapid improvements of the future shall inseparably unite them with intervening edifices of business and elegant private abodes—thus forming an immense metropolis for the great North-west!

The Falls of St. Anthony, with their mills and their factories propelled by the greatest available water power in the world, were wonderful to behold; and, by crossing the great Suspension Bridge, I might visit that colossal structure called the Winslow House, and also a certain cellar where the spirit of a dead man is said to appear. But had I seen the Falls of Minnehaha in their winter garb of ice?

No. That was something I had never seen. I could easily do so, at almost any hour in the day, by cars on the Minnesota Valley Railway; yet did not imagine that a waterfall was attractive when the thermometer stood eleven degrees below zero.

Snow had fallen during the previous night, and was then whirling in the air. So I imagined that it must be terribly cold. And that thought presented itself with an involuntary shiver when Mr. Horsey, one of the proprietors of an extensive livery establishment near the Nicollet House, in Minneapolis, insisted that I should drive one of their spirited teams down to Minnehaha.

To that proposition, I ejaculated something like "Good gracious! I'd be frozen stiff when I arrived there, if I drove down while the thermometer indicated such a frightful depression!"

Horsey laughed at my fears, and said that if I would accept a pair of stylish and nimble roadsters, one of his expert drivers should "put them through." He did not explain what he meant by "through;" but I readily comprehended the "put;" and finally decided to venture, upon one condition.

A ride of four miles, with the thermometer eleven degrees below zero, to look at Minnehaha, without a lady companion to cheer and inspire me on the way, would be a prosy exit from life; and I at once thought of *Louise*. Perhaps she might be induced to share my fate. I shall not mention her other name in this connection. Though the reader must not imagine her to have been a *myth*. She was real and living, with an avoirdupois weight of just one hundred and thirty-two pounds, and picking up half a pound or so more every day. There is something very pretty in the name of "Louise." It always comes musically to my ear. And I particularly admire a certain bright-eyed lady, who invariably responds with a sweet smile when I interrogatively articulate the vowel melody of its dual sound. Well, Louise's home is somewhere near the Hudson River. She visited Minnesota for her health, and then asked permission to reside there forever.

"Minnehaha!" she cried. "Yes, I'll be ready in no time!"

"That's quick enough!" thought I. And she seemed highly delighted at the prospect of freezing herself to death in such a very romantic excursion. So I said to Horsey, "We'll go!"

"All right!" he responded, with that pleasant twinkle so frequently seen in his eye. And, accordingly, Louise and I were soon seated together in a stylish vehicle, *en route* to the Falls. My fair companion securely covered her ears; and so did the son of Ethiop who managed the reins; while my whole attire remained simply and precisely as I wear it at home in New York City. I put nothing over my ears; yet a warmly-lined buffalo robe enveloped our feet and otherwise protected us from the cold. And, after an hour's ride, we were snugly toasting ourselves by the fire at *l'hôtel de shantie*, while criticising the melancholy remains of a despoiled register which lay upon a table in the public room, from the suggestive contents of which an ingenious writer might glean enough for a very readable volume in either comic poetry or melancholy prose. But Louise was impatiently anxious to realize the satisfaction of contemplating the beautiful cascade, and I closed the mutilated volume very abruptly in response to her persistent exclamation of "Do come!"

And then, arm in arm, out in the cold, with pleasantly anticipative emotions, we cautiously descended the slippery path to that particular stand-point near the mystic tree, against which so many thousands have leaned, one

Suspension Bridge across the Mississippi River, from the City of Minneapolis to Nicollet Island, just above the Great Falls of St. Anthony.

by one, for safe support while abstractedly lost in rapture with their first glimpse of the loveliest waterfall in all the world. I need not relate how we shivered in speechless admiration; for the tongue of a stranger seldom disturbs the exquisite silence of the soul, which is sure to be enjoyed at that particular moment, and perhaps never experienced so sweetly again in any emotional pleasure of remaining life.

"Is that all?" at length bursted Louise, in a sadly disappointed tone. I could not help regretting her lack of enthusiasm; but the comical expression just then pervading her countenance from the effects of such a lengthy exposure in unaccustomed cold, and suddenly "blasted hope," threw me into a violent fit of laughter, which in turn so startled her that she grasped my arm with a desperate violence that came very near precipitating us both together head foremost over the rocks into the abyss of water apparently boiling beneath the ice below. Her pretty cheeks were tinged to the hight of rosy red; yet her melting eyes seemed rather dim; and her luscious lips were tightly drawn and palely blue. An odd semblance for sanguine beauty to wear. But she was *Louise*, nevertheless. And I fancy that a similar adventure would temporarily distort and discolor the face of any other lovely woman.

Poets and authors have exhausted themselves trying to picture Minnehaha, without a word touching its sublimity in winter. And Louise was too full of ideal expectancy to realize satisfaction from what she then beheld.

"You must not reproach me!" said I. "What Longfellow wrote was no fault, or merit of mine!"

Nor could I remove those huge columns of ice which had crept up around the gorge until only a small portion of the upper part of the cascade was visible to her sight. It was too bad, after she had been for years picturing in her imagination

>How the *Laughing Waters* sweetly dance and play
>In the joyous sunshine of a summer's day.

But she looked again; and then saw something grand to admire. For the surrounding objects below the Falls were all covered with ice, presenting the most singularly sublime spectacle that I ever beheld. Perhaps the reader can imagine a world of pure, white glass, or rather a magic scene of earth, rocks, stones, bushes and trees, with every leaf and limb congealed into a brightly-crystallized form, while a million sparkling lights, reflected from the rays of the blazing sun, are gleaming with gorgeous splendor in the frosty air! Such a picture will disclose an ideal vision of what the external features of Minnehaha represent when its eternally showering mists have frozen in their fall! So, instead of hastening away, we lingered on in contemplation of the novel scene, which seemed to grow more and more enchanting as we gazed. And during the remainder of our lives, neither of us can forget the strange delight experienced then. But there was a sadness in the roaring of the Falls. For, shivering

>Together there, beneath that wintry sky,
>We heard the *Weeping Waters* gurgle and sigh,
>While clad in funeral shrouds of drifting snow,
>They darted to their icy tomb below.

But our toes were getting numb with cold; and so we scrambled back to the quaint little hotel standing near. Then, promising to repeat our visit again the following summer, we returned to the Nicollet House, after an absence of only four hours. And, although the weather must have been very cold, we each admitted that our suffering was less than it would have been with the thermometer twenty degrees above zero in the raw atmosphere sometimes experienced at home.

I also discovered a great mistake on the part of the colored boy who drove us to the Falls. He tied up his ears so warmly with "comforters" and furs, that they became moist from perspiration; and then, when a displacement of the covering let in the outer air, they were not only all the more susceptible to the frost, but liable to instantly freeze. This hint may serve to caution "white folks" against too much fussy bundling up instead of endeavoring to keep the exposed features dry, and warm from within.

Hon. Lieutenant-Colonel W. R. Marshall, the present very popular Governor of Minnesota. (1868.)

Impatient "Sight-seers," Starting on a Tour.

Many tourists who annually visit St. Paul are sure to stop at *Park Place Hotel*, which is generally filled with gay cavaliers and charming belles from Eastern and Southern cities. The edifice stands upon Summit avenue, in the vicinity of the State Capitol, and nearly all its two hundred windows overlook the city. The waters of the majestic river, and the colossal bluffs beyond, give a picturesque and singularly romantic background to the extended view. The apartments are all well-furnished and airy, and many of them especially arranged for the convenience and comfort of families. And there is a shady park adjoining the house, in which the ladies may amuse themselves at croquet and other health-improving games, while the little ones drive "goat-carts" and extemporize circuses, if they will. And then at even-tide, when tell-tale blushes are hidden from sight, and the honeyed words of panting ardor fall in accents soft and low, "the old love or the new" may sigh or dream there beneath the foliage of the trees. Many pleasant hours were spent in the Park Place Hotel by some who now have passed away. But in their places another and another throng of buoyant hearts return from year to year.

A *Hungry* Tourist Left Behind.

The *Summit House* commands a fine view of the city and surrounding country—the panoramic perspective reaching eight to ten miles down the Mississippi, four miles up the same river, and at least fifteen miles up the enchanting valley of the Minnesota, which lies between frowning high hills, where the flashing steel-blue waters of its serpentine stream resemble a poetical vision of beauty, appearing and disappearing among the green verdure of fairy meadows and miniature trees. The old trading-post of Mendota is plainly in sight; and the quaint little church of St. Peter's can also be seen. In Dakota dialect, the word *mendota* signifies "meeting of the waters." And there we can behold the great Father of Rivers caressing his beautiful daughter, as she seems to come laughingly and lovingly unto his panting, broad bosom. The Summit House is a large, comfortable, and well-kept hotel, situated upon the very verge of the great bluff overlooking the mighty river, and immediately upon Summit avenue, the *boulevard* of the aristocratic part of the city, with its magnificent residences and suburban villas, all continually enlivened by equipages dashing along the beautiful and shady drive. It is not a commercial house; being more particularly frequented by wealthy tourists and pleasure-seekers, whose refined tastes enable them to realize the enjoyment of such a delightful retreat.

Commercial people, business men and hurrying travelers, frequent the *Merchants' Hotel;* which, though immensely large and "roomy," was never known to have an empty bed. Its contiguity to the levee and railroad depots, is some inducement to strangers. But the great popularity of Col. Shaw, the "jolly landlord," would keep any house continually filled, if his acquaintances expected to find him there. When I say his acquaintances, I mean all those who have once tested his hospitality. It is now a generally admitted fact that many hotel proprietors are entirely too autocratic for their position. And I once overheard the unsocial monarch of a great *caravansera* in his closet-sanctum bewailing a lack of the popularity he so much craved! But Col. Shaw is always to be *seen*. And he is sure to have a welcome smile and a cordial shake of the hand for either rich or poor who seek food and shelter in his house. The reader will remember that Lady Levasseur and Fleurette made their home at this hotel for several months after arriving in St. Paul.

It was at the Merchants' Hotel where I became acquainted with his highness (?) *Po-go-na-ghe-shick*, the erratically misanthropic Chippeway chief, whose familiar title, from some analogical inference totally beyond my exploration of "Injun lore," is admitted even by himself to be Hole-in-the-day. He was partly inclined to assist in the extermination of the white race as demonstratively proposed by the Sioux in '62; but fortunately his hereditary abhorrence for Little Crow deterred him from joining in the slaughter. And thus he escaped the vengeance that would have overtaken him as it did his mortal enemy. With bitter contempt he informed me how his (Chippeway) grandfather bestowed that ornithological sobriquet upon the grandfather of his late foe because the old fellow was so proud of wearing a *crow's skin* across his breast like a shield. He also expressed much delight when alluding to the manner of Little Crow's death. That wicked old Sioux perished in the vicinity of *Minne-Wakan*, or Devil Lake, whither he fled, vainly hoping to escape pursuit. And visitors to St. Paul may now see his skeleton among the curious relics on exhibition in the rooms of the Minnesota Historical Society. He was formerly chief of the Light-foot Band, who inhabited the village of Kaposia, a locality on the opposite side of the river, a few miles below the city, and now called Pig's Eye. His Indian name was *Tah-o-ah-ta-doo-ta*, His Scarlet People."

But whenever Hole-in-the-day visits St. Paul, his excessive inebriety is sure to terminate in jail. He said to me, "Chippeway chief love rum. White man, stranger, much-whiskers (long-beard), come drink with Injun. No? Augh! Then big Injun drink for white man too. Rum! Big Injun drink much rum!" He soon kicked up a pleasant little row, and somebody called in two strong policemen to represent the municipal law. His correct portrait is on the next page.

PO-GO-NA-GHE-SHICK; or "Hole in the Day." The number of Eagle Plumes on his head indicate how many murders he has committed; but tell us of no good he ever did.

CHAPTER XXVI.

The Drives around St. Paul are numerous and delightful. They include views of transparent lakes, rapid streams, verdant mountain ranges fading away on the distant horizon, leaping cascades, wild and rugged ravines, primeval forests, cool bubbling springs, vine-embowered cottages, dark gloomy caves, vast rolling prairies, grain fields and farms, gigantic bluffs, and the great Father of Waters—more wonderful than all!

By driving three miles to the south-east, a panoramic view may be had from the top of Mount Prospect. But to be realized, the eye must see all that as it really is. Description will fail to paint its beauty here. There is the city, away down below, apparently a variegated cluster of miniature abodes, where Liliputians might dwell near the banks of the grandly beautiful stream which bears upon its silvery bosom those floating palaces, with their banners of "red, white and blue" streaming in the breeze, while bands of music pour forth sweet lullabies or melodiously inspire the balmy air. And then, through dim distance far beyond, the enchanting scene becomes "absorbed, like memory in a dream!"

"The Round Trip" is about twenty-three miles in all. First, up the river-drive; and while dashing out Summit avenue there is a grand view of the mighty stream and the great, long bluff beyond. That solitary pine, beneath which I sat so long in reverie one November night, may also be seen away over there near the curious mound of round blue stones, where, at the rising of each full moon, Old Betz is sure to add still another silent memento in evidence of eternal grief for her first-born child. Then, a few minutes at Fountain Cascade, with a peep at the mouth of that unexplored Cave, out of which ever flows a bright rivulet of delicious water. The "Fairies' Glen," with its tiny *jet d'eau*, and also the romantically spurting *Mazas-ka*, or "silvery fall," point the way to Bridal Veil, Silver Cascade (which I have had drawn and engraved for the reader), and the Mineral Springs. The roaring of "many waters" will break upon the ear, as the beautiful cities of St. Anthony and Minneapolis appear, with a showery mist sparkling in the sunlight between them, to startle the beholder's mind after calmly dreaming upon the river scenery of gorges and bluffs that were passed in the delightful journey thither.

Then across the Suspension Bridge (which, I am told, was originally devised and erected by the intrepid Frank Steele, that pioneering gentleman who built the first saw-mill in the State, near the great Falls. He also started the first lumber-train in that region, by hitching a single ox to a rude cart, and now virtually owns a large tract of land on the other side of the river, including the Falls of Minnehaha, Fort Snelling, and the Ferry near the fort, worth nearly half a million dollars).

While crossing the river at a compulsory gait of "not faster than a walk," there is a fitting pause to call up the legend of Anpetusapa, whose jealousy was aroused by the presence of a rival wife, whom her husband brought into his teepee. She took her infant child in her arms and entered a canoe above the Falls. Then, pushing the frail bark out into the swift current of the mighty stream, she chanted a death-dirge while plunging down among the boiling waters below. That was many years before the first pale-face saw the Falls; and in the morning mist the Indians believe that they can still perceive the spirit of the mother, with her child clinging around her neck, while her wailing death-song swells above the loud cataract roar of the element into which she disappears.

I fancy there is no Indian wife now living in Dakota Land who would consider the presence of one or a dozen rivals in her husband's teepee sufficiently aggravating to warrant the immortalizing of her name in that tragically romantic way. The Indians originally called the great falls *Kaboh Bikah*, which signifies "Broken Rocks;" and they now bestow that name upon the Falls of Minnehaha. Having crossed over, the next enjoyment should be a sumptuous dinner at the "Nicollet House." After which, while smoking a cigar (if the ladies do not object), an extensive view of the City of Minneapolis and its surroundings may be obtained from the lofty cupola of that grand hotel. A glance at the aqueous and mechanical wonders of those immense roaring and rumbling mills need not take long; and then the coachman will announce that he is ready for motion again. In turn, the "Laughing Waters," Fort Snelling, the valley of the Minnesota River, and Mendota will be seen. There is another legend connected with Pilot Knob, that great, dark bluff beyond where the rivers come together.

More than a hundred years ago, Eagle Eye, the son of a great war prophet, won the love of a maiden called Scarlet Dove. And while on a hunting expedition near the "Lake of Tears," he was accidentally killed by a friend. But he uttered the name of Scarlet Dove with his last breath. After mourning a few days and cutting her flesh, she subsided into silent grief, and wrapped the corpse of her lover in skins to carry upon her back all through the long day's march. At night she laid it out upon a scaffold erected with her own hands. And thus she continued wearily carrying the ghastly corpse by day and mourning beneath it at night, for more than a hundred miles!

Finally arriving at Pilot Knob, Scarlet Dove built her last scaffold overlooking the spot where the antique chapel of St. Peter now stands. Placing the remains of Eagle Eye thereupon, she took her *portage* strap with which she had been carrying them so far and so long, and then hung herself to the scaffold and died.

After crossing the "Magic Ferry," the road may be up the high hill, or along the meandering glen. In either choice, the mind will be entirely lost in rapture made delicious with a mental comparison of the poetically romantic names of *Osceola* and *Minneineeopa* while rolling back into the bright new City of St. Paul, scarcely conscious whether the past six hours were enchanting reality or a kaleidoscopic delusion; and all at a trifling cost, as proven by the reasonable charges of the livery men, who, smiling, inquire "How were you pleased?"

Lake Como is three miles to the north, through a rolling and romantic "oak opening," which terminates at a remarkably pleasant spot. The waters of the lake are the clearest I ever saw. And millions of fish may be seen darting and leaping in those scaly pastimes peculiar to the finny tribe. Hotels, summer residences, and rural cottages adorn the vicinity, and wealthy citizens love to congregate there. Equipages, quite as stylish as anything in New York City, are frequently met going to or returning from the lake.

The track is particularly delightful on a summer evening. Lovers choose it after sundown, in the soft twilight, or beneath the gentle rays of the silvery moon.

A twilight drive out there is very pleasant in November. I ascertained that fact by riding thither with Mr. Webb, the owner of that celebrated team, *Beauty* and *Fashion*, as shown in the illustration at the beginning of this chapter. *Beauty* is a superb iron-gray, and *Fashion* a splendid black. They flew out to the lake in fine style; and so swiftly, that I was obliged to shut one eye and hold on to my hat. It was a dashing flight, and terminated very unexpectedly to me in a contest and a sensation.

Just beyond the hill overlooking the city, I noticed that Webb seemed rather uneasy, and I asked him the cause.

"He's coming!" said Webb, in a feeble tone of voice, followed by an encouraging chirp to *Fashion!*

"Who's coming?" quoth I, with a look of inquiry through the corner of my open eye.

"Farmer Denton! I hate to let him pass; but his team beats anything I ever saw!"

I heard a terrific clattering of hoofs in the rear, and began to feel my own blood rising.

"Pull tighter!" I suggested, with a nudge.

"Can't pull any tighter than I am!"

"Then sing out, and let 'em go!" was my next suggestion.

"That won't do; they'll break and run!"

"Keep 'em steady, then!" I said. "And look alive, now!"

Quickly doubling up my forefinger, I thrust it into my mouth. The clattering of Denton's team behind us seemed to come nearer and nearer at a very rapid gait; and Webb groaned:

"By George! I believe he's bound to pass!"

At that instant, I blew with all my might. And such a blast! *Beauty* and *Fashion* must have fancied the shrill scream to be an Indian war-whoop, or some other sudden premonition of terrible destruction. It was at least a tolerable imitation of a full-grown locomotive signal.

"Hall'ow!" ejaculated Webb, as his horses shot ahead like two wild arrows.

But the alarm that put his horses down to a quicker gait, broke up Denton's team. And so we arrived at Como first.

Farmer Denton afterward said: "That wan't fair!"

Perhaps not. Yet fair or foul, it forever settled the contest between his bays, and Webb's gray and black; and I am quite sure that the gentleman farmer will never pass *Beauty* and *Fashion* again, while Webb holds their reins.

But that same evening, after our return to St. Paul, I

saw Farmer Denton, and Mr. Dalrymple, who is commonly called the "Minnesota Farmer," "confidentially" seated *vis-a-vis* in the remotest corner of the gentlemen's parlor at the International Hotel, and evidently discussing the merits of some new enterprise. I judged what the nature of their *tete-a-tete* might be from the meditative attitude of Dalrymple, whose wide-brimmed hat of "Southern dimension" and style, slantingly concealed his features, while Denton vigorously manipulated the tip of his nose—a very inelegant but apparently soothing habit, to which he always was addicted when absorbed in speculative deliberation. Perhaps it would interest the reader to learn that Dalrymple had something of a wheat crop last season. From *only* one thousand and seven hundred acres of land, he gathered over thirty-five thousand bushels of grain; which, at the price then ruling the market, certainly netted him a comfortable little income. No wonder they call him the "Minnesota Farmer!" And tourists who are interested in modern agriculture will be pleased to form a personal acquaintance with him, and learn to what an immense extent he is carrying it on. He is an unassuming, intelligent and pleasant man. I may add that he and Denton are very intimate friends.

And while those representative farmers were maturing their plans for greater aggrandizement in the future, I luckily slipped into a current of simple events, which unexpectedly led me on to an interesting, if not actually startling discovery.

In the second chapter of this extemporaneously written volume of heteroscian characters and agglomerated scenes, there is an allusion to a *Lost Key*, which I accidentally found one day. I will here explain what that means; and at the same time reveal how it enabled me

The "First Shanty" erected by a white man on the romantic bluff of Im-in-i/as-ka, that beautiful locality where the "Bright New City of St. Paul is so grandly flourishing now.

to unlock the mystery which had been so long concealing the ultimate fate of Pierre Parrant, the notorious old whisky-trafficker, who impiously retarded the good results labored for by the better part of the community identified with the early history of St. Paul.

But first I will simply recur to that adventure near the square rock below Mendota, where Kaskadino and Old Betz each played a part in lieu of Florinda. During the encounter of the treacherous half-breed and Parrant, the latter was supposed to have been killed. But almost immediately after the tragedy his body and his canoe disappeared. And the following day he was seen back again in his whisky-shanty at St. Paul. His head was bandaged, and he looked remarkably pale. He seemed to be unusually active; but during the entire day was not heard to speak. At night, a candle was left burning near his bed until it flickered out at the end of the wick. The next morning Parrant could not be found.

Nearly a quarter of a century had elapsed after the disappearance of the old whisky-trader, when, while Denton and Dalrymple were discussing their plans, as already stated, I made the acquaintance of an "Overseer," who was superintending a gang of laborers engaged in the work of opening the route for the upper division of the St. Paul and Chicago Railway, at that time just begun. The Overseer was a good-natured man, and kindly invited me to drive down and see how they got along. But the invitation did not strike me as being a very tempting one. However, just then Professor Dodge chanced to join us; and he said, "Go, by all means!" I accordingly thanked the man, and promised to come.

The name of Ossian E. Dodge is familiar to almost

every one in the United States. As a poet, a musician and a wit, he is quite inimitable. Thousands remember him as the editor of the "Boston Literary Museum!" At present he is one of the most enterprising geniuses in St. Paul. He went to Minnesota, some years ago, for the health of one of his little boys. The lad was soon afflicted with very rosy cheeks, and the father enthusiastically concluded to stay. Having already laid up a snug fortune by the exercise of his talents as a writer and a vocalist, not only in this country, but nearly all over the world, he said to himself:

"I'll travel no further! Paradise is here!"

But Professor Dodge is endowed with one of those extraordinary intellects which are too irrepressible for inactivity anywhere. And he is remarkably fond of blending ideality with the substantial requirements of life; in which rare peculiarity he is more than a match for a dozen "wiseacres" who persist in ciphering out original problems by exploded or obsolete rules. He has invested largely in city lots, and also built a number of model cottages, each one of them being ornamentally designated by an appropriate name. Indeed, he is never at a loss to find the right name for anything. He dwells in *Alpine Cottage*, an unique edifice, constructed to suit himself. His extensive Cabinet of Indian relics, curiosities culled from nature and produced by art, including many antiquities and modern inventions, is not surpassed by that of any other gentleman in this country. Among the relics of historic interest treasured up by Professor Dodge, is the "sacred pipe," or *Calumet of Peace*, formerly owned by Winnesheik, the war-chief of the Winnebago nation. (The pipe is seen in the hands of the chief as he "squatted" to have his photograph taken for the engraving which adorns the second chapter of this volume.) It was made from a very fine-grained, soft red-stone, quarried from the "Red-stone Ledge" of the Yellow-stone River. There are two colors used for Indian calumets. The *blue* represents the "good spirit of peace;" the *dull red*, that of the "evil spirit of war." The "evil" is esteemed more than the "good." Indian like! They call the red-stone *eyanshah*. When thoroughly polished, it is not only impervious to acids, but perfectly infusible.

So sacred have the Indians considered this stone, that for nearly fifty years they guarded the quarry night and day from the approach of white men. But, since the great massacre of '62, there is no holy ground to the foot of the pale-face in any part of Minnesota. The Winnesheik pipe, for many generations, was used by the head chiefs at the close of their hostilities with other bands, as a pipe of peace or treaty contract. A few years ago, Hon. A. T. Sharp, then Mayor of Wabasha, by legal skill and many months of untiring labor, succeeded in saving to Winnesheik and his band a large and valuable tract of land, which had been "jumped" by speculative sharpers. In gratitude for that service, Winnesheik called upon Mayor Sharp one morning and said:

"You serve poor Indian and refuse gold! Indian heart big! warm! grateful! Indian give as pledge of endless love what money no buy. Take this pipe, hundred years in my family, and remember Winnesheik!"

Major Sharp subsequently presented the pipe to Professor Dodge. But, aside from the innumerable curiosities in *Alpine Cottage*, it is a peaceful sanctuary of domestic bliss, made bright and happy by the perpetual smiles of a beautiful and loving wife.

Dodge dined with me the day after I accepted the

17*

Overseer's invitation. We fared sumptuously at the International Hotel, and then drove down to look at the workmen on the line of the new railway.

Just before our arrival at the scene of operation, there had been quite an excitement among the men in consequence of discovering some portions of a human skeleton, which they unavoidably exhumed while delving at a point near the bank of the Mississippi River. They were then in the act of replacing the bones in the earth, just beyond the line, as we alighted.

"What's that?" cried Dodge, at the sight of such a crowd around one spot.

"Ah, an' be dad, your honor, ets the decayed remanes uv a bhloody Injun baste, shure's me metherr's name wus Biddy Mucklevarney!" replied a Celtic individual attached to the very short stem of an inexpensive but unpleasantly odoriferous pipe.

"That's so!" coincided the Overseer. "No doubt we shall find lots of 'em between here and Hastings. The Injuns did nothing but fight and kill one another hereabouts, for I don't know how many hundred thousand years 'fore us white folks made 'em stop!"

"Put that down!" Dodge murmured in my ear. "Item one. Fine enough for a large book anywhere in Minnesota!"

After viewing the pieces of grim and frightful anatomy, we proceeded to inspect the locality where they had been found. And there I trod upon a curiously shaped object and stooped to pick it up. Upon close examination, it proved to be a formidably large knife. With considerable hammering we removed the adhesive rust, and saw an unintelligible inscription. Then I looked at Dodge for some suggestion.

"Here's another!" said the Overseer, handing us what

proved to be a very much neglected double-barreled pistol. I thought it was sadly out of repair. And, engraved upon the upper stock-plate of that, we saw another alphabetical signum. And then Dodge looked at me for my opinion. But I had arrived at no conclusion.

Dodge and I continued to exchange glances, until at length he said, " If you don't keep them I shall!"

Thereupon I expressed much gratitude for his suggestion, and threw the old weapons into the bottom of the buggy, saying, "We'll take them home and decipher those inscriptions!"

"I comprehend!" shrugged Dodge. "You want to find the plot for another one of those marvelous stories which you are addicted to writing."

I smiled as ghastly as usual. We then lighted fresh cigars; during the process of which I mumbled, "You're very clever at surmising."

"Just so! I 'tended guessing school once—half a day," was his quick retort.

Hastening to *Alpine Cottage*, Dodge and I immediately began to scour the old pistol and the rusty knife.

Dodge's curiosity equaled mine; and we went to work unfastidiously, in true scullion style. Indeed, he was much delighted with the promise of a solution to something perhaps worth knowing.

" What *are* you at?" cried the sweet voice of Mrs. Dodge, who came into the kitchen rolling her pretty optics with inquisitive surprise.

"That's a mystery to be got at by soap and sand!" said Dodge in grave response, and at the same time casting a side wink for me to see.

" More of those horrible Indian traps, I'll be bound!"

continued Mrs. Dodge with a "Humph!"—from which I inferred that she did not cherish a very exalted opinion of the aboriginal race. "If you intend greatly increasing the number of such horrible objects, it will be necessary to erect a building expressly to hold them. The house is now entirely filled with curiosities. Perhaps you and the Colonel had better establish a hypodramatic museum in St. Paul.* He might introduce the performing dogs and horses, and other living animals, while you exhibit the inanimate wonders of the world, extemporize poetry, and make funny speeches!"

"Bravo! And 'twould pay, too!" cried Dodge. "You see, Fannie, dear——"

He did not finish his sentence. My scouring at the old knife was successful; and I abruptly broke in, "Look here; I have it now! The first letter is T. The next A. Then s, and, and——"

"And HAE!" Dodge articulated for me.

"Why, it spells *Tashae!*" I cried. "That was the name of a fur trader who lived at Selkirk Colony, twenty-five years ago!"

"And here's the other name!" exclaimed Dodge. "P-a-r-r-a-n-t—'PIG'S EYE!' sure as you live!"

And there it was, engraved in plain English upon the upper stock-plate of the old pistol.

"You're a lucky fellow!" Dodge remarked to me the next day. "Mr. Williams, Secretary of the Historical Society, would have given anything for Parrant's old pistol."

"Can't help that!" was my reply. "After I came here all the way from New York, for the avowed purpose of compiling and writing up an illustrated history of St. Paul, he announced in the editorial columns of

---

* Since then, Dodge *has* taken a lease of "INGERSOLL HALL."

the 'Pioneer' that he intended to do the same thing. And then another gentleman made a similar announcement in the 'Daily Press.' Mr. McClung published a like intention. And, as if to frighten me off entirely, a country editor added his name to the list of my rivals. Thus at least four members of the Minnesota press, each of them infinitely better posted than I am, and much more competent in every other respect, have opened their 'masked batteries' upon me, while I have not even a squib-cartridge to pop or 'fizzle' in return."

I paused at this period for Dodge to reply. But he continued to smoke his cigar without any sign of speech, and so I went on to say, "*Five* Histories of St. Paul at the same time, will be rather too many; and, therefore, I shall unvalorously, but expediently, retire!"

Then Dodge took a long pull at his cigar, and hurriedly blew out a mouthful of smoke to say, "Go ahead and write your book, old boy. I'll bet on you!"

I bowed in acknowledgment of his kindly-intended response, and suggested that he should have a fresh cigar. He approved of the suggestion, and I resumed:

"Mr. Williams can send down and get what is left of old Parrant's bones. They'll do to place in the rooms of the Historical Society, beside the skeleton of Tah-o-ah-ta-doo-ta, alias 'Little Crow,' for the inspection of inquisitive people. But, with your permission, I shall retain the pistol and the knife, and leave to him and his equally ambitious contemporaries, the coveted and remunerative task of doing up St. Paul, separately or conjointly, in as many *histories* as they please. Meanwhile, I *can* retire to the peaceful quietude of that obscure little village sportively called Gotham, but anciently known as New Amsterdam, and more recently sobriqueted New York. And as a denizen of that remote hamlet, I might boastingly say that it has some prominence in connection with the current events of the day because of its contiguity to the more noted localities of Hoboken, Coney Island, Tilletudlum and Tubby Hook. There, in undisturbed seclusion, I will write—aye, write a book! Nor shall the 'subject matter' thereof 'even ever' so slightly interfere with the grand project which the aforesaid gentlemen 'collectively' have in view. And *such* a book!" I jocosely emphasized, for the amusement of Dodge. "Such a book it shall be. And the name ——"

"What?" interrupted Dodge, suddenly roused to a demonstrative pitch of inquiry. "What will be the name of your book?"

"*Dakota Land!*" I spouted, in mock theatrical display.

"Good! The best idea you ever had in all your life!" Dodge exclaimed in a similar melodramatic style. "And 'if 'twere done when 'tis done, then 'twere well 'twere done quickly!' And, what's more, I'll help you if I can!"

A few days after that conversation, I left St. Paul. And since then, Dodge has proven, in more ways than one, that he is not only a true friend to me, but also the friend of every honest man! His frequent encouragement by letter has inspired me in the task and considerably lightened the tedium of my toil. May God bless him and all that he loves in this life, and not forget him when he dies!

But neither he nor I can tell how old Parrant's body came to be buried in that lonely spot, through which the track of the St. Paul and Chicago Railway now runs. And if Mr. Williams, or "any other man" should meet with better success than we have in elucidating the problematic fate of "Old Pig's Eye," I trust that the public will be duly informed of the singular facts.

The "ghost story" which I have heard in connection with the old whisky-shanty will not be doubted by credulous people who believe in spiritualism. For my part, I am unable to arrive at any satisfactory conclusion in reference to what they say. Those who knew him intimately before he went away, still persist in saying that a strange light frequently glimmered in the room where he slept the last time in St. Paul. And my informant assures me that he can remember hearing old Parrant's voice late one night several months after he disappeared. He thought it sounded as if the old miser was then in a violent encounter with some person. "Let me have it, or you die!" was uttered perfectly plain. At least, so my informant declares. He was casually passing by the shanty at the time, and also observed a dim light through the small window. But when he approached to learn the cause, the voice was silent, and the light vanished with a fitful flicker, like that of a tallow candle burning the last particle of grease at the end of the wick. Another time he saw a light at the window when there was every reason to believe that no living being could be in the shanty. Again he approached, more cautiously than before, in hope of solving the mystery. But, just as he came near enough to see through the window, one or two feeble flashes extinguished the last glimmer, and left him in a frightened state of feeling for several days afterward.

Perhaps when the gentleman here alluded to learns what I have disclosed in this volume, he will come to the conclusion that old Parrant's spirit did actually return to the shanty every night in quest of some treasure concealed there. Most likely this will be his theory, inasmuch as he has always differed from a general belief that the ill-fated wretch was extremely poor. He has contended from the first that Parrant was rich; but, being miserly in the extreme, carefully buried every piece of gold that came into his grasp. Therefore, if he became the victim of an assassin, it is probable that his buried treasures will never be obtained.

The knife found with Parrant's skeleton was undoubtedly the same that Kaskadino stole from Tashae—and which he unintentionally dropped in the sandstone gorge of the bluff near the square rock below Mendota, where he had such a desperate struggle to rob the old whisky-seller of the gold intended for Florinda, as had been agreed upon that day at the shanty in St. Paul—now almost a quarter of a century ago.

An individual supposed to be Kaskadino was among the savages who escaped justice after participating in the massacre of '62. But the laws of mortality will shortly bring him to a final account. He is getting old, and must soon yield up his life. From the perpetration of that remorseless crime, instigated by Florinda, which sent Leonore's mother to a grave near the waters of the Red River, he went on with bad deeds, until eventually deserting his numerous family by flight, to join a marauding band of outlaw Indians, who were the cruelest demons engaged in that work of death and plunder attributed to the Sioux.

Tashae has already gone to settle his account. Since writing those allusions to his *liaison* with Florinda, his unsuccessful design upon Leonore and her mother, and his subsequent discomfiture at Mendota, I have discovered the existence of a very estimable gentleman of the same name, who is now living in the settlement at Red

River; and in justice to the latter, I shall here state that there was no relationship between them.

But I am obliged to leave future historians the task of unraveling the mysterious connection previously existing between Parrant and the incomprehensible Florinda, who subsequently committed suicide in the Levasseur mansion, before its destruction by fire.

And I will merely suggest, in consideration of the everlasting benefit which he conferred upon future generations, that the skeleton of "Old Pig's Eye" should be carefully preserved as a companion to the anatomical deformity representing "His Scarlet People!"

Verily, everything about St. Paul is *marvelous* to see or hear. And tourists voyaging thither on board the *white collar* steamers of the "North-western Union Packet Company," are here informed that much of their enjoyment has been provided for by the enterprising liberality of *Commodore Davidson*, the monarch of that immense concern. His magnificent residence is situated upon Dayton's Bluff, the gigantic hill which seems to be towering immediately above the steamers as they make their final turn just before arriving at the levee of the bright new city. And in the once sacred Cavern of Wakan-tebee, all wrapt in funereal silence, those mysterious relics of the ancient dead are yet lying, far down beneath the cozy chamber where the Commodore now sleeps at night. And he is a "whole soul" man, whose popularity has won for him an enviable reputation, while recording his name among the millionaires of Minnesota. His private office, banking-house, and the executive offices of the "Company," entirely fill that elegant new block which stands directly opposite the Merchants' Hotel, and adjoining the extensive "Livery Establishment" of *Messrs. Cook & Webb.*

An Ex-Consumptive Invalid taking comfort in Minnesota. He weighed little over a hundred pounds on arriving there, but when the Author last heard from him, his weight was not less than two hundred and thirty-six.

One more paragraph, and then this chapter will be done. To avoid the inconvenience of answering anticipated applications for photograph pictures of Tashae's old knife or Parrant's old pistol, I will state that I deposited them in Barnum's Museum, on my return to New York. They were hung up near the collection of Indian Portraits, just at the top of the first flight of stairs—as I then thought, all nice and secure. But alas! a fire broke out during the coldest night in winter, at that unseasonable hour when editors and authors are generally supposed to be in bed and asleep. I rode down Broadway about noon the next day; and where the Museum so gaily stood the evening before, I then saw only a magnificent spectacle of ruin, all enveloped in strange and fantastic forms of ice. So I am sorry to say that those singular relics are now unavoidably mixed up with the ashes of snakes and bears!

Happy Tourists **Homeward Bound.**

Scene on the Minnesota River, from near Fort Snelling. The Chippeways call this stream *Ashkibogisibi*, or "Green-Leaf River."

CHAPTER XXVII.

NOTWITHSTANDING the apparently indifferent and contemptuous feeling of Madame Zorah at the time of her abrupt departure from the house of Levasseur, it was but a turbulent prelude to bitter regrets. For the Major had scarcely quit Paris when she began to realize the deplorable consequences of her folly. In the perpetual whirl of excitement, intensified by novel extravagances and costly pleasures, she seemed to have forgotten the existence of any possible uncertainty that might sustain the then exalted position of herself and Leonore. When they both indignantly flouted from the presence of the then irate man, and defiantly scorned his support and protection, neither of them seriously estimated the enormity of their individual losses. The demonstrative episode was not merely one of those periodical freaks of passionate ebulliency which immoderately idolized beauties are specially privileged to by their doting and indulgent lords, and therefore necessarily susceptible of that delicious reconciliation generally associated with the terminal crisis of a lover's quarrel or a family jar. It was too serious for that. Madame's untimely impertinence widened the trifling breach to the impassable width of a boundless chasm, and thus destroyed all opportunity for connubial restoration by the personal exercise of an *entente cordiale* between them.

A novelist has the power of creating characters at will, and placing them in any conceivable position that his fancy may choose; and if I were now writing a romance, instead of narrating a series of biographical events, the relative circumstances of Major Levasseur and Leonore should be vastly different from what the reader finds them here. And the devoted grandma would accordingly occupy a less prominent position in the story. But then, if all these seemingly preposterous realities were omitted, I would not have any remarkable developments to make. So, with a strict adherence to the most extraordinary facts, I shall proceed to state that when Leonore abandoned Levasseur at Madame's command, she was unconsciously opening the first scene in the last act of the petit drama of her own life, which destiny seemed to have marked for a double tragedy in the end!

It was quite natural that Madame should rave, and that Leonore should go wild with grief, when they discovered how the forsaken father had taken Irene from the convent. And why not take her with him? He innocently and sincerely believed them when they told him that she was Lady Levasseur's child. And thus at length they perceived the fatal consequence of that long-fostered lie!

Tears will destroy facial beauty in a very short time;

and Leonore's great, lustrous, black eyes were transformed into optical frights. Madame said that would never do. She could not be seen in such a plight by the gallant nobleman who admired her so.

"Let the nobleman go, in welcome!" she wept and stormed. "I want Irene! Oh, it's all your fault, grandma! He has left us forever; and even Irene will never love me any more! You have made me incur his hate! Oh dear, there is no one to love me now! But, grandma, I say you must and you shall bring Irene back! And I can not live with the thought that, perhaps, he has returned to the arms of his beautiful wife! Oh, I'm sure she will forgive him; for he is so handsome, so noble, so good, and so loving and kind! Grandma, I must get back the treasures of my heart or die!"

A speedy repentance, a frantic struggle, and then the dreary curtain would fall in mental darkness brought on by despair!

And so they followed Levasseur across the sea. Madame knew that he was a client of the great law firm of Crane & Burr; and, upon their arrival in New York, she inquired at the office in Wall street to find out where he was. Unluckily, they had just been notified of his supposed death in Tennessee, and without any hesitation told her all they knew. She asked only one more question, and then hurried back to Leonore, carrying the fatal news.

"Well, well," impatiently cried Leonore. "You found him; and we shall meet again very soon! Why don't you speak?"

Madame related what she had heard, and Leonore fairly shrieked, "No, no! Not dead! That can not be!"

But Madame bowed her head and murmured, "Alas, they say it is true!"

"I will not believe it," persisted Leonore. "They told you what they knew was false, to prevent our meeting! Yes, yes; I see what they want to do! A *ruse* to deceive me. Ah, they'll fail in that. But Irene! Where is she?"

"Gone! They say she can not be found!" sighed Madame.

"It's all a lie!" screamed Leonore. "I will go and see them myself! They dare not tell me so. Come, quick!" And she seized Madame violently by the arm, ejaculating, "Now! Now!"

Madame could not appease her short of immediate compliance with that sudden resolve to go. And as they went forth, Leonore half deliriously reiterated, "Be quick! Come, hurry! Oh, why don't you run?"

They reached the law office, and were shown into a private room. The great Mr. Crane received them with some condescension for a man like him; and he certainly had a particular motive when *he* was so respectful to the former mistress of his wealthy client, whom he supposed to be dead. Perhaps there would be additional litigation, and that was whereof he rapidly accumulated abundant riches. Yet, despite Leonore's impatience, he leisurely replied to her questions; and when he felt his dignity touched by her doubting insinuations, he imperiously said:

"If you desire anything more than the truth, apply to some other counsel. We never prevaricate here. I repeat that Major Levasseur is dead, and his daughter has not been found!"

To that Leonore mildly replied, "Husband dead! Irene gone!" For a moment she seemed to reflect;

and then, as if gradually realizing the solution of a difficult problem, her eyes expanded to their utmost capacity, while every muscle in her face harmonized with the startling expression. Drawing a heavy breath, she uttered a slight shriek, and smiled with a vacant stare. The next moment Mr. Crane bounded from his chair, while he and Madame were both appalled to hear her neighing a maniac's wild laugh.

Leonore was insane!

Mr. Crane sent for a carriage to take her home; and all that day, and for many days to come, the fair lunatic continually wandered about her chamber as if seeking some one. Occasionally, she would burst into hysterical paroxysms of insensate laughter; but she was much oftener heard mournfully articulating:

"Irene! Husband! My child—*not hers!* He is dead! And *she* killed him, because he loved me so! Now they are both gone! Irene was to be the heiress; and they have lost her somewhere in the great world! Lost! Dead! Oh, this choking at my heart and this pain in my head! I feel it here, and here! The day is very tiresome and long. Will the night come soon? Ah, grandma made me do it all!"

The beautiful maniac could moan, and talk, and laugh; but she would never shed another tear!

Madame visited the great law office again to inquire if they had any tidings of Irene; and then they told her that Levasseur was *not* dead! They said he was still living, and had taken Irene with him to the City of St. Paul. And, without learning what he had gone there for, she gladly hastened back to tell Leonore the joyful news! But alas, reason had entirely left that beautiful form. She could not understand. Oh, how sad it was to see those magnificent eyes all swollen and staring like

18

globes of glass! Her lips were blue, and a strange pallor o'erspread her cheeks. Yet her heaving bosom was soft and warm, and her heart went on throbbing as it did when she felt happy with conscious love. But now it was utterly devoid of any manifestation to indicate the slightest emotion of a soul! Pity it was that Levasseur could not look upon her then, and contemplate the speedy transition of loveliness to that inevitable doom of even the fairest of the fair.

In vain did Madame try to make Leonore comprehend the joyful news. She uttered endearing words and lavished caresses; but the only uttered responses she could get were like live coals of fire heaped upon her own head.

"Yes, lost!" laughed Leonore, as though with joy. "Away in the boundless world! My child—not hers! She would have been his heiress, too. Dead! And I loved him so much!" Then she would look sad, and continue, "They are all gone now! But grandma made me drive them away! Oh, my head! And there is such a weight on my heart!"

Madame was an old woman. She would soon be threescore and ten! Her faculties were failing fast, and the terrible results of a misspent life began to palsy her senses, too. One moment she thought of appealing to the law, and the next she resolved to personally see Levasseur, and either coerce his return, or upon her knees beg and implore him to take pity on Leonore. She would confess her crime in substituting Leonore's child for that of Lady Levasseur's, and go and seek the true heiress. And then she recoiled from all those propositions. She was undecided what to do, and really powerless for any decisive action.

At that juncture Levasseur returned to New York.

The letter of Messrs. Crane & Burr, which he received previous to his departure from St. Paul, announcing the arrival of Madame and Leonore for the avowed purpose of settling certain matters in the courts of law, would have caused most any other man in a similar strait to prudently avoid the needless risk of an unpleasant collision between the parties interested. And the safest guarantee for avoiding that risk would seem to be in their wide distance apart. But Levasseur never did anything like other men. He had his own way, and in all cases predicated by personally selfish decisions. It would be no injustice to say that the Major was a determinedly self-willed man. An individual possessing that predominant trait of character is more than likely to incur no little unhappiness for himself while creating an abundance of trouble, if not downright misery, for those who become associated with him in any position of life. And the past, present and future events connected with Levasseur's existence would ultimately satisfy even him that there is "a right and a wrong," which, in the choosing, leads one way to sunshine and another way to impenetrable gloom.

Having already started when the letter came to hand, he resolved to continue on. And it was quite possible that the chances of a collision would really be less in the great city, though they were near together, than by remaining at the mercy of scandal-mongers, whose thirst might not be quenched with an ocean full of tears. But, anxious to remain incognito until a secluded abode could be obtained, he took the precaution of recording an assumed name at the hotel. Yet even that did not avert the wrath to come.

And while Madame was not aware of his presence, he did not suspect the deplorable condition of Leonore.

He was in no haste to meet coming events by a visit to the office of his attorneys, where intelligence of his discarded *proteges* awaited him. But even though he was tardy in that particular inquiry, the agglomeration of variform fatalities rapidly thickened about him unawares.

Irene acted very strangely, and he could not help noticing the fact. She had changed greatly since her sojourn in Louisville, during his adventure in Tennessee; but he attributed it all to the inharmonious feelings pervading his newly organized family, and accordingly endeavored to decide upon some plan of permanent reconciliation. And while he thus exercised his mind in her behalf, she stepped out of the hotel to take a walk, leaving a letter addressed to him, in which she intimated a preference for sharing life with some one whom she loved!

He never was more astounded than when reading the contents of that letter. But still Lady Levasseur did not seem to worry herself much about Irene's choice. And Fleurette whispered, "Ma, dear, perhaps it is very wicked in me to do so, but I can not help wishing that Irene would never return!"

"Hush, darling!" was the warning reply. "Be careful that *he* does not hear what you say!"

The father then had a heavy heart, indeed! He sought Irene, but she was not to be found. With whom and whither she had eloped he could not even conjecture, much less ascertain. And the apparent apathy of his wife was so painful to him that he quite readily accused Fleurette, in his own mind, of steeling the mother's love against her natural child. Thus he permitted an ugly feeling of jealousy to enter his mind.

Yet he no longer loved Leonore. From that fatal moment, when she turned her back upon him in Paris, he had been shuddering with vivid reminiscences of the past. The mad spell was broken. And his fond wife, who was waiting for him, said that he would return just as he had done. She also said, that as he left her at night, he would reappear to her in the twilight of evening. How fully her prophecies were verified in his final restoration to her arms. She said that her spirit would not leave him—and that the old love must triumph when his heart grew sad. And thus all her predictions had come to pass!

But if Levasseur really did not wish even to see Leonore again, what would be the final consequence of his oath? Had he entirely ceased to remember the nature of that vow, while his wife was listening at the door, and Leonore unconsciously lay in his arms? And what did Madame say to him when he swore to cherish Leonore in future instead of Lady Levasseur? With his hand raised and his arm tightly grasped by the old woman, he articulated: "I solemnly swear that Leonore shall be my only love to the end of life!" Then she responded: "Your oath is recorded in the Book of Fate! Violation of it will be death!" And the sacrifice was then before his eyes.

But atonement and repentance were not both one! He had repented. Atonement would follow soon. If the words of his wife came to pass, why not dread those uttered by Madame? Yes; he would realize the terrible end, all in a very short time. Even then a strange event was about to happen. And Fleurette would be instrumental in accomplishing that. She saw a melancholy item in a morning paper, which read thus:

"Among the bodies now lying at the *Morgue* for

Prairie-View around Pembina Mountain, on the Canadian Frontier of Dakota Land.

identification, is the corpse of an apparently beautiful young lady that was discovered, some time yesterday afternoon, floating in a dock on the East River."

Fleurette could not banish that sad announcement from her mind; and the answers she received in reply to numerous questions only increased her desire to know more. And, at the solicitation of Lady Levasseur, the Major half reluctantly ordered a carriage to visit the *Morgue*. She naturally shrank from such associations; but in that instance some irresistible inspiration seemed to be urging her on.

The porter at the *Morgue* informed them that the corpse of the beautiful young lady had been identified and taken away. But whither? Fleurette must see that one in particular. She did not so much as pause to view the other bodies lying there.

The porter wrote the street and number upon a blank card, and evidently wanted to be paid for the favor. Lady Levasseur placed a dollar bill in his hand, and then he took off his hat to bow and blarney: "Thanks! You are a lady, I'm sure!"

"This is the place!" said the coachman, opening the door of the vehicle for them to alight. "A boarding-house. Mrs. Cline keeps it. Her name's on the door!"

They rang the bell, and were admitted.

"Front room, up first flight of stairs!" grunted the servant girl who received them. She did nothing more. Quite the style of reception in many boarding-houses where the scale of prices would certainly warrant some respect from the mistresses, and a little more attention, if not civility, on the part of the Celtic females who superintend the domestic performances necessarily required. But as the front room door was slightly ajar, it did not seem necessary to knock.

The Major softly peeped in, and then started back all pale, and gasping "Leonore!"

Lady Levasseur shrank from the door with the intention of quitting the house; for she remembered that name, alas, too well!

The corpse lay with its face uncovered; and those who had ever seen Leonore alive, would recognize her in death.

"You must not leave!" said the Major, in a hoarse whisper, as he tightened his fingers around his wife's arm. "She is dead! Do not permit your feelings to overcome you now. Heaven—"

"Who comes here to talk of Heaven?" wailed Madame Zorah, lifting her head off the bosom of the corpse, where she had been crouching in tearless grief. "Hah! Major Levasseur! Then you are here to exult in mockery over the destruction of my child! But you come too late; for the poison is here!" and she pressed her finger against her throat!

"Peace, woman! The occasion is unsuitable for recrimination or random talk, by you or me!"

Then, perceiving Fleurette, she naturally mistook her for Irene, and exclaimed: "So, so! And you've brought her back with you to look at her mother now!"

"I am not Irene," promptly answered Fleurette. "She has fled!"

A shadow crossed the Major's brow; and Madame started up as if to inquire for explanation, when a severe spasm pulled her down. But she muttered in half-strangling accents, "No m—mat—er! It w—will all be—be over very soon! That stuff is wor—king home! There, upon—the—the table!"

She pointed while writhing in pain; and they beheld an empty vial that told too plainly what she meant.

And with a violent effort she rose and staggered forward upon a chair.

Rousing herself, she endeavored to say something else; and began with, "Lady—lady!" and pointing at Leonore's corpse, "I ch—changed *her* babe—babe for—for *yours!*" And there she failed again.

"Oh, what is she saying?" cried Fleurette. "Do listen, ma, and try to understand!"

Then Madame hysterically resumed by saying, "I took—tock your child—child to the orphan—phan asylum—and forgot to remove—move—move!"

"What—what?" frantically implored Fleurette. "What did you forget to remove?"

"That neck—lace—of Job's—tear beads! Engraved upon—pon the locket, was the name—of my—my own child! Leonore's mother! Ah! I am dying! Hold me! Air! Oh, I want air! I am blind! Let me breathe!"

"The name upon the locket?" they cried all together, as the miserable old woman fell back into the Major's arms. "The name? The name?"

"Fleu—*Fleurette!*" came in a scarcely articulated groan. And then almost immediately a sudden and violent spasm raised her up once more, to fall back upon the corpse. Quivering there a moment, her muscles all relaxed, and her body slid down in a heap upon the floor.

"O, merciful Father!" exclaimed Lady Levasseur, kneeling in horror.

With her also knelt the Major and Fleurette!

Neither of them prayed aloud; but when they rose again, a flood of tears was streaming from each of their eyes!

"I can at least see that they are decently buried!" groaned the Major.

"Yes. I forgive them as I have already forgiven you!" replied Lady Levasseur.

And, after that terrible scene, what else could there be yet to find?

Husband and wife! Parents and child! They were all restored, while other hearts would beat no more!

But poor Irene! Where was that rash and wayward girl? Though, while reflecting upon the circumstances in which she was reared, I am more inclined to pity than to condemn! The blame rested with her mother, or rather her mother's grandma, who was an unwise preceptress for a beautiful girl. The old creature's love and affection might have been very deep and pure for the offspring of her darling grandchild; but alas! she thought too much of the vanities of the hour to instill, into the susceptible young heart such lessons as would serve to guide her happily through the temptations and vicissitudes which must inevitably come!

And Levasseur did not become aware of the actual consanguinity of himself and Leonore until after he had put her and her grandma in the grave. He then discovered all from a perusal of some letters which were among Madame's hoarded treasures. The terrible truth staggered his very reason. But it was then too late for any purpose except to make his unhappiness all the more complete; and he resolved that the secret should remain in his breast and go with him to oblivion when that grew cold. Yet, a short time before her death, Madame had also learned the fraternal relationship of Leonore's father and the man whom she so dearly loved; and in her complaints against Levasseur, at the office of Crane & Burr, she divulged the singular fact. And from that mere chance I was enabled to unravel the entire web of their fate, which may be discussed here without fear of wounding the feelings of those particularly interested, or in the least compromising any one, since a sharp contest at law has already made known to the world what Levasseur and his living wife would have concealed for the sake of Fleurette.

Nearly four years have elapsed since the flight of Irene, the accursed child of that almost incestuous alliance! And still her father does not find any one who can tell him where she is. Possibly she will never know the curse of her origin, nor how her mother became a maniac, nor yet the manner of her death. She may also remain ignorant of the melancholy fate of her great-grandma. And indeed, even now, her own soul may have already gone to join theirs beyond the grave!

Major Levasseur is failing fast. There is a fixed sorrow in his eye, and his hair is almost entirely gray. He tries to be happy; but recollection haunts him so that there is very little pleasure in what he realizes now. If wealth could smooth his path, he might pleasantly glide along to the end. If the devotion of an angel heart, which is throbbing warmly near him, could destroy the canker eating into his own, some earthly hope might be left for him still.

He perceives that Fleurette is more affectionate to him than Irene ever was. And then their wonderful resemblance haunts him. What a contrast between two lovely sisters, so perfectly alike in all the external beauties of life! And what a sorrowful reflection for their father. Yes; and far more painful *to me* than my readers will believe—for I once saw them both together; and could here relate much that is left unsaid, for reasons not necessary to explain! The world will never know all!!

But now, whenever I meet a young lady whose head

is adorned with a great profusion of exquisite, light golden hair, I inquiringly scrutinize her face. I am irresistibly and perpetually seeking for Irene. And I have seen very many tresses of light golden hair; but none so beautiful as that of the prototype daughters of Major Levasseur.

I often see Fleurette! She was married some time ago; and is now a fond mother herself, as well as a happy wife. Her husband was formerly a Navy Captain; and he did much good service at the bombardment of several of those strong fortifications defended by the rebels during the war. But he resigned when he saw her.

Their nuptial ceremony was performed at a fashionable church in New York City, and chronicled in some of the newspapers the following day. The joyful husband proposed a voyage to Europe, a tour of the Continent, and a visit to the Paris Exposition. But his bride much preferred a trip to St. Paul, where she might revel once more in the delicious atmosphere of Minnesota. And never having been there to "see and feel," of course he reluctantly assented to her choice.

Yet, instead of going direct to St. Paul, Fleurette suggested the Nicollet House, in Minneapolis, until she could settle her nerves, as she said. The circumstances of her departure from St. Paul had been rather peculiar; and she trembled somewhat at returning. However, they quietly went down to the Summit House one day. And when the Captain asked permission to "scratch his name on the register," Mr. Carpenter did not for a moment dream that he was the husband of Fleurette, "The Beauty of St. Paul." But when he saw her in the parlor, he could hardly believe his eyes. Of course he wanted to tell everybody "who had come." And such a guest would have made the other landlords in the city just as proud as he was. But that very evening Fleurette had a delightful call. Farmer Denton drove up with his "double team," not only bringing Miss Jane, but also the dog Goliah; and the Captain was amazed to see the enthusiastic meeting of that sagacious quadruped and his lovely bride. The next day there was a continual coming and going of the *élite*, who were "ever so much pleased (or delighted) to see her, though 'ma' did not come along!" Indeed, some of them were determined that she and her husband ("the Naval Officer," as Carpenter persisted in calling him) should go home with them and *stay*.

"That's all very well!" said the Captain to his bride. "But I never was fond of *staying* to test the hospitality of my friends. We'll return their calls, and dine, sup, dance, or ride, or drive, or hunt, or fish, or 'pic-nic' with them, and gladly, too. But I prefer lodging at a hotel, or on shipboard, unless it is in my own house."

Fleurette replied that there were some ladies in the city whose kindness to her dear ma and herself she could never forget. And she must visit them immediately.

"But that terrible dog!" said her husband. "I can no understand why you should make such a time over him!"

"Goliah my old preserver," laughed Fleurette. "He surely doesn't make you jealous. Remember, I have told you how he once saved my life."

"That may all be," persisted the Captain. "But it would have been quite as well if some of the *men* on board had done so in his stead."

"But they didn't, though!" retorted Fleurette, with slight derision. "And I shall always believe that no other assistance would have been in time to rescue me from drowning. Those heroically gallant gentlemen who plunge into rivers at the risk of their own lives to save others, are less numerous than you imagine. Goliah had me out of the water while Dr. Passion was still struggling in the current, and vainly shouting for help!"

"Speak of the 'Old Nick,' and he's sure to appear!" observed Mr. Carpenter, who casually entered the parlor while the Captain and Fleurette were in conversation. "Dr. Passion has just passed the window. I believe he is coming in. And here he is!"

The Vampire softly glided in, like a feline monster, fearful of making the least noise. As he removed his hat, the whole of his face suddenly dissolved into a great confusion of wrinkles and smiles. And he made a short, queer bow, while smoothly uttering, "Ah, how'de do? Ehem!" And his fat hand carefully ran through the greasy black hair upon his very round and very large head.

Then Fleurette raised her eyes with a shiver, and the Captain stared. Whereupon Mr. Carpenter courteously articulated the words of a formal introduction.

"Oh," said the Vampire, with a pathetic smile of sentiment which made the Captain frown. "I purposely came to congratulate the beauty of St. Paul! It gives me intense pleasure to see her still looking so beautiful and fair!"

Fleurette courtesied coldly in reply; and motioning to her husband that she wished to retire, he politely led her to the door, where she whispered something in his ear.

"I understand," he murmured in reply. And then, turning to Mr. Carpenter, he said: "Now then, if you are ready, sir, we will go down into the city. I wish to call on Bishop Grace and also see Father Ireland!"

"Of the Catholic religion, I presume?" inquisitively quoth the Vampire.

"No, sir; not at all. My visit to one is strictly a matter of business; the other I became acquainted with elsewhere some years ago."

And when they walked down the avenue toward the city, the Vampire did the same thing. But Mr. Carpenter felt sorry for his cool reception, and kindly inquired how long he intended to remain in St. Paul.

"Oh, business is very dull up here, now-a-days. So many *quacks;* they disgust all the invalids, and leave *us physicians* nothing to do." As the Vampire spoke thus, Carpenter quietly smiled with a slight twitch of his mustache, in his own comfortable way. But the great man also said, "I arrived here last night, and shall take a steamer back again this evening."

Since then the newspapers have published a startling case of criminality in St. Louis which seriously involved a notorious "quack," whose description corresponds with that of Dr. Passion!

But Fleurette's visit was a very pleasant one; and when they left, the Captain acknowledged that he would need no coaxing to return.

Poor Irene has not been heard from, since the hour when she fled. Where she is none can tell. And her father's mind continually wanders out into the world after the absent one. He begins to court solitude, and restlessly walks the chamber-floor while his thoughts are living over the past.

Pity mingles with love in every look and action of Lady Levasseur, when she sees how melancholy he is. And while her own eyes seem to brighten more and more, she frequently weeps for him when alone.

They travel in the summer, and visit pleasant scenes;

and yet no place nor view has attraction enough to divert **his** troubled mind. Associations of what "has been," will intrude to cast a pall upon the surface of every glad picture that meets his gaze.

But when at home, he frequently steals off to Greenwood Cemetery. And he goes there alone. He generally chooses a stormy day, when no other visitors are likely to be there. And lest his wife might know of his going, he even does not ride down in his own carriage. The coachman would talk about it, if he did. Therefore he hires a livery coach to convey him, and takes a different one each time. The gate-keeper has become accustomed to his eccentricity of a stormy day, and invariably salutes him with a nod and a smile. And while the shivering coach-horses and driver wait for him, all wet with rain, at a particular crossing of the avenues in the city of the dead, he wanders away among the tombstones and monuments, with a huge umbrella hoisted over him to effectually hide his face from the scrutiny of other visitors, if any should chance **to pass** ever so near.

A strange fancy, to steal away in a great cemetery on **a** stormy day and stroll among the sober white columns and the elaborately chiseled obelisks, which are more spectral than otherwise to an imaginatively superstitious mind. To meditate there alone beneath an immense umbrella, while the pouring rain patters down upon the marble slabs, and floods the bending grass, and washes the graveled walks so clean.

A **sad** enjoyment for one like Major Levasseur! The world would say it **was**. But the world does not know **what** is passing in his unhappy mind. The world does **not see** him wandering or standing in silent contemplation of the memorials sculptured by the living for the loved who are lost in eternal decay. Yet, he **knows and he feels** what the world cares nothing about.

And God is watching him there all the time, when he imagines himself entirely alone. Yes; and **God and his soul** go down there together with him, to commune in that retired spot upon the steep hill-side facing **the water of New York Bay**—there, not far from the **old vault near the weeping** willow tree—there, in the vicinity of that grand **floral design, carved upon** a colossal monument of **polished** marble—there, at the foot of a plainer, and seemingly sadder, *memoria technica* of white stone, upon which **he can read** the simple words of "*Zorah and Leonore!*"

And near that spot there is now an empty **tomb, entirely new,** in which a living victim of bitter remorse has willed that his own body shall be laid when he dies. **There is abundant** space in that new empty tomb **for others beside** himself. So that, perhaps, **in time to come,** those who live may also read another inscription on marble there, in which the names of Levasseur and his more than faithful wife shall both appear!

Then, perhaps, by and by, the dust of the lovely orphan victim and her avenging grandma will mingle in the earth together with that of the beautiful " angel heart" and her destroying husband, while their souls have gone to meet the **great Judgment which is Forevermore!**

I now pause in a sad reverie, and mournfully wonder if **Irene** will ever visit Greenwood, and there, on the hillside beneath the weeping willow, shed tears over the spot where her devoted grandma and **her misguided mother** both lie in the same grave?

The "Silver Cascade," between Minneapolis and St. Paul.

www.ingramcontent.com/pod-product-compliance
Lightning Source LLC
Chambersburg PA
CBHW020545300426
44111CB00008B/798